The Princess and the Philosopher

The Princess and the Philosopher

Letters of Elisabeth of the Palatine to René Descartes

Andrea Nye

ROWMAN & LITTLEFIELD PUBLISHERS, INC.
Lanham • Boulder • New York • Oxford

ROWMAN & LITTLEFIELD PUBLISHERS, INC.

Published in the United States of America
by Rowman & Littlefield Publishers, Inc.
4720 Boston Way, Lanham, Maryland 20706

12 Hid's Copse Road
Cumnor Hill, Oxford OX2 9JJ, England

British Library Cataloguing in Publication Information Available

Library of Congress Cataloging-in-Publication Data

Nye, Andrea, 1939–
     The princess and the philosopher : letters of Elisabeth of the
  Palatine to René Descartes / Andrea Nye
       p.   cm.
     Includes index.
     ISBN 0-8476-9264-7 (cloth : alk. paper). — ISBN 0-8476-9265-5
  (pbk. : alk. paper)
     1. Descartes, René, 1596–1650—Correspondence.   2. Elisabeth,
  Countess Palatine, 1618–1680—Correspondence.   3. Philosophy,
  Modern—17th century.   I. Title.
  B1873.N93   1999
  193—dc21   98–44821
                                                                                      CIP

Printed in the United States of America

♾ ™ The paper used in this publication meets the minimum requirements of Ameri-
can National Standard for Information Sciences—Permanence of Paper for Printed
Library Materials, ANSI Z39.48–1984.

The late blessed Princess Elizabeth, the Countess Palatine, as a right claimeth a memorial in this discourse, her virtues giving greater lustre to her name than her quality which yet was of the greatest in the German Empire. She chose a single life as freest of care, and best suited to the study and meditation to which she was always inclined; and the chiefest diversion she took, next to the air, was some such plain and housewifely entertainment as knitting. She controled a small territory, which she governed so well that she showed herself fit for a greater one. There every last day in the week she would constantly sit in judgement, and hear and determine cases herself where her patience, justice, and mercy were admirable, frequently remitting forfeitures where the party was poor or otherwise meritorious. And what was excellent, though unusual, she would temper her discourses with religion, and strangely be able to draw unconcerned parties to submission and agreement, exercising not so much the rigor of her power, as the power of her persuasion.

—William Penn, remembering his friend Elisabeth Palatine
after her death (quoted in Elizabeth Godfrey,
A Sister of Prince Rupert)

Contents

Preface

The painting by the Dutch master Vermeer reproduced on the cover of this volume exemplifies seventeenth-century Dutch art. In an era of genius in painting, Vermeer, Rembrandt, Gerald ter Borch, and others produced luminous, acutely observed, vividly realized studies of domestic life. While Italian painters of the period focused on mythic narratives and heroic events, the Dutch celebrated life on earth. In place of pagan gods and goddesses, they pictured rich interior spaces, graced with imports from a far-flung and profitable trading empire. With the rest of Europe locked into religious enmity and murderous combat between jealous princes, provincial governments in the Dutch Republic were democratically controlled, Dutch universities tempered official Aristotelianism with research in experimental science, and religious zealotry was moderated by acquaintance with other cultures and faiths. In this refuge of relative peace and safety, two extraordinary figures crossed paths, the young Princess Palatine Elisabeth, elder daughter of the impoverished and exiled queen of Bohemia, and René Descartes, the beleaguered founder of philosophical modernism.

During the seven years that followed their first meeting, the rapport between them developed from attraction, to acquaintance, to mutual admiration, to friendship. The relationship came late in Descartes's life and early in Elisabeth's. When they met, he was in his forties, she only twenty-four. Almost immediately the difference in age seemed negligible. Elisabeth's rigorous education in science and mathematics as well as in classics, theology, and jurisprudence made her close to Descartes's equal in learning. More important, a native honesty and forthrightness allowed her to say what she thought without the flattery, manipulation, and posturing that were so irritating to Descartes in academic life. Often separated geographically, they kept their friendship alive in letters.

In the seventeenth century, writing and reading letters was a necessary element of civilized life. Artists depicted the concentration required for correspondence and the drama attached to sending and receiving letters. Popular manuals for letter writing and letter reading gave detailed directions for a letter's proper composition and diction. Letter writing was not simply a matter of conveying information; it required finesse and skill.[1] In the cover painting, a woman looks up from a letter. A moment before, settled alone at her desk, she concentrated, working to frame thoughts so that they would be intelligible to her correspondent. Now a maid has come with a message. Patiently but reluctantly, she stops writing. The letter must wait.

What she was writing about is not made clear. What we see is the painful loss of her focus, the frustrating diversion of her attention as she is interrupted by some domestic duty or pressing business. Is the subject of her letter love? An illicit encounter? Flirtation? So critics have speculated about what goes on in a seventeenth-century woman's mind. Or did the content of the abandoned letter go deeper, to scholarly aspirations, moral insights, sensitive intelligence at work on the difficult business of life? Might it even be philosophy that the woman was writing: thoughts about the nature of morality, or God, or the human soul? Certainly letters are not the traditional medium for philosophy. More usual is the treatise, or at most a dialogue, modeled after Socrates and directed toward a specific task of definition. Letters are written to be answered, are written in answer. They lack the controlling logic of a treatise, the masterful Socratic hand that guides a debate, the firm march of philosophic meditation. What kind of philosophy could it be that is expressed in personal correspondence?

The letters translated in this volume are one answer to this question. One might cite many reasons why philosophical exchanges such as that between Elisabeth and Descartes have been neglected: the image of the philosopher as an individual genius, emphasis on a few canonical figures rather than on the interpersonal genesis of ideas, simple bias against the importance of women's thoughts. In the case of Elisabeth, the loss was partly her own choice. After Descartes's death, when it was proposed to her that her letters to him be published, she refused.

She came from a famous family. Her irrepressible younger sister Sophie would be mother of a king of England, her brother Rupert was a popular military hero, her mother was the glamorous "Winter Queen" of Bohemia. The adventures of the Palatines made gripping plots for popular histories and romances. The scholarly Elisabeth, "la Grecque" as her family called her, is seldom a major figure in these romances. Depicted as severe in judgment, without humor, preoccupied by her studies, never married, Elisabeth was remembered for erudition and her friendship with an awkward scholar whom the family thought at best amusing. The main source of information about her life to date is an out-of-print 1909 biography, Elizabeth Godfrey's A Sister of Prince Rupert. Nothing is known of any published or unpublished formal writings of Elisabeth's; if they survive in the archives of some abandoned chateau or abbey, no one has yet discovered them. But her letters show her to be a gifted correspondent, weaving together personal concerns, autobiography, and theory as she probed the relation between the demands of practical life and the new scientific philosophy.

From its beginnings in ancient Greece, philosophy has taught detachment from practical life: from the corruption of politics, the pressures of business, and the appetites of the flesh. As Plato explained it in his founding allegory of the cave, the philosopher must leave the shadowy and illusory darkness of appearances and worldly affairs behind. He must ascend into the sunlit world of rational Enlightenment to contemplate eternal and perfect ideas and commune with Truth. On this view, diplomacy, civility, and prudence, to say nothing of blasphemies, murders, and executions, have nothing to do with philosophy. The philosopher serves practical human affairs, if at all, after the fact of theorizing, when he returns to earth armed with the truth to reshape always imperfect human affairs. If Elisabeth was a philosopher, she was not this kind of philosopher. For her, philosophy and science had to be lived, had to meet the test of experience. No theory of ethics and morality could be accepted if it resulted in pain or enmity.

Descartes is often credited with updating the ideal of philosophical detachment for the modern period. In an age of science, the physical world of the senses and passions is left behind, but not for metaphysical entities existing in a supersensual heaven. Withdrawing from immediate physical sensation, from family and friends, from the false views of academic authorities and social life, reflecting only on the nature of space, extension, motion, the modern scientist-philosopher concentrates on the clear and distinct mathematical ideas that are the key to physical reality,

In her letters to Descartes, Elisabeth takes a very different approach to philosophy. Here is no detached thinker opposed to involvement in human affairs. Committed to family, deeply concerned about the quality of physical life in Europe, immersed in the aftermath of the devastating Thirty Years' War, she is skeptical of the rationality proposed by Descartes as the only way to truth and goodness. Philosophy as it is expressed in her letters dictates no wisdom superior to experience but proposes theses to be constantly submitted to experience. Faced with political or natural disaster, can the mind really separate itself from the body as Descartes urged? Is detachment from passion, watching events pass as if one were in a theater, really the best way to decide on wise policy? Is positive thinking and blind trust in God's goodness really the best way to cure disabling mental suffering? These were the questions Elisabeth forced on the rationalist Descartes, questions meant not to protect academic privilege nor to further a scholarly reputation but to stimulate a better understanding of human affairs.

Most of Descartes's biographers have devoted a page or two to Elisabeth's first letter to the philosopher, in which she posed a question: if the thinking mind is separate from the body, then how can mind and body interact? If the mind is separate from the body, how can ills and upsets of the body affect the mind and the mind tell the body what to do? But few have noted the widening scope of topics discussed as the correspondence continued until Descartes's death. In standard accounts of Descartes's life, a life fairly barren of sentimentality or romance, Elisabeth provides at most a small touch of human interest. The vital practical and ethical concerns that prompted her questioning are ignored. How can one weigh one's own interests against the interests of others? How can one correct an inherited temperament? How reliable is a natural inclination either to altruism or to concern for self? Which emotions are useful or even necessary in judging what is best? Which passions disturb good judgment? Should one avoid sympathy for others, or cultivate sensitivity to others' pain? Should one act decisively and then forget the past? Or should one engage in painful retrospective examination of actions and motives? For Elisabeth, such questions were not irrelevant to the metaphysics of the new science but crucial to its vitality and usefulness.

Confronted with Elisabeth's insistence that a separation of mind and body is inconceivable, Descartes counseled her to spend less time and energy on metaphysics. Establish sound philosophical foundations, he told her, and then get on with science. It is advice that many present-day philosophers still take to heart, deferring to the "expert" opinion of science or defending a realism based on the findings of current scientific theorizing. For many philosophers, metaphysics is still rationalization of intellectual commitments once established and better left alone. Elisabeth's philosophical style is different. Caught up in human events, always conscious of the passion and inclination that can distort reason, intelligently assessing the effect of misguided medical and moral advice—for her, philosophical speculation is more troubled and more ongoing. The philosopher establishes no unshakable foundations but engages in continued and shared inquiry into changing conditions. If Descartes's tree of knowledge has metaphysics for roots, so does Elisabeth's, but it is a different metaphysics. Descartes's dualist metaphysics supports a trunk of objectivist positivist science and a derivative technological ethics. Elisabeth's nondualist metaphysics of thinking body and material mind nourishes a morally sensitive weighing of values and interests among friends and colleagues that supports human life.

At stake is the very nature of philosophical discussion. Descartes, as he filled page after page with responses to the objections of academic critics, often did so with disdain and irritation. The controversy and judicial proceedings that resulted did the new philosophy little good. The letters between him and Elisabeth represent another kind of philosophical interchange: not debate between professional rivals fighting for academic advantage, not bruising battles of wits between antagonists forced into increasingly alienated and defensive positions, but frank and open discussion between friends. These are philosophers who enliven philosophizing with practical application, who insist on bringing nominal disputes back to the interests of human life, who care enough about each other to listen and respond to what the other says. Such collaborations are never easy. Part of the drama in the letters and commentary that follow involves misunderstanding, disappointment, and sometimes just simple weariness with what the other person persists in saying. What I hope to show is that the vulnerability and patience such exchanges demand are a price worth paying for the rewards of a philosophy practiced between friends.

Acknowledgments

Permission to reproduce the illustrations in this volume is gratefully acknowledged:

Frontispiece: Zeittafel, *Elisabeth von der Pfalz, Princess Palatine, Abbess of Herford*. Courtesy of the Städtisches Museum, Herford.

Page 6: The family of Frederick, King of Bohemia, in exile. Old print. Courtesy Städtisches Museum, Herford.

Page 17: Bourdon, *Portrait of Descartes*. Courtesy of the Louvre, Paris.

Page 126: Dumesnil, *La Reine Christine de Suède*. Courtesy of the Louvre, Paris.

Page 170: The Abbey of Herford in the seventeenth century. Old print. Courtesy Städtisches Museum, Herford.

Prologue

A Terrible Grief

$\sim$

n February 1650, Hector-Pierre Chanut, French ambassador to Sweden, had an unhappy task. A guest in his house as well as a friend, the philosopher René Descartes, was dead of fever. It was up to Chanut to sort out the dead man's belongings and arrange for transport of the body back to France. To his surprise, as he went through Descartes's papers, Chanut found packets of personal letters with a royal signature. Assiduous in his duties, he mailed them back to the sender, ostensibly unread, assuring her that the letters, carefully folded among Descartes's most important documents, must have been extremely precious to the philosopher. He explained: "I think myself obliged to give you an account of a person whom you value for his rare merit, and to tell you, Madame, with a terrible grief, that we have lost M. Descartes." He went on to explain that both he and his friend Descartes had fallen sick with the same illness, a fever with inflammation of the lungs, and that although Chanut had recovered, Descartes had not. The philosopher's end, he assured her, was "gentle and pleasant." He added this plea:

> I do not doubt, Madame, that it would be advantageous for your reputation if people knew that you have had serious and learned discussions with the most clever man who has lived for several centuries, and I know from M. Descartes himself that your letters were so full of light and intelligence that it could only give you glory if they were known. Nonetheless, I thought that respect for your Royal Highness and fidelity to my deceased friend required me not to read any of them, nor to permit them to fall into other hands than by order and permission of Your Royal Highness herself.[1]

Elisabeth, Princess Palatine, whose letters they were, refused Chanut's offer of publication and told him to put the letters into the hands of the ambassador from Brandenburg to be transferred back to her possession. Shortly after receiving her refusal, Chanut wrote to her again, in answer to her queries about Descartes's last moments.

> It is not really, Madame, that I think that you are committing an injustice in that the relatives of this famous man would have an interest in keeping in their house

1

some of the marks of the honor that he received from your approval, but an injustice in that these letters would have justified to the world what Descartes wrote in the dedication of his *Principles* to your Highness. Some day it will happen that, envy having died out, no one will any longer doubt the foundations which he discovered in the structure of the world; time and experience will affirm this doctrine, which now seems to us so extraordinary. But it will be always incredible to posterity that a person of the age and condition of your Highness would have been the first, and for a long time, almost the only one to understand these truths. This is why, Madame, it seems to me that in order to clear the memory of my friend of all suspicion of flattery, it would be just for you to permit that some of your letters be seen in order to serve as a geometric demonstration of what he wrote in his Dedication to you. For even though the letters were not written with the design of making evident the wide reach of the light of your spirit, being unstudied images, they represent, with that much more purity, reason active in the search for truth.

Failing in his usual diplomacy, Chanut went on to add an appeal unlikely to alter Elisabeth's decision to keep her letters private. Along with Descartes's part of the correspondence, said Chanut, Elisabeth's letters would, as he put it, "make a very useful present, if not to the public, at least to the Queen of Sweden." The queen, he went on "well knows how to give a just value to works of this merit, and, seeing everywhere virtue without envy, would be happy to be confirmed by her own judgment in the singular esteem that she has for Your Highness."

Chanut then answered Elisabeth's queries about Descartes's last moments, describing the course of his fever and Descartes's deathbed announcement that "he had settled his account, and was resolved to leave the world without pain and with the assurance of God's mercy." Chanut concluded:

> I believe, Madame, that if he had thought, the day before, that he was so close to his end, still having the liberty of speech, he would have ordered me to carry out some last wishes, and, in particular, he would have wanted me to tell Your Royal Highness that he died with the same respect for Her he had during his life, respect which he often witnessed to me in words full of reverence and admiration. And I know that he would have charged me to render to Your Royal Highness for him, as much as is possible, all the respect and service that he owed you.

It is doubtful how comforting this well-meaning reconstruction of what the philosopher would have said on his deathbed if he had thought of her could have been to the thirty-two-year-old Princess Elisabeth. She was in need of comfort. Under her aunt's protection in Germany; conducting difficult negotiations for her sister Henriette's marriage; at odds with the head of the family, her ambitious brother Charles-Louis; permanently estranged from her mother, the exiled queen of Bohemia, she considered Descartes her closest friend. For seven years, she had corresponded regularly with the philosopher, speaking to him with a frankness and intimacy rare in the press of diplomatic and political intrigue in which she and her family were constantly embroiled. During the correspondence, the Palatines had repeatedly tried and failed to recover their home territory in the Rhineland, Elisabeth's mother had recklessly spent what was left of the family money, her brother Edward had proved traitor to the Protestant cause by marrying a Catholic, another brother had murdered her sister Louise's lover in full daylight in the streets of The Hague, and her uncle King Charles I of England was beheaded in London. Through all of this, Descartes had been her confidant and friend, an intellectual companion and a sounding board.

After hearing the news of his death, she continued to complete arrangements for her sister's marriage, saw the new couple off on their wedding trip, and then returned to her brother's household. On her return, relatives wondered at the change in her spirits. Characteristically, they did not bother to inquire as to its cause. As her sister Sophie described Elisabeth's sad demeanor in her *Memoirs*:

> The Court of Madame the Electress of Brandenburg, where [Elisabeth] had been staying had done her no good. We found her much changed in spirit and body. Prince Edward said to me under his breath when he saw her, "Where is her liveliness of spirit? What has she done with her pretty mouth?" Madame l'Electrice [Elisabeth's brother's wife] found her disagreeable also and M. l'Electeur [Elisabeth's brother] who held the marriage of the Princess Henrietta against her was of the same sentiment as his wife.[2]

As for the letters, they disappeared. Two hundred years later, copies were discovered by a French aristocrat, Auguste Foucher de Careil, in the library of a French baron at the Chateau Rosendal near Arnheim. Foucher de Careil had read Chanut's letters and had searched old bookstores in Amsterdam for remains of the correspondence. Finally, receiving a tip from a bookseller who had cataloged the chateau's library, he recovered the letters.[3]

It is understandable that the aristocratic Foucher de Careil would have found Princess Elisabeth intriguing. By birth she was related to the most illustrious houses of Europe. Her mother was a Stuart, granddaughter of Mary Queen of Scots, daughter of James I of England, sister of Charles I. Her father, Frederick of the Palatine, was descended from the line of German electors who led the Protestant resistance to Catholic domination in the Hapsburg empire. Her paternal grandmother, Juliana, was of the Dutch House of Orange, daughter of William the Silent, who delivered Holland from Spanish domination and autocratic monarchy. In Elisabeth's blood flowed the great hopes that had been attached to her parents' marriage, celebrated as the alliance between German and English Protestants that would usher in a new era of freedom and progress in Europe. Royal blood was not Elisabeth's only attraction. In her character, Stuart vitality, German steadfastness and determination, and Dutch sobriety and good sense fused with an intense and speculative mind to produce a spirited intelligence. It was this intelligence that attracted the attention of the most famous and controversial philosopher of his time, René Descartes.

1

The First Overtures

~

T he year was 1643. The Thirty Years' War dragged on, even as peace negotiations began in Münster. Like exhausted boxers, the great powers and princes of Europe, coffers empty, armies decimated, squared off yet again. The French, ineptly led and poorly equipped, managed to win back Alpine passes from Philip of Spain, who was distracted by rebellions at home. In England civil war broke out, and Cromwell formed his New Model Army. Fears of instability under the weak Louis XIII agitated Paris, where Descartes's intellectual rival, Gassendi, promoted atomism as the new foundation for science and the state.

Descartes, in semiretirement outside of The Hague, was increasingly embittered by hostility to his work that persisted even in freethinking Holland. He lived without close attachments, expending much of his energy fending off attacks from clergy and university officials. His groundbreaking work in mathematics and epistemology, the work that would later earn him the title of the first philosopher of the modern period, was in the past. His *Discourse on Method*, his *Meditations on First Philosophy*, now two of the most frequently read philosophical texts of all time, seemed still to arouse only controversy. In them he had argued, he thought decisively, for the detachment of the rational mind from a body that is a physical thing like any other and subject to natural laws. He had proven that the mechanistic science that elucidates those laws is consistent with the major tenets of Catholic belief. It increasingly rankled that in his homeland, France, he had received no official recognition. He had not realized his ambition of convincing the Jesuits, his old teachers, that Cartesian philosophy should be the basis of their education system. Nor had he managed to clear a safe place for science in the freethinking Dutch universities. His spirits were low. The fame he thought he deserved eluded him, along with fulfillment of his dream that scientific method would replace Aristotelianism as the official teaching of the Schools. He had supporters, even disciples, but he also had many detractors.

He had never married, never, as far as anyone knew, maintained a long-standing love affair with any woman. A brief liaison with a Dutch servant woman had faded into oblivion, along with an illegitimate daughter who had died in childhood. He was no hermit and was even a celebrity of sorts in Dutch circles. His

FREDERICVS. D.G. REX BOHEMIÆ.
FREDERICVS. Koning von Bohemen Pfalts
graeff an den Rhijn Hartoch van Baueren en
Silesien MarcKgræff van Moravien en van Lusaſs etc

1 Frederick   5 Mauritius   8 Eduardt
2 Carolus   6 Louiſa Hol·   9 MariaHenriette
3 Elsabeth   landina   10 Philippus
4 Robertus·   7 Lowys   11
             Namen der Konings Kinderen

ELISABETH.D.G. REGINA BOHEMIÆ.
ELISABETH Koninginne van Bohemen.
Pfalts graefſinne an den Rhijn etc Hartoginne van
Beijeren en Sileſien MarcKg: van Moravien en Lusaſs etc

Fig. 1.1. An old print shows the large, sometimes unruly family of Frederick and Elisabeth Stuart. Elisabeth is shown at her father's left hand, as the oldest daughter; the youngest, Sophie, is still unnamed in her cradle.

genial friend Palloti, or Pollot, as the Dutch called him, in service to the prince of Orange, saw to it that he met leading intellectual figures in The Hague and luminaries in court circles who might support the new philosophy and its benefits for mankind. It was in that cause that he found himself one day in the lively salon of the glamorous, exiled, and widowed queen of Bohemia.

The queen lived in The Hague under the protection of the Dutch government. Many of the leading lights of Holland found their way to her drawing room, men like the powerful and learned Constantine Huygens, secretary to the stadtholder (the official title of the prince of Orange), and the painter Honthorst, who painted the royal family many times. Also welcome were adventurers, bons vivants, and sycophants. In 1639, English Puritans visiting The Hague went by the queen's house and described it as brightly lit, with loud music coming out the windows, and "devilish Hallooings."[1] The down-at-the-heels town house, not known for sobriety or order, housed a large and unruly family. The supervision of the queen's many children was irregular at best. Younger sons, roaming the streets of the Hague with gangs of unruly aristocrats, were on occasion arrested for insulting people in the street. Young people entered the house dusty, disheveled, and without ceremony. The queen's daughters walked in the markets dressed like commoners. An artist daughter, Louise, flirted conspicuously with any visitor who caught her fancy. The queen had a taste for entertainment, crude jokes, the latest fashion, and court politics, which she manipulated with all the force she could muster.

Certainly Descartes, who had left Paris years before to escape the distractions of both high and low society, could not have found her salon much to his liking. On his first visit he might have thought only of extricating himself and have taken little notice of the quiet, bright-eyed young woman who listened so intently as he attempted to explain physics to an audience more interested in scandal than logic.

He might never have returned if it had not been passed on to him that one of the queen's daughters took an interest in his work. Flattered—what middle-aged scholar would not have been?—he wrote back to his friend Palloti. He had heard of this princess, he told Palloti, heard of her marvelous mind. That she read and approved his work showed she had better judgment than all of the Schoolmen with their Aristotles. As soon as Palloti was in The Hague, could they go again to the queen's house so he could expressly make the princess's acquaintance?[2]

The life of this princess whom Descartes proposed to get to know better had been very different from his own. For the first two years of life she had lived in fairy-tale splendor at Heidelberg Castle, where her young father, passionately in love with a beautiful Stuart wife, planted terraced gardens with English roses and commissioned magical mechanical landscape constructions. Heidelberg's pink sandstone exterior, porphyry floors, tapestries, and paintings, and its owners' patronage of the arts were legendary. At the heart of the German Renaissance, the Palatine was the most progressive of the German imperial territories. A center of learning and the arts since the fourteenth century, Heidelberg's Bibliotheca Palatina held one of the most important collections of books in Europe. Protestant intellectuals from all parts of Europe congregated in Heidelberg to escape persecution and participate in what they saw as the enlightened wave of the future.

Two years of royal infancy were all the aristocratic luxury Elisabeth would enjoy. Embroiled in the escalating conflict between Protestants and Catholics in the Holy Roman Empire, Frederick, her young father, urged by his ambitious Calvinist chaplain and his maternal relatives in the House of Orange, accepted the throne of Bohemia from Protestant rebels. Once crowned, he was further convinced to impose the dogmatic Heidelberg Catechism on the evangelical Bohemians, who again promptly rebelled. Nor was either the Holy Roman Emperor or his ally Philip of Spain willing to let the Bohemian throne go to the Protestants. Assaulted on all sides, Frederick was routed from his kingship within the year, his dethronement precipitating a war that would last thirty long years, ravage Germany, and kill off a large portion of the population of central Europe. Spanish and imperial troops overran Bohemia and the Palatine. Frederick was stripped of his electorship in the empire and all of his territory. The ill-fated "Winter King and

Queen," as the Jesuits called him and his wife, fled with their eldest son and heir to The Hague, where they were given refuge by Frederick's uncle, the prince of Orange.

Elisabeth and a younger brother, Charles-Louis, remained behind in Heidelberg. They were brought up by their sober and sedate grandmother, Juliana, the only one to advise against the Bohemian adventure, and by her maiden daughter, Catherine. Juliana moved the children from place to place out of the way of the fighting until the small family group settled on an estate in the small, remote town of Krossen. There, at the confluence of two rivers, on the border between Silesia and Brandenburg, young Elisabeth flourished under her grandmother's and aunt Catherine's responsible tutelage, developing traits of generosity, loyalty, concentration, steadiness, and good sense for which she would be known all her life.

When she was nine, the summons came for her and her brother to join the family in Holland. She was now the eldest child, and fatherless. In 1629, an older brother had been drowned in a boating accident, with Frederick, his befuddled father, unable to save him. Three years later, after fighting with the king of Sweden against Spain and the Hapsburgs in hopes of recovering his kingdom, Frederick himself, weakened by depression and the constant frustration of his hopes of recovering his kingdom, died of fever on the battlefield. Elisabeth's mother now transferred her considerable, if often misguided, energies to her second son; her goal, to recover the family property at any cost. The cost was great. Any money that came to the family from Holland or England was diverted to futile schemes to raise armies and conduct diplomacy.

Once in Holland, Elisabeth and her brother were dispatched to a "nursery palace" in the university town of Leyden to complete their education under the strict supervision of royal tutors. The Plessen family ran a *Prinsenhof*, or princes' house, with a strict hand. Lessons included math, history, jurisprudence, classical and modern languages, and theology. On Wednesday and Sunday nights, professors from the university were guests at dinner. Formal court etiquette, including long series of ceremonial bows, was observed at all meals.[3] Unlike other members of the family, Elisabeth excelled in her studies, earning the epithet "la Grècque" with which less serious siblings would taunt her. After further "finishing" in social graces at the hands of one Lady Vere, she was finally judged ready to come to live with her mother in The Hague.

The queen's interest in her daughters was minimal. A handsome widow with many admirers, she saw no particular advantage in being surrounded by a bevy of daughters, especially when they were unlikely to attract advantageous marriages. Certainly the queen had little liking for the studious young woman who now appeared in her dramatically black-draped "presence chamber" for nightly inspection. Nor was she kind. She complained about Elisabeth's serious demeanor, ridiculed her reputation for book learning, and made jokes about her nose, which had a tendency to turn red when Elisabeth was upset. Elisabeth made the best of it, helping as much as she could with younger brothers and sisters and continuing to pursue her studies when she had the time.

By the spring of 1643, when Descartes appeared in her mother's chamber, Elisabeth was a grave and comely young woman of twenty-four. As depicted in the frontispiece portrait, she was tall and slender, with dark hair and vivid coloring. Her fair skin blushed easily, her bright brown eyes were sharp under thick lashes, her nose was long and elegant above a pleasant and lively mouth. She had a keen intelligence and a refreshing—some said abrasive—honesty. Her mentor, Lady Vere, had taught her the social graces, but she had not been able to teach her tolerance of pretension and gossip.

Elisabeth had been in The Hague for fifteen years. The love and attention of her grandmother and aunt in Germany were distant memories. In the queen's household she was often made a scapegoat, expected to control irrepressible younger children, chided when she could not, pressed into service whenever there was an unpleasant task. Eight years before, at sixteen, she had turned down the only offer of marriage she is on record as receiving, from King Wladislaw of Poland, a Catholic. When the Polish Diet had refused her permission to remain Protestant, true to her faith, she refused the marriage.

What Descartes thought of the princess on his visit to get to know her better is not recorded. Busy with a move from a large villa near The Hague to a more remote country village, increasingly embroiled in an ugly dispute with Voetius, the leading theologian of Utrecht, Descartes had other things than princesses on his mind. Nevertheless, when he was again in The Hague, he called on her, only to find her out. A few days later, at a time when his affairs seemed particularly bleak, he received the following letter:

The Hague, 16 May 1643

Monsieur Descartes:

I have learned of the intention you had to see me a few days ago with much joy and regret, touching first on your charity in being willing to communicate with such an ignorant and intractable person as myself and then on the misfortune which prevented me from enjoying a conversation so profitable. M. Palloti [Pollot] has much strengthened this last passion by repeating to me the answers which you have given him to the objections [to your work] contained in the *Physics* of M. Rhegius, answers about which I would have been better instructed out of your own mouth. I also proposed a question to that same professor when he was in this town with the result that he also referred me to you for the required satisfaction. My shame in showing to you a writing style so disordered has prevented me from asking this favor of you by letter up to now.

But today M. Palloti has given me so many assurances of your kindness for everyone and especially for me that I have chased all other considerations aside other than to profit from that kindness in asking you to answer this question: How can the soul of a man determine the spirits of his body so as to produce voluntary actions (given that the soul is only a thinking substance)? For it seems that all determination of movement is made by the pushing of a thing moved, either that it is pushed by the thing which moves it or it is affected by the quality or shape of the surface of that thing. For the first two conditions, touching is necessary, for the third extension. For touching, you exclude entirely the notion that you have of the soul; extension seems to me incompatible with an immaterial thing. This is why I ask you to give a definition of the soul more specific than the one you gave in your *Metaphysics*, that is to say of its substance as distinct from its thinking action. For even if we suppose the two to be inseparable (which anyway is difficult to prove in the womb of the mother and in fainting spells), like the attributes of God we can, in considering them separately, acquire a more perfect idea of them.

It is because you know the best medicine that I expose to you so liberally the errors in these speculations and hope that, observing the oath of Hippocrates, you will bring to them remedies without publicity, which I ask you to do as you suffer the importunities of

your affectionate friend at your service

Elisabeth

2

Body and Soul

~

“Extension,” “immateriality,” “thinking substance”—hardly terms that a young princess might be expected to bandy about, and it is surprising that someone so young would be capable of so forceful and practiced an argument—“for the first two conditions,” “for the third.” Certainly, this was diction more to be expected from a professor than a princess. How can the mind move the body if it is an immaterial thing? A question that would not occur, one would think, to a young aristocratic woman, taken up with balls, needlework, and finding a husband.

Her opening compliments are modest: Will the famous philosopher be willing to read her nonnative French? The question is somewhat disingenuous, since she and her brothers and sisters had spoken French between themselves from birth. Would he resent her persistence in asking for immediate answers? Even in this first letter, her apologies are tempered. She has been afraid to write, she says, because her style is so disordered, but she goes on confidently to exploit the complex resources of French grammar. She apologizes for her ignorance, but her closing reference to the “Serment de Hipocrates,” newly published at Leyden with a commentary by the scholar Meibomius, as well as her apparently close contacts with Rhegius, a well-known professor at the University of Utrecht, are hardly consistent with ignorance.

This is a highly educated young woman, trained by a succession of tutors and governesses who did not limit her studies to religion and morality but gave her rigorous training in Greek, Latin, and mathematics. Once graduated from the Plessens’ princes’ house to her mother’s town house in the city, she profited from the freedom of The Hague, where she supplemented private academic studies with drawing lessons at the studio of the painter Honthorst and university lectures in natural science and mathematics with her friend Anna van Schurman.[1]

In this first letter, as in many to come, sound two voices. One is the voice of a stateswoman skilled in graceful pleasantries who, when she wishes, manipulates the elaborate compliments of court etiquette. The other has a deeper timbre; armed with reason and unadorned with rhetoric, it presses a question just to the edge of civility. Typically, as here, even a polite opening flourish has an edge to it.

Elisabeth confesses to the weakness of intractability, but she warns that she will continue to press her objections as long as Descartes does not answer them to her satisfaction. Descartes will soon learn that this is a young woman not content with pleasantries and polite dismissal, one who requires thought and care with the issues she raises.

Nor were her questions easy to answer. The problem of the relation between mind and body was at the heart of the new science that Descartes and others were proposing as successor to the Aristotelianism of the medieval Schools. For science to be grounded in certain and necessary truth, independence of the rational mind was crucial. An objective, rational approach to knowledge of the physical world could do away with prayers, miracles, and God-created essences that get in the way of science. Science would henceforth be dependent, not on clerical authority, but on mental conceptions untainted by human interest or desire. If with his dualism Descartes proclaimed the autonomy of the modern scientific mind from any external authority, including the church, he also demanded its independence from a man's own emotions and appetites.

It was this last that troubled Elisabeth. A challenge to clerical authority was neither new nor shocking to this daughter of a long line of Protestant activists. Her studies had long since taken her beyond the dogmatic Calvinism of her father's zealous chaplain, creator of the Heidelberg Catechism. Yes, you might question the teaching of a cleric or minister, who is after all only a man, just as you might declare independence from any institutional authority. But how is a person to be free of herself? That, it seemed to Elisabeth, was another issue altogether.

How is it, she asked, if the mind is separate from the body, that it can move or affect the body? How can the mind of a man, or a woman, attached to a physical body and infected with all the emotion, passion, and desire that go with that body, achieve the rational autonomy Descartes declared necessary for objective, disinterested knowledge?

Elisabeth was not the first to raise these questions. Descartes's dualism—the view that there are two kinds of things in the world, physical things and minds or souls capable of knowing those things—was under attack from many quarters: from theologians fearful that spirits separated from bodies would inevitably be discarded to leave only godless materialism, from Scholastics determined to retain their university positions teaching Aristotle, from spiritualists who denied that the material world is made up only of physical things and forces. Elisabeth's argument, for all its academic framing, came from different sources, from the concerns of life, concerns of a young woman presented with challenges that taxed both soul and body.

If the human body is to move, it must be impelled; and to be impelled, it must be touched by something extended in space. But the mind of a rational scientist is not supposed to be extended or to be material in any sense. How then is voluntary action possible? Can you not know rationally, in your mind, what is expected of you, yet find your body resisting, even refusing to obey? It is not enough, Elisabeth told Descartes, to know what the mind does, to know what we happen to be thinking. In order to understand the mind's effect on the body, you have to know what thinking is, what the mind or soul is, whether it is separable from the body, and what are its links with the body. In this first letter, there is a personal urgency not found in the academic disputes that seethed around the new science.

Descartes's scientific method, as well as his research, depended on disinvolvement, on putting the body to one side and concentrating on intellectually generated mathematical concepts. It was a philosophy that Descartes lived out, with his judicious retreat to Holland away from the distractions of Paris, with his insistence on avoiding political disputes, with his isolation in the Dutch countryside. As he explained in his autobiographical *Discourse on Method:*

> It is just eight years ago that this desire [to concentrate on rational inquiry] made me resolve to remove myself from all places where any acquaintance were possible, and to retire to a country such as this, where the long-continued war has caused such order to be established that the armies which are maintained seem only to be of use in allowing the inhabitants to enjoy the fruits of peace with that much more security; and where, in the crowded throng of a great and very active nation, more concerned with its own affairs than curious about those of others, without missing any of the conveniences of the most populous towns, I can live as solitary and retired as in the most remote of deserts.[2]

Descartes had chosen well. Having won independence from the autocratic Spaniards and achieved a degree of popular rule, Holland was a peaceful Protestant country, relatively tolerant, a traditional refuge for French freethinkers and expatriates.[3] The sober mercantile Dutch, as Descartes observed, minded their own business; the government did not interfere in citizens' private matters or in scholars' researches. The universities at Utrecht, Leyden, and Gröningen were under secular and not clerical control, and they attracted students from all over Europe, especially in the sciences. At the same time, there was no need to do without the amenities that Descartes always enjoyed. The successful struggle of the Dutch to escape from the domination of Spain and a flourishing foreign trade resulted in marvelous prosperity. Companies like the Dutch East India Company governed overseas territories, controlling luxury imports such as pepper, cinnamon, nutmeg, mace, cloves, tea, porcelain from China, cotton from India, silk from Persia. Dutch ships did a profitable carrying trade in slaves from Africa and grain from the Balkans. In and out of the great harbor of Amsterdam six hundred of them came and went in a day, bringing carpets from Turkey, spices from Indonesia, and exotic tropical fruits, all without the civic disorder, assassinations, beheadings, throat-cuttings, ambushes, and robberies that troubled the rest of Europe.

Best of all, in the federated Dutch Republic there was no autocratic central government to monitor scholarship. Power was concentrated in town councils dominated by practical men with interests in business and trade. Elisabeth's relatives in the House of Orange, the stadtholders, ruled as modern executives, on sufferance, more or less under the control of commoners, with exclusive power only over the military. Even foreign policy was monitored and checked by assemblies whose interests did not always conform to those of the royal house. In Holland, Descartes could work in studious isolation, free from distracting involvements, far from his family, with whom he had never been close. Even his closest friends respected his privacy.

Elisabeth's life was very different. The questions she raised came not from isolated meditation but from involvement: from painful experience, emotional upset, intellectual turmoil, struggles with self and a recalcitrant body, conflict between her own desires and the will of others. She was not concerned, as were so many of Descartes's critics, with defending an academic reputation or scoring points. Unlike her friend Anna van Schurman, she had no ambition of lecturing in the universities nor of becoming a leading light in literary circles. Nor did conventional piety drive her to approach the philosopher. Elisabeth, although she was a staunch Calvinist, saw no inconsistency between critical thought and theology. Of primary concern to her, then and later, were more immediate matters: the fate of fatherless and homeless brothers and sisters, the revival of the Protestant cause in war-ravaged Germany, the restoration of peace to Europe. These were the worries that, even if they began in her conscious mind, soon found their way to her body, making her physically ill.

Can we also think that more personal concerns might have contributed to this young woman's decision to conquer her shyness and approach someone so known for his merciless intellect? When she was called each evening to present herself before an irritable and indifferent mother, why did her nose turn red with nervousness? "Poor thing," her mother is reported to have grimaced in an aside, "she will never make a marriage with that nose." More important than an unreliable complexion, the pomposity and pretense of court life that her mother maintained with such energy gave Elisabeth her debilitating headaches. Slights or ridicule by her family, common enough, roiled in her stomach for days.

Even more troubling might have been other, still more personal feelings. Dressed like ordinary Dutch citizens, she and her friends walked the streets, explored the stalls at market time, marveled at elephants at fairs, visited galleries. On fine spring days they went out in the carriage, down to the docks where gaily decorated boats with striped awnings waited. They mingled with crowds of prosperous merchants, wives in brightly colored silks and Paris hats, men in tall top hats and white ruffs, groups of students on a lark, and young men of all classes, simple people, working people, all embarking on the riverboats, floating worlds of pleasure where differences in station and birth no longer mattered. So they would slip between green fields planted in spring with the scarlet-and-canary-striped tulips that, even even after the collapse of "tulipmania" in 1637, were still a great wonder in Europe. Gossip about Elisabeth and her friends was recalled by the arch tattler, Sorbière.

> At the same time, which was 1642, in Holland it was a diversion for the Ladies to go by boat from The Hague to Delft or Leyden, dressed en bourgeoisie and mingling with the common people, in order to hear what was being said about the nobility on topics to which they would steer the conversation. And it would often happen that they would hear various things being said about themselves, and even, their gallantry being something extraordinary, it would also happen that they would hardly return without having found some cavalier who would offer them his service and who, on embarking, would see himself fooled in the little hope he had that they were courtesans, when he saw the carriage that was always waiting for them there.[4]

How was she to make sense of that irrepressible elevation of the blood when one of these handsome young commoners misunderstood the freedom of her conversation and tried to follow her home? For days, a young woman might have felt an excitement that no degree of rationality could calm, with every night the image of a young man's face coming into her mind, along with other thoughts, less pure, more disturbing to the body. She had never been allowed to love, had never seen in person that one rejected suitor, Wladislaw.

Could the philosopher Descartes, in middle age, embittered by the poor reception given his work, perched in the country village of Egmond-den-Hoef, looking out over brown fields to the staid dunes of the North Sea, have been troubled in quite the same way? Foremost on his mind was controversy in the universities and indignation at what he took as the increasingly libelous and scurrilous attacks on his work.

3

The Scent of a Rose

❧

*D*escartes's answering letter (21 May 1643) was immediate and effusive. Despite the outcry about his radical philosophical views, he was a prudent man, well aware of the advantages of having friends in high places. Elisabeth might be a minor princess exiled from a small principality, but she was of royal blood, granddaughter to James Stuart, niece of Charles I, king of England, intimate of the House of Orange. Certainly this was not someone to be offended.

But Descartes was no practiced courtier. As a youth in Paris, he was by reputation associated more with beer and gambling halls than with court society. His opening compliments are overblown, awkward if not stumbling:

> The favor with which your Highness has honored me in allowing me to receive your commandments by letter is far greater than I could ever have dared hope. And it makes my defects easier to bear than the one event that I would have fervently wished for, that is to have received them from your own mouth, if I would have been able to be admitted to the honor of paying you my respects and offering you my very humble services when I was last in The Hague. Because there I would have had so many marvels to admire all at once, seeing a discourse more than human come from a body so like those painters give to angels, I would have been in the same rapture it seems must be those who, coming from earth, enter for the first time into heaven. All of which would have made me even less able to respond to your Highness, who without doubt has already remarked in me this defect when I had the honor to speak to you before. Your clemency in leaving me the traces of your thoughts in writing would make me hope that, reading them several times, and getting used to considering them, I will be, in truth, less overcome. But in fact I only have that much more admiration, remarking that your thoughts not only seem to be ingenious at the first reading, but even more judicious and solid the more one examines them.

Had there been more congress between these two than a few introductions and stilted drawing-room conversations, as some have surmised? Had Descartes's recent move from a villa at Endgeest near The Hague to the more remote village of Egmond-den-Hoef actually been flight from an inconvenient romantic entanglement with this princess? Had the trips on the riverboats had a secret destination:

Fig. 3.1. René Descartes is shown in a portrait by Sébastien Bourdon.

disembarkation near Descartes's villa and a series of clandestine private visits? Had this attractive young woman intruded on the famous philosopher in his rented château, ventured up the tower where he kept his study and laboratory to be tutored in private intimacy in mathematics or in more personal subjects?

So Foucher de Careil, the discoverer of Elisabeth's letters, speculated. And what a heyday Descartes's biographers have had with such an interesting conjecture.[1] It makes a romantic scene. Young women in their cloaks, scarves drawn up over their faces lest they be recognized, sway up Descartes's long brick-paved drive like a gaggle of geese. Giggling, they are invited into the house; Descartes is hard at work upstairs. Leaving her escort downstairs, Elisabeth is ushered up the long flights of stairs. The embattled scholar turns from his manuscript; his face lights up, flattered to see this dark-haired girl at his door, tempted by her obvious admiration, Elisabeth shy but burning with desire for knowledge and more.

Descartes is hardly the usual hero of romance, but he had his own brooding appeal, as is clear from his portrait. He was a little below average in height, with a head rather big in relation to his torso. He had a large and prominent forehead, almost always covered with rather straggling hair. With the underdeveloped body of a scholar, thinning hair that in later years he always was careful to cover with a wig, sporting a neatly trimmed moustache beneath a pointed chin, Descartes was not the typical ladies' man. His best feature was his eyes. Large, farsighted, sad, they are the eyes of an orphan, wanting, waiting, never receiving a mother's love. Why is he still so pilloried, so unappreciated? Why, when he has selflessly given everything he has to science, to the pursuit of useful knowledge? Why, when friends and admirers like Pollot know that he is a genius, know that he is the foremost intellect of his age, why has he had so little recognition? Why, when he has sacrificed any private life he might have had, removed himself from all distractions so that he could concentrate on science, judiciously avoided family obligations, detached himself promptly from a dangerous entanglement with the servant girl that might have disrupted his work and ruined his reputation? His father and sister are dead—not that he had ever been close to them. He maintains no permanent house, no home, in fact has never lived anywhere more than a few years. Selflessly, he has dedicated himself to truth.

Why might his head not have been turned by this young person already reputed to be the most learned woman in Europe? She stands beside him at the table where he examines a specimen, their two heads, both dark, hers almost level with his, coming closer together. Then, the dark times. A realization late at night, sitting alone in his dressing gown by the light of a single candle: too much of his mind is taken up by her. Waiting for her visits is distracting him from his work, as he listens for the sound of laughter below, of footsteps on the stairs. No, he must flee, move away from the rented villa with its comforts and its invitation to visitors, move further out into the country, past where the riverboats call, to a small cottage where he can work free of temptation.

But whatever the appeal of such a scenario, Descartes's move from his villa farther away from The Hague was not a flight from love. This was no withdrawal from a woman who forced herself on him. The slowly developing friendship between these two was considerably more complex and interesting than this evocation of a salacious incident between monkish tutor and seductive student. And Descartes's mind, as he changed residence, was taken up with more prosaic matters than flirtation. Prudently removing himself from the jurisdiction of the civil authorities at Utrecht, he narrowly escaped the summons that would shortly be issued for him to appear before the council. He expected it and dreaded it, this order to answer to charges that he had made slanderous attacks on his archenemy, the foremost theologian and professor of Utrecht, the "Pope of the Dutch Reformed Church," the hated Voetius.

No; reading his first letter to Elisabeth carefully, one cannot think that this man is yet on very intimate terms with a young woman tired to illness of the hypocritical hyperbole of court life. His inflated compliments serve only to excuse his failure to satisfy her doubts, a conceit that might have pleased someone more vain than the princess but that anyone close to her might have realized would not be to her taste. In the philosopher's apology may be already the realization that he has underestimated this young woman, taken her for a shallow *femme savante* like those he often encountered in the salons of Paris, Certainly he did not discourage the interest of fashionable women, remarking several times to friends that he had written his works in French so that "even women might get something out of it."[2] Still, "getting something out of it" is not the same as understanding. And Elisabeth, it seemed from her letter, was not so easily impressed and satisfied as he might have thought she would be as he sat beside her in the queen's shabby drawing room with its torn brown velvet drapes and threadbare tapestries, a cup of Indian tea balanced on his knee. Had he too quickly brushed off the girl's conversation as of little note and unworthy of serious response?

More gentle than was his usual style with academic critics, he muses on her questions. Yes, she has put her finger on the problem, so that he cannot slip anything by her. Yes, he talked much about pure thought but not much about how the mind acts and suffers with the body. Yes, while we have only the bare idea of the union between soul and body, we have no idea with which to understand that union in the same way we understand physical bodies as extended and the soul as a thinking thing. In a burst of ingenuity, Descartes proposes a creative, if perplexing, solution to Elisabeth's difficulty.

> So I believe that up to now we have confused the idea of the power with which the soul acts in the body with the power by which one body acts in another body. And that we have attributed both the one and the other, not to the soul, for we do not understand that yet, but to various qualities of bodies, such as heaviness, heat, and others, which we have imagined to be real, that is, we have imagined them to have an existence distinct from that of the body, and by consequence to be substances, even though we have named them qualities. And we use these ideas, just as we use ideas which are in us to understand bodies and ideas that are in us to understand the soul—according to whether we take them to be material or immaterial. For example, in supposing that heaviness is a real quality—of which we have no other acquaintance than that it has the power to move the body in which it is toward the center of the earth—we avoid the trouble of understanding how it moves the body, or how it is joined to it, and we think only that it is done by a real touching of one surface against another, for we look in ourselves to see if we have a particular idea to conceive of that. I believe that we use that idea badly if we apply it to heaviness, which is not really anything distinct from the body—as I hope to show in my Physics—but that this idea has been given to us to conceive the way in which the soul moves the body.

In other words, a mistaken idea of qualities like weight and heat as separate substances that move bodies can be recycled to explain how the soul works in the body. Perhaps it is not surprising that Descartes, even as he might have hoped that such ingenuity would please a royal dilettante, immediately has some doubt that this solution is "entirely satisfactory." He finishes with a small flourish of additional compliment. He will hoard her letter as "misers do their treasure which they hide the more they value it, so that, keeping it out of view of all the world, their greatest contentment is in contemplating it."

A middle-aged scholar, not known for his looks, dissipated in his youth, recovered from an unfortunate alliance with a servant girl, estranged from his family—can we blame him for playing the courtier from the safe distance of Egmond? But still with a hint that he will come or write whenever he is summoned to her royal presence?

> I would witness to not have sufficiently understood the incomparable spirit of your Highness, if I would have used more words to explain, and I would seem too presumptuous if I dared to think that my response would be entirely satisfactory, but I will try to avoid both one and the other, in not adding anything more, unless it is that, if I were able to write or to say anything more that would agree with her, I would take it always as a great favor to take up the pen, or to go to The Hague for this purpose. There is nothing in the world so dear to me as to be able to obey her commandments.

Imaginary clandestine visits aside, perhaps this sober, rational man has caught a fleeting, tantalizing scent of romance as he sat in Egmond in yet another rented garden. Might he have savored it as he would the odor of a particularly fragrant old rose? Did he dream just a little that this young woman might indeed be the one, as one of his biographers will poetically imagine, to "reflect his thoughts, as if in a magic mirror where his ideas would dress themselves with grace and femininity"?[3] Had he finally the hope of finding the feminine "cogito," soul mate to the modern rational man?[4]

4

An Initial Disappointment

~

_A_ few weeks go by before Elisabeth answers.

The Hague
20 June 1643

Monsieur Descartes

Your kindness is apparent not only in pointing out to me and correcting the faults in my reasoning, as I have understood them, but also in that trying to make their recognition less upsetting you attempt to console me—to the prejudice of your own judgment—by false praise, which might have been necessary to encourage me to work on the remedy for my faults, if it were not for my upbringing. In an environment where the ordinary fashion of conversing has accustomed me to listening to people incapable of telling the truth, I presume to be always sure of the contrary of their discourses, which makes the consideration of my imperfections so familiar to me that they give me no more emotion than is necessary for the desire to undo them.

This makes me confess, without shame, to have found in myself all the causes of error which you have remarked in my letter, and to not be able to banish them completely. The life I am forced to lead does not leave me the disposition of enough time to acquire a habit of meditation according to your rules. So many interests of my family that I must not neglect, so many interviews and civilities that I cannot avoid, batter my weak spirit with such anger and boredom that it is rendered for a long time afterward useless for anything else. All of which will excuse my stupidity, I hope, to not have been able to understand the idea by which we must judge how the soul (not extended and immaterial) can move the body by an idea we have in another regard of heaviness, nor why a power—which we have falsely attributed to things under the name of a quality—of carrying a body toward the center of the earth must persuade us that a body could be pushed by something immaterial, especially when the demonstration of a contrary truth (which you promised in your Physics) confirms us in thinking it impossible. This idea of a separate independent quality of heaviness—given that we are not able to pretend to the perfection and objective reality of God—could be made up out of ignorance of that which truly propels bodies towards the center of the earth. Because no material cause represents itself to the senses, one attributes heaviness to matter's contrary, the immaterial,

21

which, nevertheless, I would never be able to conceive but as a negation of matter and which could have no communication with matter.

I confess that it is easier for me to concede the matter and the extension of the soul than to concede that a being that is immaterial has the capacity to move a body and to be moved by it. For if the former is done by giving information, it is necessary that the spirits which make the movement be intelligent, which you do not accord to anything corporal. And although, in your *Meditations*, you show the possibility of the soul being moved by the body, it is nevertheless very difficult to comprehend how a soul, as you have described it, after having had the faculty and habit of good reasoning, would lose all that by some sort of vapors, or that being able to subsist without the body and having nothing in common with it, would allow itself to be so ruled by the body.

But since you have undertaken my instruction, I do not entertain these sentiments except as friends which I do not count on keeping, assuring myself that you will explain the nature of an immaterial substance and the movements of its actions and passions in the body, as you have all the other things which you have wished to teach. I pray you also to believe that you could not perform this charity for anyone more sensible of the obligation she owes you than

your very affectionate friend,
Elisabeth

Pleasantries, but the barbs are not so subtle now. It was a skill in which Elisabeth would prove adept, this cushioning of gentle rebuke in an elegant tangle of compliment. Did she expect better from the great philosopher than tired clichés, high-flown comparisons to angels and hoarded gold? A certain sharpness of tone infects her repeated questioning. This is no game of manners.

How is someone like herself, not a cloistered academic and not a professional scholar, but a passionate and intelligent woman, involved with family interests and public affairs, how is she to practice Descartes's detached rational method? How is anyone, for that matter, active in public or communal life to put body and bodily emotion away and attend only to clear and distinct ideas? Most of all, how is it that a mind, her mind for example, if it is truly separate from her body, finds it so difficult to detach itself from the stupidities and hypocrisies of court life? How is it that she cannot float comfortably above her perfumed corseted body, as she sits and listens to beribboned flatterers turning her mother's and sisters' heads with hopes of recovering the lost territories of the Palatine, all the time wanting—she would never say anything so crude to Descartes—to get under their skirts?

Her mother. Called the Helen of Germany, because she prodded her besotted young husband, the father Elisabeth had never known, to take the throne of Bohemia and so bring down on Europe the Thirty Years' War. Called the Winter Queen, because one winter was all her enemies rightly predicted her husband's incompetent rule and her own contempt for Bohemian piety would be tolerated. At her mother's mock court in The Hague, the young and judicious Elisabeth watches and suffers. She has no friend there, no one to advise her about the emotional turmoil she feels, no one she can trust. A supporter and confidante, one Mrs. Croft, has been sent packing, with her mother scornfully charging that Elisabeth was too ready to be "governed by one person." Croft was not tolerable, not when she encouraged Elisabeth to be critical of the queen's household.

Elisabeth had been steadfast in religion and in family loyalty. She had refused the offer of marriage from Wladislaw, she had been loyal to her dead father and the long line of Protestant princes who were her ancestors—not that Wladislaw was much of a personal loss. Widowed, elderly, chronically adulterous, he would hardly have made a good husband. Nor was it clear that she would have been happier in a ruling court where intrigue and civility might have completely distracted her from philosophy and the sciences that she had come to love. But, love aside, as reigning queen she might have accomplished something, had an effect on policies, built a library, established a university.

What really rankled was the insult to her intelligence. Descartes gave her an answer that could satisfy only a dilettante. Again, she marshalled the force of argument, surprising in someone so young. If we "make up" an independent immaterial "heaviness" to account for the motion of objects, might we not similarly have made up a fictitious soul to account for the movements of the body? Might not both be a result of ignorance? Why not simply say that the body itself is intelligent? How else would it heed the directives of the mind? And why would the mind, her mind for example, if it is so independent, be so troubled by her body, so constricted by the low-cut bodices that pushed up a woman's breasts and made it difficult for her to breathe, so dulled sitting cramped on the hard seats of drawing-room chairs hour after hour, listening to "people incapable of telling the truth," so bothered by irritating calls, meetings, conferences that left her exhausted both in spirit and in body.

Just like the woman in Vermeer's painting, Elisabeth must have looked up in irritation at yet another interruption as she sat at her writing table. The news from England was not good. The profligacy and autocracy of her uncle, King Charles, had brought the country to the brink of civil war. Her mother's disordered and extravagant household, constantly in debt, lived from hand to mouth, selling off the few remaining family treasures. How in such circumstances was it possible to exercise the mental detachment that Descartes the philosopher prescribed? But still it is from the foremost modern practitioner of philosophy that she expects an answer.

5

The Uses of Metaphysics

~

*D*escartes answered promptly, apologizing for his failure to explain his philosophy to Elisabeth's satisfaction. Again the tone is respectful, a change from the irritation and contempt he often expressed with academic critics. Is this only prudence on his part, deference to royalty? Does he see Elisabeth's favor as a way to legitimize the new philosophy, give it credence, just as he will soon have to appeal to Elisabeth's relative, the prince of Orange, to smooth over troubles with the Utrecht magistrates? Or is it a more personal quality that attracts him to the princess, a sense of human concern rather than just another challenge from an academic rival? In a second and longer letter (28 June 1643) he omits the extravagant compliments and gets more quickly to the point.

> I am under a very great obligation to your Highness, in that after having found that I had so badly explained myself in my preceding letter on the question that she was pleased to propose to me, she deigned again to have the patience to hear me on the same subject and give me a chance to comment on things which I had omitted. The main thing seems to be this . . .

Descartes goes on to lay out his argument in more properly philosophical terms. Yes, having isolated three kinds of primitive ideas—of body, mind, and their union—he should explain more clearly the differences between them. And, yes, he must explain why he used the analogy of heaviness. There are three kinds of understanding, he tells her: first, pure metaphysical understanding, which conceives the soul alone; second, mathematical scientific understanding aided by imagination, which can understand physical bodies; and, last, the understanding of a common person who draws only "on life and ordinary conversations." Common persons, who "never philosophize and only use their senses," are the ones who conceive the union of mind and body most clearly and mistake them as one thing.

Descartes catches himself, perhaps aware of the possible effect of this statement on his correspondent. Might he be construed as saying that Elisabeth is common, a rube incapable of abstract thought, only concerned with animal appetites? "I almost fear that your Highness will think that I am not speaking seriously here, but that would be contrary to the respect that I owe her." No, he assures her, even he spends only a small amount of his time philosophizing.

> I can say, with truth, that the principal rule that I have always observed in my own studies and that I believe I have made most use of in acquiring knowledge has been that I have only been occupied a very few hours each day in thinking that occupies imagination, and for only few hours per year in thinking which occupies the understanding alone. And I have given the whole rest of my time to relaxation of the senses and the repose of the spirit. I even count among the exercises of imagination all serious conversations, and anything which requires attention. It is this that made me retire to the country, for even though in the busiest city in the world I could still have as many hours to myself as I now use in study, I would not be able to exercise them so usefully, when my spirit was tired out with the amount of attention the traffic of life requires.

Disingenuous? Can we really credit this account of Descartes's short working day? Indeed, contemporary accounts of his daily routine included a careful attention to cuisine, an interest in gardening, a late rising. But only a few hours a day for serious matters and only a few hours a year for philosophy? It is difficult not to read condescension in this reassurance from an intellectual celebrity to a fan hardly on his level.

> I take the liberty here to write to your Highness, to witness to her that I admire truly that among the affairs and the concerns that are never lacking with people of both great spirit and high birth, that she has been able to devote herself to the meditation that is required if one is to understand correctly the distinction between the mind and the body.

Carefully, if rather clumsily, Descartes maneuvers. Actually, he writes, he began with the assumption that she had to some degree managed the attention necessary for philosophy and that she had read his *Meditations* and accepted the reasoning there that proved the separation of mind and body. He assumed it was this that allowed her to see the apparent inconsistency between the separation between mind and body and their union. And it was actually because he thought that her grasp of philosophy was so sure and unshakable that he was not concerned that the separate quality of heaviness he likened to the soul was not in fact real. He only meant to give her a convenient way to bypass the apparent materiality of the soul and so to return to the hard philosophical ground of the soul's separation from body. As he explains it:

> It would then be easy for her to consider that the matter which she had attributed to the mind is not really the mind, and that the extension of matter is of another nature than the extension of the mind, in that the first is fixed at a certain location,

by which one excludes all other bodily extension that does not make a second thing. And thus your Highness would be able easily to return to the knowledge of the distinction between soul and body, without being prevented from conceiving their union.

Expressing his conviction that his "frankness" will not offend, Descartes hastily concludes. But it is a bad thing to continue to worry metaphysical matters; rather, one should "be content to retain metaphysical principles in your memory, believe in the conclusions that one has at one time drawn, and then employ the rest of the time available for the study of thoughts where understanding acts with the imagination and sense."

Almost in midsentence, he breaks off this difficult letter. A messenger is at the door. Another letter has arrived, the dreaded letter, the letter he has been expecting. He has been accused before the Utrecht magistrates of libeling Voetius. A commission has been nominated. He is ordered to appear to defend himself. He signs off. He can say no more. The infuriating official document with its red seal now requires his immediate attention.

Elisabeth responds quickly to her new friend's troubles, apologizing for adding to his burden.

Monsieur Descartes

1 July 1643

I know that you receive as much inconvenience from my esteem for your instruction and my desire to profit from it as you do from the ingratitude of those who deprive themselves of that instruction and wish to deprive the human race of it. I would not have sent on a new result of my ignorance before you had finished with those of the latter opinion if [your publisher] Van Bergen had not obliged me by being willing to remain in this city so that I could send on with him a response to your letter of 28 June. That letter made me see clearly the three primary ideas we have, their objects, and how we must use them.

I see also that the senses show me that the soul moves the body, but that they do not show me really (any more than the Understanding or the Imagination does) the way in which it does. For that, I think, there are properties of the soul, unknown to us, which could, perhaps, overturn what your *Meditations* persuaded me of with such good arguments: that is, the nonextension of the soul. This doubt would seem to be founded on the rule which you yourself laid down in speaking of truth and falsity: that all errors come from forming judgments on matters that we do not see clearly enough. Although physical extension may not be necessary to thought, it isn't repugnant to it either, and could derive from some other function of the soul, one not less essential to it. At least attributing extension to the soul avoids the contradiction of the Scholastics that all soul is entire in all of the body or that it is entire in each one of its parts. Know that I do not excuse myself for confusing the soul with the body for the same reason as the vulgar. That conjecture in no way cures my first doubts.

But I despair of finding certainty in any thing of the world, if you don't give it to me, which is all that keeps me from the skepticism to which my first reasoning led.

Still I owe you this confession, to give you the grace of it. I believe it would be very imprudent if I did not recognize—as much by the experience I have already had of it as by your reputation—a kindness and generosity equal to the rest of your merits. You cannot witness it in a more obliging fashion than by the clarifications and counsels to which you make me a party and which I prize above all the greatest treasures which could be had.

Your very affectionate friend at your service,
Elisabeth

"Know that I do not doubt because of the reasons of the vulgar." Elisabeth, vulgar, common? Unreflectively accepting the unsophisticated arguments of "common" farmers or merchants? Was Descartes perhaps referring to the adventures on the river "en bourgeoisie" that were talked about in town? Indeed, as Sorbière noted, one purpose of those trips was to investigate the views of the "common man" taken up with "trade and provisioning," so important in Dutch politics. And one can see why Elisabeth might want to know what was said about her family's protector, the stadtholder, the prince of Orange, as well as about the Palatines, who were often the butt of irreverent satires and cartoons in the free press of the provinces. In Holland privilege was attached to nobility, but privilege strictly within bounds, associated as much with responsibility as with license. Elisabeth would want to know how her family was viewed, how its cause was perceived. She would want to know how the Dutch people felt about the allowance paid to support the queen of Bohemia and her many children, just as she might have been interested in news from abroad that might not be included in official diplomatic dispatches—the real course of the war? secret communications afoot between England and Spain or France and Sweden? On these topics the commoner, the merchant who traveled Europe, the sailor who visited foreign ports might be more knowledgeable even than her "noble" cousins in the stadtholder's palace.

No, Elisabeth was not confined to the company of the aristocracy. Not only did she travel incognito on the riverboats, but also she attended lectures with Anna van Schurman, visited and studied at the studio of the painter Honthorst. In her freedom of movement, she emulated the distinguished Dutch women painters of her time, Judith Lyster, the pupil of Frans Hals; Rachel Ruysch, known for her paintings of flowers; Elisabeth's own sister Louise, an accomplished painter of flowers and landscapes. The Hague was a busy, bustling city, a modern city, where wealth was leveling many of the distinctions between "vulgar" peasant, churchman, scholar, and privileged aristocrat. Dutch women enjoyed the freedom of the streets, ran businesses, participated in family concerns, learned accounting. All kinds, colors, races, Arabs, Turks, Africans walked the streets of Amsterdam and The Hague and did business in this "mart of Europe."

Elisabeth rejects Descartes's condescension. The common man, he tells her, the nonphilosopher, thinks of the soul and body as one. Is she to think that this is where she should stop with her reflections, because she must be, like common people, too little involved in intellectual life, too much involved in the physical and its distractions to appreciate the higher life of the mind? And if so, is she to accept on faith his arguments for the independence of the soul and get on with whatever superficial studies time and interest allow, think no more about the deep questions, leave them to the philosophers, to men like Descartes, and not make her own inquiry into "first philosophy"?

Certainly Descartes was not the first or last man to give a woman that kind of advice. One remembers the castrated monk Peter Abelard advising his former student and lover, Heloise, to accept his superior theology of divine love,[1] or the French philosopher Jean-Paul Sartre in the Jardin de Luxembourg urging the young Simone de Beauvoir to leave metaphysics to him and get on with applying existentialism to practical problems like the situation of women. But to see here only the condescension of a learned man to a female protégée is a mistake. The advice not to worry about metaphysical questions was advice that, to some degree, Descartes seemed to have taken seriously even for himself. As he explained it in his *Meditations,* once he had removed himself from Paris and set-tled quietly in the Dutch countryside away from visitors and controversy, he sat down once and for all to establish the foundations of knowledge. Then, sure of his ground, he got on with science, without sickly rumination or continual wor-rying of deep questions but with resolution. Establish foundations and then build on them. But the advice, even if it was advice that Descartes took himself, was not acceptable to Elisabeth. The questions that troubled her were not so easily settled.

She will be, she is afraid, as much a nuisance to the philosopher as Voetius and his theological cronies. Still she persists in raising questions. But even as she con-fesses her unwillingness to accept uncritically his teaching, it is clear that he has already become a kind of lifeline, a lifeline of careful, disinterested reason, of attention to issues that transcend the petty personal grievances and grudges of court life. Here was the real promise of philosophy, a discourse that is not caught up in the flow of appetite and desire but that reflects intelligently on its own con-cerns and commitments.

Still, Elisabeth, this extraordinary twenty-four-year-old, cannot hold her sharp tongue. Can he really be suggesting that they leave the muddle alone? Was it not he who laid down in his *Discourse on Method* the rule that one should take noth-ing as true that is not clear and distinct? Should he really have glossed over this difficulty with mind and body? Even more important: might not the uncertainty, if allowed to stand, endanger the whole argument of the *Meditations* and with it the integrity of the new science?

At the end of her letter come again apologies and gratitude that are sincere enough. Where else in that benighted court of the spendthrift queen of Bohemia could she have had this kind of conversation posing deep, frank, careful, engaging questions fundamental to human life? Where but in philosophy could she have found a forum for such inquiries? Where else could she live the life of the mind, which she prized above all of the pleasures and privileges coveted by her mother and sister? Even the learned and celebrated Anna—with her literary pretensions, her mysticism, her reading of the Bible in Hebrew, and her courting of Voetius—did not offer as much as this man.

6

A Test

〜

here was a marked pause. Was Descartes weary of questions, weary of this youthful stinging fly on the back of the great steed of Cartesianism? Or was he simply too busy fighting off Voetius and the Utrecht magistrates to think about the princess? Certainly letters to his male friends were filled with panic. Will he be arrested? Will his papers be seized? His friends reassure him. This is not Spain, or Rome, this is Holland. Galileo's views are openly taught. No one is put under house arrest as Galileo was in Italy. The fact is, outside of Utrecht, he is in no danger. He should let the controversy die down, which it will.

But Descartes cannot leave it alone. He demands satisfaction. The insults eat at him. He turns to Gröningen University, urging its scholars to defend his physics. Controversy flares there too. He maneuvers behind the scenes, complaining bitterly about his treatment. Discouraged, when his lease is up in May, he threatens a return to France. So depressed and angry is he at the Dutch that his friends worry that he will leave Holland for good.

They also might be forgiven for thinking that some of his problems were his own fault. Under Descartes's direction, his follower Rhegius, the professor whom Elisabeth mentioned in her first letter, introduced Cartesianism at Utrecht aggressively and with little skill or tact, which resulted in the escalating and hostile dispute with Voetius. When Voetius was elected rector of the university and Rhegius was forbidden to teach Cartesianism, Descartes himself entered the ring, publishing *Objections to Septima*, in which he describes a theologian, obviously modeled after Voetius, who is bigoted, stupid, pompous, and ignorant. In response to Voetius's heated protest, he aimed even more direct and abusive insults in a public *Letter to Voetius*. It was only then that, claiming libel, Voetius appealed to the Utrecht city council. When Descartes refused to honor the council's summons, arguing that the council should be investigating Voetius's libels against him and that anyway he was out of their jurisdiction, a commission was duly appointed to investigate. While the commission deliberated or, more likely, stalled, hoping the dispute would blow over, Descartes traveled to France.

He returned in the fall, this time to another Egmond, Egmond-binnen, not far from the first one but slightly farther from Utrecht, where he rented a modest villa. In the meantime, the commission issued its verdict. His *Letter to Voetius* was declared libelous and banned. In renewed panic that all of his books might be censored or that he might be expelled from Holland, Descartes launched an all-out war, using all the contacts he had at court with Elisabeth's relatives to lobby for more favorable judgment. He traveled regularly to The Hague, asking that his friends intercede. The prince of Orange intervened, with Elisabeth probably adding her voice. The council reconsidered. The result was a split vote and no decision. The council, attempting to dampen increasingly destructive controversy, declared a moratorium. From then on, nothing could be publicly written either for or against Descartes.

In this atmosphere of tension, Descartes visited the princess in The Hague, no doubt complaining to her about the unfairness with which he was treated. By now they were close friends. He avoided the queen's drawing room and went straight to Elisabeth. It was her he wanted to see, not fashionable visitors who might be enemies or at best waste his time. On one occasion he writes apologies to Pollot, for whom he was to have waited at the princess's apartments. As he came out of Elisabeth's rooms, he explains, he saw some French gallants coming from the queen's apartments and rushed away so as not to be drawn into long, useless conversation and lose his sleep.[1]

What went on between Elisabeth and Descartes in these private sessions we cannot know. Certainly Elisabeth would have given him a sympathetic ear. To distract him, she may have asked him for instruction, if not in metaphysics, at least in mathematics, in which he made so many brilliant innovations. Perhaps, given such a request, he might have worried that he would waste his time tutoring a dilettante. Whatever the pretext, in October, through their old friend Pollot, Descartes assigned to Elisabeth a test problem: given three circles, find a fourth circle that touches all three.[2]

It was an old and difficult problem, one that challenges even professional mathematicians. Descartes, his mind increasingly occupied with the injustice he thought he was suffering at Utrecht, immediately had second thoughts about assigning it to Princess Elisabeth. After more bitter complaints to Pollot about his treatment at Utrecht, he adds at the end of a letter on 21 October, "For the rest, I have much remorse for proposing the problem of the three circles to Madame the princess of Bohemia, because it is so difficult that it seems to me that an angel who had only the algebra taught her by St. [Descartes's mathematical rival Stampioen, Elisabeth's math tutor] would not be able to solve it without a miracle." Even though Pollot has told him that Elisabeth is working on the problem and thinks that she has found a solution, Descartes is still skeptical. Stampioen is clearly ignorant of Descartes's superior innovations in algebraic technique.

Worrying about Elizabeth's possible embarrassment, Descartes sits down to write to her his own solution using two unknowns: "Having learned from M. Pollot that your Highness has taken the trouble to find a solution to the problem of the three circles, and that she has found a way to solve it, with only one unknown, I thought that I ought to put down here the reason why I had proposed several." In considerable detail, Descartes outlines a lesson in algebraic method and its advantages in saving "laborious calculation." In conclusion he adds a dose of flattery: he is afraid that he might have bored her by detailing "easy" things that she knows as well as he, but still these are the keys to "his algebra" as opposed to the algebra of her teacher.

But no, having written that elaborate explanation with all its carefully drawn diagrams and detailed formulas, he demurs. Perhaps, in assuming she will not be able to solve the problem on her own, he will offend. No, he will not send his solution after all. Finally, he decides on a middle course. He writes to Pollot in November, enclosing the unmailed letter of instruction to Elisabeth:

> On what you wrote me last time about Mme. the Princess of Bohemia, I had thought that I should send her the solution to the problem that she thinks she is looking for, and the reason I do not believe that one can solve the problem well by supposing only one unknown. But I do that nevertheless with some scruples because perhaps she would like better to look more herself than to see what I have written. And if it is that, I ask you not to give her my letter right away. I have not put a date on it. Perhaps she has found the solution but not been able to do the calculations, which are long and tiring, and in that case, I would be very glad to have her see my letter, because in it I try to dissuade her from taking so much unnecessary trouble.

What a flurry over a math problem! Has geometry taken the place of love poetry in this "amour intellectuel"? Has math, the very prototype of rational, clear, and distinct ideas, itself been colored with anxious attraction, hurt feeling, the tender longings of love?

As soon as he has written, he is reassured by Pollot. Princess Elisabeth has solved the problem by the old method and sends her solution to Descartes. In a few days, Elisabeth writes to him herself:

> Monsieur Descartes,
>
> 21 November 1643
> If I had as much ease in following your advice as I had trouble, you would find already the effects of your charity in the progress which I have made in reasoning and in Algebra, of which, to date, I have shown you only faults. But I am so accustomed to show to you what comes to me, as a young angler might show an old fisherman his catch, that to omit it would be a shame. I decided to show you the solution to the problem that you gave me, by the method that someone else had taught me, more for the purpose of making you show me its shortcomings than because I was not well versed in your own. For I knew perfectly well that in my solution, there was nothing clear enough to result in a theorem. And I would never have found the reason without your last letter, which has given me all the satisfaction that I asked, and taught me more than I would have learned in six months with my tutor. I am

very indebted to you, and have nothing to pardon M. Palloti for if he had acted according to your order. He would give your solution to me only on condition that I send you what I had done. Do not take it wrong then that I give you a further inconvenience, since there are few things that I would not do to obtain the effects of your good will, which is infinitely esteemed by

your very affectionate friend at your service,
Elisabeth

"Old fisherman"? A bit harsh. Is that how Descartes thought of himself, as a stooped-over grandfather to whom an eager youth holds up the trophy of a math-ematical fish? Was he so old then? But whatever the slight to his vanity, it is over-shadowed by delighted surprise at Elisabeth's mathematical abilities. Descartes responds:

The solution that it pleased your Highness to give me the honor of receiving from you is so just that no more could be desired. And I was not only bowled over with astonishment in seeing it, but I cannot help adding that I was ravished with joy and I couldn't help the vanity of seeing that the calculation that your Highness used is very much like the calculation I proposed in my Geometry. Experience has taught me that most people who have facility in understanding the reasoning of meta-physics cannot conceive those in Algebra, and reciprocally, that those who compre-hend easily the latter are normally incapable of the other. But I see that is not true of your Highness, to whom all things are easy. It is true that I have already so many proofs that I could not have doubted it, but I thought only that she might lack the patience that is necessary in the beginning to overcome the difficulties of calcula-tion. For it is a quality that is extremely rare in people of excellence and great estate.

Now without any hesitation, Descartes proceeds, page after page, to explain and diagram his new method using two unknowns, no longer making any conces-sion to aristocratic or girlish ineptitude. Elisabeth has passed a test more crucial than metaphysics. She has an aptitude for mathematics, the key to Descartes's universe.

7

The Philosophic Muse

~

or almost a year after Elisabeth solved the math problem, Descartes is busy traveling, arranging the publication in Holland of his *Principles of Philosophy* and visiting France to distribute and introduce his book. No doubt there are visits to Elisabeth as he passes back and forth through The Hague. Then the visits stop. Descartes is away in France, out of touch. That next summer Elisabeth falls ill, the first of many illnesses that would plague her throughout her life.

It was a trying time for the Palatines. Henriette, wife of the king of England, disturbed the peace of the Orange court with a long visit, requiring not only pomp and ceremony but also funds to support the royalist cause for her beleaguered husband. She was finally gone, but not until Elisabeth's favorite brother, Rupert, along with her brother Maurice, had been dispatched with her in a Dutch warship to fight for the king. At home, Elisabeth's older brother, the heir, Charles-Louis, was infuriating her mother by showing sympathy with the parliamentary side in England, and family dissension rocked the brick town house on the Lange Voorhout. In the meantime the situation of King Charles in England worsened. Elisabeth, worried about her younger brothers' safety and trying unsuccessfully to intercede between her mother and her older brother, came down with fever.

When he heard of her illness, Descartes wrote a letter of medical advice from Paris. Gradually Elisabeth recovered, but without much of her old spirit. Her philosopher was gone. There was no more private tutoring, no more math lessons, no more interesting metaphysical speculations. She languished in the queen's drawing room, trying to mediate between warring factions and usually succeeding only in bringing someone's anger and irritation down on her own head. Soon, however, she had more startling and public proof of Descartes's regard for her. When his *Principles of Philosophy* appeared in print, it was prefaced by a public letter in which Descartes dedicated the book to "To the Most Serene Princess, Elizabeth, Eldest Daughter of Frederick, King of Bohemia, Count Palatine and Elector of the Holy Roman Empire."

If dedications to royal patrons were commonplace, the explanation that Descartes appended was unique. Not only did his praise for Elisabeth have a sincerity missing from the usual stock eulogy to a patron, but it was grounded in a philosophy of virtue. The great reward from publishing his writings, he said, was that he had come to the princess's notice and had been able to converse with her. To describe her, he said, he did not have to use the arts of flattery; he needed only to describe and explain the unvarnished truth about her merits. Some virtue, he theorized, is the fault of ignorance—a person may be kind simply because he is simple-minded; but true virtue is a combination of both the knowledge of what is best and the will to carry it out. This is the virtue that Elisabeth possessed. Not only was she kind, modest, brave, but also, unlike most princesses, she had a taste for learning and was adept in geometry and metaphysics, the greatest proof of which is that she understands his writings. Descartes recalls his pleasure in her friendship. What a surprise it was for him to find intellectual virtue not in some dried-up professor but in "a Young Princess whose face and years are more representative of the Graces than either a Muse or a wise Minerva." And in addition to beauty of body and mind, she had the other component of virtue, strength of will. Though fate had injured her unjustly, she was not bitter or dejected.

The latter compliment was more wish than description. Descartes must have known how disturbed Elisabeth was at the state of her family, her mother railing at her brother, the prince of Orange sending arms to England against the stated policy of the Dutch government, Rupert in danger, the family finances in ruins. In addition, the indiscretions of her sister Louise, high-spirited, artistic in temperament, unstable in behavior, continued to subject the family to ridicule and gossip. In the background was always war, maiming, killing, and destroying her homeland. Eventually even darker events would test the princess's courage and fortitude and turn a lively dark-haired girl in a light-colored gown cavorting on the riverboats into a sober matron. Now, before the worst came, Descartes's praise of her might have been enough to restore her spirits and her health.

She was grateful, not just for the public acknowledgment of her abilities, but also for the sense that she had been part of such important work. She writes to Descartes, still in France distributing his book.

The Hague
1 August 1644

Monsieur Descartes,

The present [of the *Principles*] which M. Van Bergen has given me on your behalf obliges me to render you grace and my conscience accuses me of not being able to do so according to its merits. If I only received the good which has come of your book for our century—the century which owes you everything that previous history has paid to the inventors of science since you alone have demonstrated that there is a science—it would be enough. But to what proportion will mount the debt of someone to whom you give, along with your instruction, a part of your glory in a public testimony to me of friendship and approval.

Pedants will say that you have been forced to create a new morality to render me worthy. But I take that morality for a rule of life, only feeling in the first person what you approve: the desire to inform the understanding and the will to pursue the good that it recognizes. It is to this very will that I owe my understanding of your work, which is only obscure to those who examine it by the principles of Aristotle, or with very little care. The most rational of our doctors have confessed to me that they do not really study your work, because they are too old to begin a new method, having used up the strength of their body and mind in old age.

But I believe that you will justly retract the opinion you have of my understanding once you find out that I do not understand how quicksilver is formed, both so full of agitation and so heavy, contrary to the definition you have given of heaviness. And also when the body E, in the figure on page 255, presses it when it is above, why does it resist this contrary force when it is below, any more than air does in leaving a ship which it has been pressing?

The second difficulty which I have found is that of making the particles curved like a shell pass by the center of the Earth, without being folded or disfigured by the fire which is found there, as they would be in the beginning in order to form the body M. It is only their speed that could save them, and you say on pages 133 and 134 that it is not really necessary to be formed in a straight line and in consequence, that these are parts least agitated by the first element which flows there by the globules of the second. I am equally surprised that they make such a grand tour in leaving the poles of the body M and pass by the surface of the earth to return to the other, since they can find a shorter path by body C.

I only represent here the reasons for doubts about your book, those for my admiration are innumerable, as are also the reasons for my obligations to you, among which I count still the kindness that you have had in letting me know your news and giving me prescriptions for the preservation of my health. These give me much joy for the good success of your journey and for your continuing plan to return, as well as profit for me, since I have experienced already the kindness to myself of that return. You have not shown to M. Voetius the danger to him in being your enemy, the way you have shown to me the advantage in your beneficence. Otherwise, I would not have as much the title, as I try to merit it, of being

your very affectionate friend at your service,
Elisabeth

A new ethic invented for her, invented to do her honor: virtue in knowing what is best and having the will to act on that knowledge as far as it is in one's power? Gratifying, but hardly the truth, as Elisabeth knew. This was no ethic invented for her. It was Descartes's own "provisional ethic," outlined in the *Discourse on Method*, tacked on in response to critics who charged that his method of doubt could lead to an inability to act at all, provisional until science delivers complete knowledge and the best thing to do becomes certain. What irony that this great public praise is not invented for her, is not for her own proper virtue at all, but for a virtue she will now persistently disclaim. Know the best, have the will to carry it out, be content and untroubled by guilt or painful hindsight. Whatever Elisabeth's virtue, it was not this.

Adroit and grateful nonetheless, she turns Descartes's counterfactual praise to reciprocal compliment. If indeed she has the supposed virtue of detachment, she exercises it with his work: she has seen the best in it and tried to make it her intellectual guide. In defense of her friend, she upbraids the laziness of the Utrecht professors who have disturbed his concentration. They would not even take the trouble to read his work. She expresses gratification that she, no professor and only an amateur scholar, has been able to make up in some small way for their stupidity and laziness. Just as Descartes acknowledged the difficulty of her situation, she deplores the draining, vociferous, mean-spirited struggle in which he is involved. Voetius, to her regret, has turned even Anna van Schurman against Cartesianism, thus ending her friendship with Elisabeth.[1]

Again Elisabeth is a close and careful reader, capable of a sophistication of thought that allows her to make technical criticisms of the detail of Descartes's physics, as well as address larger philosophical problems. The inconsistencies she points to in her letter are particular and specific, fruit of her own scientific understanding. Is this still a humble pupil, or is she more a coworker? At first courtier and princess, then tutor and pupil, now writer and editor, even collaborator in ongoing work. Certainly Elisabeth is no transparent mirror reflecting a famous man's philosophy. Instead, she is something more valuable, a woman on her own account worried about the accuracy of the "new philosophy" of modernity and all it promises. The developing mutual promotion of progressive thought can no longer be confused with flirtation, or tutelage or patronage, but is an interchange of ideas and thoughts based on mutual respect.

It is something she must have longed for. She had never been popular at her mother's court. Too studious, too little interested in keeping up appearances, too little in sympathy with extravagant display, she constantly irritated her mother and her sister with her silent and not so silent criticisms. Years before, when she first arrived at her mother's side at fifteen, she was greeted with derisive laughter. "The very image of the Electress Juliana" was the reported response of the prince of Orange to the grave face in which he saw a resemblance to the sometimes inconvenient sobriety and good sense of Elisabeth's grandmother. Certainly in Palatine affairs Juliana had been a lone voice of caution.

In her mother's household, Elisabeth was quite alone. She was out of sympathy with her sister Louise. Her irrepressible little sister Sophie was still at the children's house in Leyden. She had no allies. Her studiousness, her habit of reading late at night, her reputation for learning, what was taken as her defeatist attitude to family fortunes, most of all her disapproval of flirtations and excessive expenditure angered her mother, as it did her sister Louise. Who wanted such a gloomy professorial presence around, when there were balls, admirers, promises, intrigues to enjoy?

In the midst of it all, Descartes's dedicatory preface, as full of kind hopes for her happiness as of overestimation of her ability or willingness to accept his Stoic ethic, might have brought a rush of tears. She knew that there would be a dedication, but not that it would have so linked her character and achievements to philosophy.

8

Doctor-Philosopher

~

escartes answered her acknowledgment promptly in August 1644. He was still in Paris, drawn into worrying disputes, tired to death of debate with people for whom he has little respect or admiration; Elisabeth's friendship offers him a welcome respite.

> The favor which your Highness has done me in not having found it disagreeable that I have witnessed in public how much I esteem and honor her, is too great, and obliges me more than anything I could have received elsewhere. And I do not think that anyone will accuse me of having changed anything of Morality in making known my sentiments on the subject. For what I have written there is so true and so clear that I am assured that no reasonable man would deny it. But I am afraid that what I have put in the rest of the book, is more doubtful and obscure, since Y.H. [your Highness] finds difficulties.

He goes on to explain and qualify his theories but apologizes for his lack of concentration. He is always traveling now, which makes it hard to think, and he has not got with him the copy she marked with her annotations, but he hopes that in two or three months he will again be in The Hague and they can meet and discuss at leisure the points she raises. His friends are trying to persuade him to stay and establish residence again in France. Elisabeth's letter recalls him to his old peaceful life in Holland and the pleasures of companionship. In November he is back in Egmond-binnen, exhausted.

He confessed to Pollot a great weariness. Paris had taken more out of him than he thought. He must recoup his strength, study nature on his little farm, surround himself with plants and animals. Resting, absorbed in his researches, happy in the peace of the countryside, he did not write to his friend Elisabeth nor call on her. Then, in May of the next year, he heard that she was ill again, this time gravely ill.

Throughout that winter, with Descartes back from France but incommunicado in his country retreat, there had been continuing concern for Elisabeth's health. When Descartes finally heard about her illness from Pollot, he asked whether he should make the trip to inquire in person. Pollot reassured him, probably on Elisabeth's orders, that she was better and that he, Pollot, would write to Descartes if there was any real problem.

Still claiming exhaustion, Descartes gave the matter little more thought. He shut out the world that had disappointed him, he concentrated only on his work. Receiving no further word from Pollot, he assumed that Elisabeth was well. Then he again had reports of her illness. For three or four weeks she had been ill with fever and a dry cough, even delirious for four or five days. Again Pollot reassured him that she was doing better. With perhaps some pangs of guilt at his self-absorption, Descartes answered Pollot on 18 May 1645 with more excuses. He was very concerned before to hear about the princess's illness, so concerned that he "would have gone" to The Hague as soon as he had heard if Pollot had not added that the princess was doing better. Indeed, he himself was not very well. As he explains to Pollot,

> I must tell you that, since my trip to France, I have become twenty years older than I was last year, so that now it is a greater voyage to go to The Hague than before it was to go as far as Rome. It is not so much that I have any illness, by the grace of God, but I feel myself more feeble, and feel that I have more need to seek out my own convenience and rest.

Given, however, that his medical advice had been taken favorably the summer before, Descartes sat down to write to Elisabeth on 19 May 1645 to offer again his medical opinion.

> I have been extremely surprised to learn, by letter from Pollot, that Y. H. has been sick for a long time, and I blame my solitude for making it so that I did not know this sooner. Even though it is true that I am so much withdrawn from the world that I know nothing of what is happening, still the zeal which I have in the service of your Highness should not allow me to go so long without knowing the state of her health. I would have gone to The Hague expressly to enquire about her if Monsieur Pollot, writing to me in haste about two months ago, had not promised to write again by the next mail. And since he never omits to tell me how your Highness is doing, and since I did not receive any letters, I had supposed that you were always in the same state. But I have learned in his last letter that your Highness has had for three or four weeks now a slow fever, accompanied by a dry cough, and that after being delirious for five or six days, the illness returned and that, anyway, at the time that he wrote to me—which was close to fifteen days in transit—your Highness began a second time to do better. With this I detected the signs of a serious illness, and even though it is one from which your Highness will certainly recover, I cannot keep from sending her my regards. For though I am not a medical doctor, the honor which your Highness gave me last summer, of wanting to know my opinion on another indisposition that she had then makes me hope that such a liberty will not be disagreeable to her.

The letter of medical advice that Descartes wrote the previous summer was the first of many that Descartes would write advising Elisabeth about her health. For Descartes, a science free from superstition and metaphysically grounded in the separation of the mind from the body was not only a speculative study. If the mathematical representation of reality reveals the truth, it must also show what is best to do. Science would, he believed, clearly indicate the most efficient way to weave cloth, the most accurate way to grind lenses, and the best way to treat illness. In that spirit, in the next three years, Descartes took on the job of doctor-philosopher as Elisabeth struggled with a variety of health problems. She would not always take his advice, for reasons she would explain, but she was continually grateful for what must have been more important to her than medicine—a real and disinterested concern for her and her welfare, a concern all too rare in her mother's household.

Obviously worried, although still not worried enough to warrant a trip to the city, Descartes brings the full weight of his science to bear on Elisabeth's condition, introducing philosophical and moral topics that will be a constant source of discussion and dispute between them in the years to come. He writes with some confidence:

The ordinary cause of a slow fever is sadness. The perseverance of Fortune in the persecution of your house brings on you continually irritation so public and so striking that it is not possible to use much conjecture or to be very much involved in these matters to judge that this is the principal cause of your indisposition. And it is probable that you would not be in such a delirium if only, by the power of your virtue, you would make your soul content in spite of the disgraces of Fortune. I know that it would be imprudent to want to persuade a person to feel joy when every day sends her new subjects for displeasure, and I am not one of those cruel Philosophers who wish their sages to be without feeling. I also know that your Highness is not so affected by what regards her in particular as she is by what regards the interests of her House and the persons she cares about. That I esteem as the most likable of virtues. But it seems to me that the difference which there is between great souls and base vulgar souls consists principally in that vulgar souls give themselves up to their passions and are only happy or unhappy insofar as the things that happen to them are agreeable or displeasing. Whereas noble souls have arguments that are so strong and so powerful that, even when they, too, are suffering from passion, and even from passions more violent then the usual ones, nevertheless their reason remains the master, and even makes those afflictions serve it and contribute to the perfect felicity which they enjoy thereafter in this life. For on the one side considering themselves immortal and capable of receiving very great contentments, and on the other side considering that they are joined with a mortal and fragile body subject to many infirmities which cannot not help but perish in a few years, they do everything they can to make Fortune favorable in this life, but at the same time they value it so little in regard to Eternity that they almost think of events only as acted-out dramas. And just as the sad and lamentable Histories which we see represented in the theater often give us as much entertainment as happy Histories, even as they bring tears to our eyes, so the greatest souls, of which I speak, have a satisfaction in themselves from all the things which happen to them, even the most infuriating and unbearable. Feeling grief in their heart, they work to bear it patiently, and this proof that they have of their own power is agreeable to them. Seeing their friends in great affliction, they sympathize with their trouble, and do all that is possible to help them and do not fear even death in this endeavor if it is necessary. Meanwhile, however, the witness their conscience gives them that they are doing their duty, and are performing actions that are lovable and virtuous, make them more happy than all the sadness which compassion inflicts on them can make them sad. And, in the end, just as the greatest good Fortune does not inebriate them, and does not make them more insolent, so the greatest adversities cannot strike them down or make them so sad that the body to which they are joined falls ill.

Her illness Descartes diagnoses as depression, not surprising given the tragic events of her life. For such an illness, his dualist metaphysics is the cure. The separation between mind and body allows a "noble" rational soul to be in opportunistic control of passion. Noble souls can even get a pleasurable feeling of power as they master emotion, a pleasurable satisfaction that they are doing the right thing. This morality, a further elaboration of the provisional morality of the *Discourse*, now medicalized to give a prescription for Elisabeth's illness, is flower and fruit of Descartes's metaphysics.

Descartes reiterates his conviction that Elisabeth will be able to profit from her condition because she has an "elevated soul." Because of that, he writes, she "ought to be among the most happy, and she will be that in fact, provided that she turn her eyes to what is beneath her, and compare the value of the goods she possesses which never can be taken away, to the good things Fortune has deprived her of and the disgraces with which she is persecuted in the person of her relatives." He concludes with a final assurance: "Then she will see the great reason she has to be content with her own advantages."

To this rather extraordinary advice, Elisabeth responds immediately, defending a very different ethics that she will continue to elaborate.

24 May 1645
The Hague

Monsieur Descartes,

I see that the charms of the solitary life do not rob you of the virtues required in society. The generous kindness you have for your friends and for me witnesses to the concern you have for my health. I am angry that they would have involved you in making a trip all the way here given that M. Palloti told me that you have judged that repose is necessary to your health. And I assure you that the doctors, who see me every day and look at all the symptoms of my illness, have not found the cause, nor have they ordered remedies as salutary as those you have ordered from a distance. If they had been sufficiently wise to suspect the part my spirit plays in disordering the body, I would not have had the frankness to confess it to them. But to you, Monsieur, I confess it without scruple, assuring myself that such a naive recitation of my defects would not lose me the part I have in your friendship but would confirm it all the more, since you will see how necessary it is to me.

Know then that I have a body imbued with a great part of the weakness of my sex, know that it registers very easily afflictions of the soul and does not have the strength to be quit of them, being of a temperament subject to obstructions and remaining in a climate which contributes to them. For persons who cannot do much exercise like myself, a long oppression of the heart from sadness is not necessary to disrupt the spleen and infect the rest of the body with vapors. I think that the slow fever and dry cough which is still there even with the heat of the season and the walks which I take to rally my forces come from this lack of exercise. It is this which makes me consent to the advice of the doctors, to drink in a month's time the Spa waters (which will be brought here without letting them spoil), having found, by experience, that they dispel obstructions. But I will not take them before I know your opinion, since you have the kindness to wish me to cure my body along with the mind.

I continue to confess to you that although I do not place my happiness only on things which depend on fortune or on the will of men, or think myself absolutely unfortunate, when I see that my house will never be reinstated or my dear ones far from misery, I cannot consider the sad accidents that befall them as other than evil, nor can I see the actions I take to serve them useless without much inquietude, which soon as it is calmed by reason is aroused by yet another disaster. If my life was completely known to you, you would find it more strange that I survived so long with a sensitive spirit like mine and a weak body, given that I have only the counsel of my own reason and only the consolation of my conscience, that very conscience which you make the cause of my present illness,

I was employed all last winter in affairs so infuriating that they kept me from using the liberty which you granted me to present to you the difficulties I found in my studies and gave me other difficulties which would require even less stupidity than mine to get out of. I only found a little leisure before my indisposition to read the philosophy of M. Chevalier Digby, which is written in English, from which I hoped to take arguments to refute yours, since the summary of the Chapters shows two places where he pretends to have done so. But I was very surprised when I got to it to see that he had not at all understood either what he approved in your sentiment of reflection or what he denied in your sentiment of refraction, not making any distinction between the movement of a ball and its determination, and not considering why a soft body which gives retards the one, and that a hard body only resists the other. For a part of what he says on the movement of the heart he is more excusable, because he has not read what you wrote about it to the Louvain doctor. Doctor Johnson has told me that he will translate for you these two chapters, and I think you will not have great curiosity about the rest of the book, because it is of the caliber and follows the method of that English priest who gives himself the name Albanus. Even though he has there some very beautiful Meditations, one would have difficulty expecting more from a man who has passed most of his life in following the designs of either love or ambition. I would never be more strong and more constant than in being, all my life,

your very affectionate friend at your service,

Elisabeth

P.S. In rereading what I have written of my own affairs, I see that I forgot one of your maxims, which is never to put into writing, anything which would be wrongly interpreted by unfriendly readers. But I trust so much to the care of M. Palloti that I know that my letter will be well delivered, and to your discretion, that you will avert by the fire any chance that it might fall into bad hands.

Again there is the subtle mixture of compliment and reproach. Had the charms of solitary life—Descartes's well-tended garden, his accomplished cook, his leisurely researches—robbed him of the virtues of sociality? Of friendship? A harsh judgment, one that Elisabeth is charitable enough to allow his letter to dispel. But the suggestion remains, and in the succeeding correspondence it is exactly these virtues of sociality that are defended by Elisabeth and undermined by Descartes.

Is there a pinprick in the reference to his health, to the malaise that keeps him in the country, only a short way from the city where she is suffering a serious, even potentially fatal, illness? Can weariness really be compared to what she is going through? Is there irony in her concern that Pollot might have urged him to come to town when he needed his "repose"?

There is no doubt that she is in need of friends. Tension at court grows. Royalist defeats in England cast doubt that the family will recover any money from that source. Cromwell and his army are a more efficient opponent for the king than the ineffectual Parliament. In The Hague debts mount as the queen indulges her pet dogs and monkeys and her favorite servants. The stress is evidenced by Elisabeth's new caution. Spies, intrigues, enemies are everywhere. Descartes should burn her letter to prevent it from falling into the wrong hands. The family has fewer and fewer friends. The peace talks at Münster are looking more like a dividing of the spoils than a restitution of Palatine territories. Three of her brothers are in danger. Her mother's attention is riveted on Charles-Louis, the eldest son and heir, now in complicity with parliamentary interests.[1] Her old friend Mrs. Croft is berated regularly at the house in The Hague for telling tales back in London of the frivolity and wastefulness of the Palatine household.

Elisabeth, gracious as always, compares her doctor-philosopher favorably to her medical doctors, and compliments him on his diagnosis, a diagnosis that, nevertheless, she does not let go unchallenged. "Know that I have a body." Was Descartes in danger of forgetting it? Not the imagined body of an angel but the body of a woman, a physical body, prone to "obstructions," with all the "weaknesses" of a woman's body, with its menstruations, ovulations, constipations. Even more important, a body that registers a marked sensitivity to events, to other persons and their troubles, a body forced to live in exile from its native land, in the damp chill of a Dutch winter with poor heating, forced to breathe city air polluted with smoke and dirt. Add the restrictions of class and sex: outings on the riverboats outlawed by bad health, walking the streets by impropriety, the only permissible movement a pacing back and forth in the small walled back gar-den or a quick circuit of the lime-tree-lined square to try to dispel the worry of the latest news from abroad.

As she wrote, she might have imagined him in very different circumstances. He works in his garden, strolls down to the river in the fresh air. He is free to do as he wishes with his time. Really, she tells him, metaphysical dualism is not nec-essary to understand the physical causes of her illness. Even now, when she tries to walk in the warm weather, she is still troubled by a cough. Given this inactivi-ty, she thinks a physical cure, a purgative, may indeed be most useful.

So much for medical advice. The moral advice, well, there she is even less tractable. In fact, she cannot see that he understands her situation at all. With some frustration, she accuses him of misdescribing and diminishing her condition. There is much that she cannot write about, at least by mail. Perhaps if he would come, visit, take the trouble to inquire in person and not rely on Pollot. But she does not say that.

Clearly she has not taken his advice to stay away from books but is continuing to be of service to the new philosophy, this time reporting to Descartes on the writing of Sir Kenelm Digby, an aristocratic English writer, whom Descartes had met on his visit to France. Digby, though a declared supporter of the new mechan-ical science of Galileo and Descartes, claimed to note some errors in Descartes's physics. Because Descartes was not able to read English, Elisabeth, good colleague that she is, takes on the task of assessing his arguments. Should Descartes worry with them? Her answer is no. She promises to arrange some translations for him.

Descartes writes back from his retreat at the end of May or the beginning of June expressing a degree of understanding of her situation.

> I can easily conceive the many displeasures that constantly present themselves to your Highness, and which are that much more difficult to overcome in that often they are of such a nature that there is good reason not to oppose oneself directly to them or try to pursue them. These are domestic enemies, with which one must con-verse and therefore be constantly on one's guard so as to keep them from doing harm.

But still, he says, he knows only one remedy: withdraw the imagination and sense from tragic happenings and consider them only when necessary and then only with the mind alone.

> I believe a person who would otherwise have much reason to be content, but who sees continually played out in front of her Tragedies whose Acts are funereal, but who still only occupies herself in considering objects of sadness and pity that she knows to be deceitful and false and that must draw tears from her eyes and move her imagination without touching her understanding, this, I say, alone is sufficient to accustom such a person's heart to constrict and to throw out sighs.

Descartes goes on to describe at some length his account of the physical effects of sadness on the organs of the body. Again he advises that if she refrains from thinking of such things and only considers nice things, and if she takes some mild medicines such as spa water to relieve the physical symptoms, she will not only restore her health but also will be able to make judgments that are "saner." Foreshadowing nineteenth-century medical advice to "hysterical" women, he advises against intellectual work. "[I]t is necessary to deliver the spirit of all sorts of sad thoughts, and also of all sorts of serious meditations regarding the sciences, and occupy oneself only in imitating those who, in looking at the greenness of a wood, the colors of a flower, the flight of a bird, and such things which require no attention, persuade themselves that they are thinking of nothing."

Descartes adds an uncharacteristic personal confidence. He too has been troubled by emotional illness like hers:

> I have experienced in myself that an illness, almost identical to yours and even more dangerous, can be cured by the remedy I have just told you about. Being born of a mother who died, a few days after my birth, of an illness of the lungs caused by some unhappiness, I inherited from her a dry cough and a pale complexion that I had until I was twenty years old and that made all the doctors who saw me up to that time condemn me to an early death.

Descartes was doing some staging of his own for Elisabeth's benefit. According to the parish records in Descartes's native Touraine, he was born on 31 March 1596, but it was not directly after his birth that his mother died. Instead, according to the records, she died thirteen months later, after giving birth to a second infant son who also died soon after.[2] Glossing over this discrepancy, Descartes testifies to self-cure by his method of positive thinking: "I believe that the inclination that I have had always of regarding the things which present themselves with a bias which makes them more agreeable than not, and insuring that my principal happiness depends only on myself, made this indisposition, which was natural to me, little by little entirely disappear."

Descartes's advice is to ease the pain. Without the arsenal of drugs that will eventually flower from the new science to release emotion's hold on the suffering body, Descartes's medicine is the force of will—the will to see only the positive, to concentrate on one's own happiness, the will to forget and ignore.

Elisabeth answers.

22 June 1645

Monsieur Descartes:

Your letters always serve as an antidote for melancholy, even when they do not instruct me—by turning my spirit away from the disagreeable things which are furnished to it every day—how to make it contemplate the happiness which I possess in having the friendship of a person of your merit to whose counsel I can commit the conduct of my life. If I could follow your last advice, I do not doubt that I would cure myself right away of the maladies of my body and weaknesses of my spirit. But

I confess that I have trouble separating sense and imagination from things which are continually represented in discussion and letters, because I do not know how to do it without sinning against my duty.

I understand well that in taking away from an idea of an affair everything that makes me angry (which I believe is only represented by the imagination), I would judge more sanely and would soon find a remedy for the emotion I bring to them. But I have never known how to practice this except after passion has played its role. There is something surprising about misfortune, which, even when foreseen, I can master only after a period of time and which disorders my body so strongly that I need several months to put it aside, months which never pass without some new subject of trouble. Regardless of the fact that I make myself govern my spirit with care and give it agreeable objects, the least weakness makes it fall again on subjects which affect it adversely. I know that if I do not do this at all while I take the waters, it will not make me less melancholy. If I could profit, as you do, from all that is presented to your senses, I would divert myself but without ridding myself of it. This is when I feel the inconvenience of being a little rational. Because, if I was not at all rational, I would find common pleasures with those with whom I must live, and take that medicine with profit. And if I were as rational as you are, I would cure myself as you have done.

In this, the malediction of my sex prevents the contentment I would get from a trip to Egmond, to understand at first hand the truths which you draw from your new garden. Nevertheless, I console myself with the liberty you give me to ask from time to time for news, in the quality of

> your very affectionate friend, at your service
> Elisabeth

It is his concern, she tells him, the concern evidenced each time he writes with his advice, that is the best cure for her melancholy. How she must have longed for such attention. Her welfare was of little interest to her mother, who seemed to want her only as a convenient supervisor of younger brothers and sisters. Her father was dead, her older brothers away. Her mother, never warm, was critical of Elisabeth's dress and demeanor and impatient with her illnesses. What is balm is Descartes's caring, not the advice, which she cannot really take, will not take, except to extract from it the tonic of gratitude for disinterested friendship.

How different they are. Descartes, involved, yes, but in acrimonious intellectual disputes that he conducts from a safe distance, surrounded by the well-ordered household of a single life, free to walk, to observe nature, to pick pears and cherries in his orchard, to ease his mind in contemplation. Elisabeth, in contrast, living in the midst of a large unruly family with little respect for her privacy, a family whose neglect makes her that much more vulnerable to their demands.

Descartes says she should separate imagination and feeling from thought, look at painful events with reason only, do what is necessary, and then return to pleasurable pursuits. She should do as he does: live for the simple pleasures of the table, the "green of a wood, the colors of a flower, the flight of a bird." Elisabeth's reply: I cannot do this without sinning against duty. What keeps her from the supposedly therapeutic separation of mind and body is not lack of will but rather a will not to forget her obligations. The context of Elisabeth's virtue is life in time, life in history, a life from which Descartes has removed himself. In the surprise of events, she says, unless one is completely insensitive, there is no avoiding pain, a pain that lingers in the mind and body long after a crisis is past. Deep worry brings pain that no diversion can erase, pain that surfaces no matter what remedial plea- sure one tries to procure. Are the events of a life to be lined up in a row, so a per- son can pick and choose which to care about, which to ignore? Elisabeth exists in a flow of events, negotiating unpredictable currents that are never completely foreseeable. In that flow, it is never possible to be completely rational. But neither is Elisabeth, like so many around her in public affairs, unreflective, reactive, manipulative. She is between rationality and emotion, she is both body and mind. A difficult condition to maintain, but the key to virtue as she conceives it.

Oh, the pathos of that last wish. She would like to see his new garden, share the good table with which he never failed to provide himself, walk out with his guests after dinner, smell the flowers, and see the newborn lambs. She would like to take that trip that the "malediction" of her sex forbids, enjoy what her doctor- philosopher takes for granted, his freedom and autonomy. Is there another regret? The regret that men, not only evil men or abusive men but loving and caring men, men like Descartes with both virtues and faults, have such trouble imagining the restrictions on the life of a woman. Could she hope that he might notice the small scope of the "liberty" with which she consoles herself, the liberty of asking him for news of the life of an independent scholar living at ease in isolated comfort?

9

A Life Blessed with Happiness

~

*B*ut perhaps he has noticed, because immediately he responds, turning his neglect into a compliment. She must forgive him for not feeling bad about her illnesses when he gets her letters: her thoughts are so "clear" and her reasoning so "firm" that he cannot believe that such a strong spirit could exist in an infirm body. He has so much faith in her knowledge of illness and medicines that he knows that she will know the right treatments. He defends his previous advice against her objections.

> I know that it is almost impossible to resist the first pangs of pain that new misfortunes excite in us, but even though it is ordinarily the best of spirits whose passions are the most violent and act strongest on their bodies, still it seems to me that the next day, when sleep has calmed the heat which comes in the blood in such encounters, one can begin to put down the spirit and make it calm. One can do that by trying to consider all the advantages which can be drawn from the thing which one took as a great unhappiness the day before, and in turning one's attention away from the evils which one has imagined. For there are no events so dreadful, nor so absolutely bad in the judgments of people, that a person of spirit cannot look on them with a bias which makes them appear favorable.

For an added dose of positive thinking, Descartes adds a caveat about the dangers of prosperity. Those who are fortunate can become drunk with success. Adversity, on the other hand, gives one the opportunity to exercise one's spirit. Much as the tone of this advice might be dismissive, Descartes's persistence and repetition sound a genuine note of concern. He does not want Elisabeth to suffer. And to that end he will even leave his retreat and come to The Hague if she thinks that he can help to distract her with intellectual matters. "I have more desire to come to The Hague to learn the virtues of Spa waters than to learn here the virtues of the plants in my garden," he tells her.

Descartes, true to his word, visited, finding the princess still not completely well. Back at his country retreat, he writes again. She has told him how much his letters mean to her, how much they make up for her suffering. But from now on there will be no tiring mathematics; instead, he prescribes a tonic he will administer himself. The weather has been so cold that he, like her doctors, is afraid that spa waters may not be good for her. Since the doctors have forbidden her demanding reading so as not to impede her digestion, and because she has told him how much pleasure his letters give her, he announces his intention: He will write to her regularly but only for the purpose of her pleasure and entertainment. Is she so accustomed to bad news that she reads it into any letter that comes to her now? If so, she can be assured there will be nothing disturbing in his letters. Descartes writes almost playfully, a philosophical troubadour amusing his lady.

> I imagine that most of the letters that you get otherwise give you emotion, and that even before reading them, you fear that you will find in them some news that displeases you. The malignity of fortune has accustomed you for a long time to receive so very often such news. But for those letters that come from here, you are at least assured that, even if they do not give you any occasion for joy, at least they will not give you anything to be sad about. You can open them at any time without fearing that they will disturb your digestion of the waters that you are taking. For since I learn in this unfrequented place nothing of what goes on in the rest of the world and have no thoughts more frequent than those which represent to me the virtues of your Highness and make me wish to see her as happy and as content as she deserves, I have no other subject with which to entertain you than to talk of the ways that philosophy teaches us to acquire sovereign happiness, that which vulgar souls wait for in vain from fortune but that we know we have in ourselves.

He will write about philosophy because he has no other subject. But no more metaphysics, and not mathematics, either. Something lighter, less demanding, and less disturbing. Descartes draws on the past, on an ancient tradition of philosopher sage discoursing on the good life. Not Epicurus, whose revival is the trademark of Descartes's rival Gassendi. No, he chooses a less fashionable figure, Seneca, on the *vita beata*, the blessed life, the happy life. They will read Seneca together—that is, unless she has another book to suggest. And he can learn from her, too. If she is willing to give him her thoughts, she will help him to clarify his own ideas. For another troubadour, it might have been love songs. Descartes's offering is philosophy, a gentler philosophy this time than mathematical science, aimed at the good and happy life.

He writes again in early August, already unhappy with his choice. He chose Seneca because of reputation, but now he finds that Seneca does not approach the topic of the good life with sufficient "exactitude." He proposes a new plan. Instead of discoursing on what Seneca wrote, he will tell her what he thinks Seneca should have written. Seneca wrote, "Everyone wishes to live a happy life, but as for having a view of what brings about the happy life, they are in the dark." Wrong, said Descartes. What makes for happiness is very clear: It is "perfect contentment of spirit" and "an interior satisfaction" that does not depend on being favored by fortune. Yes, if you take two men, equally wise and virtuous, one rich and well born and one poor, the rich man will have the most perfect contentment.

Nevertheless, just as a small glass can be as full as one that is bigger even though it contains less liquor, so, taking the contentment of each as the fulfillment and accomplishment of his desires as regulated by his reason, I do not doubt that those who are poorer and more disgraced by fortune or nature can be just as completely content and satisfied as others are, even though they cannot enjoy as many goods.

All they need to do, he goes on, is to observe the three rules he laid down in his *Discourse*. First, try as far as possible to find out rationally what is the best thing to do. Second, have a "firm and consistent resolution" to do what reason has counseled without letting passion or appetite get in the way. Third, do not want anything outside one's power to obtain. The only thing that can take away the contentment that results is desire and regret. But "if we do always what our reason dictates, we will never have anything to repent, even when events later make us see that we have been mistaken, since this is not by our fault." If this had been what Seneca had written, concludes Descartes, his would have been the best book a "pagan" philosopher had ever written. But what does Elisabeth think?

Elisabeth responds.

16 August 1645

Monsieur Descartes,

I have found in looking at the book you have recommended many lovely passages and sentences, designed to give subject for meditation if not so much for instruction, because the study is done without method and the author does not follow through with what he has proposed. Instead of showing the shortest route to happiness, he is content to make it seem that riches and luxury make it impossible. I am obliged to write you this so that you will not think I am of your opinion out of prejudice or laziness. Also I do not ask that you continue to criticize Seneca because your way of reasoning is so extraordinary. Actually it is the most natural that I have encountered and seems to teach me not something new, only that I draw from my own spirit an understanding I had not yet grasped.

But I do not know how to get rid of doubt that one could arrive at the happiness of which you speak without the assistance of what does not depend entirely on one's own will. There are illnesses which prevent people from reasoning at all and consequently prevent any rational satisfaction, and other illnesses which diminish the power of reason and keep us from following maxims that good sense has forged and which make man more moderate, illnesses which make him subject to letting himself be carried away by emotion and less capable of disentangling himself from accidents of fortune which require prompt resolution.

When Epicurus tells a lie at his deathbed, assuring his friends he is well instead of crying out like an ordinary man, he lives the life of a philosopher, not of a Prince, Captain or courtier. He knows that nothing outside himself can make him forget his role and prevent him from acting according to the rules of philosophy. But on these occasions, it seems to me that repentance is inevitable. One is not able to defend oneself with the knowledge that failure is as natural for a man as being sick. For one does not know that one can be exempted from each particular fault.

But I assure myself that you will clarify these difficulties and many others of which I am not aware at this moment, when you teach me the truths which must be known when facilitating the use of virtue. Do not abandon, I beg you, the design of obliging me by your precepts and believe that I esteem them as much as they merit.

It has been eight days since the bad humor of a sick brother has prevented me from making this request in keeping me always at his side to oblige him either to submit to the regime of the doctors because of the complaisance he has for me or to recount to him my own regime to try to divert him from his pain because he is persuaded that I am capable of it. I wish to assure you that I will be, all my life,

your very affectionate friend at your service,

Elisabeth

Poor Elisabeth, no longer sick herself, has been immediately called on to nurse a younger brother, the headstrong Philip, who will not take his medicine or stay in bed. Again she is filling in as mother for her younger siblings.

Gently, she signals a certain lack of interest in Seneca. She has done her assignment dutifully. She does not want Descartes to think that she does not accept his gift wholeheartedly or that she will passively rely on his exposition instead of doing the reading herself. But actually she has little to add to his critique. She is more interested in his own thoughts on the subject, his own view of the good life. There is a new rapport in these letters, a sympathetic intimacy not of bodies but of minds, minds that are different, able to disagree, but also able to reason together. To live the good life together, no, that would not be possible, but they can enjoy the next best thing: thinking together about the nature of happiness.

But for all their newly found common ground, Elisabeth's style of reading is very different from Descartes's. He reads expecting to find his own views; when he does not find them, he loses both patience and interest. The openness of Seneca's approach to the question of the good life and the indeterminacy he tolerates in people's opinions are alien to Descartes. Elisabeth, on the other hand, reads Seneca as literature, as conversation. In his discourse on happiness, she finds subjects for "meditation," if not for "instruction." She admires his graceful, evocative style. The problem she finds is not with his logic but with practicality. How useful is the detached life of the mind that philosophers have promoted since antiquity? How useful is it to her, a woman involved in public life, or to any prince, courtier, or captain? Perhaps a man living the unusual, even unnatural, life of a philosopher might lie on his deathbed, claiming that he is happy to die. But a woman involved with public and family life, with all its ambiguities, is she likely to be able to afford that luxury? Yes, to err is human, but this truism does not help to absolve one of particular mistakes, whose effects can remain to the end of one's life and that one has only to the end of one's life to correct.

Elisabeth is no more willing to accept on faith the ethics of ancient Greek sages than she is Descartes's stoicism. Can the virtuous man detach his reason from the troubles of his bodily life in time? This, Elisabeth argues, is impossible. Happiness is not, and cannot be, a matter of pure will. Not only do unforeseen tragedies occur, physical illnesses derange the mind, and nervous states make it difficult if not impossible to control the passions, but, most important of all, the effects of past faults and failures can continue into the future.

Descartes, still the faithful courtier, sends more diversionary discourse even before he gets her reply to his last letter. On 18 August 1645 he writes:

> Even though I do not know if my last letter has reached your Highness—and I know that I cannot write anything on the subject I have taken up for your entertainment that I ought not to think you know better than me—I am not delaying to continue, because of the belief I have that my letters will be no more importune than the books in your library. Because they do not contain any news in which you must immediately take an interest, nothing compels you to read them in the hours when you have other business, and I hold the time I take for them very well employed if you give to them only that time which you would have wished to lose.

She must treat his letters like books in her library, says Descartes, to give diversion when she is free from other duties, when she is alone in her room or walking in the garden behind the tall hornbeam hedges that separate the house from the street.

Having laid out in his last letter what Seneca should have written, he now turns to what Seneca did say, critiquing the text chapter by chapter, line by line. Clarity, singleness of meaning, definition, generality: these, the touchstones of the philosopher's art as Descartes understands it, are now pressed into service for Elisabeth's amusement.

In his first chapter, Seneca recommends asking advice from others but also emphasizes that we must also examine that advice for ourselves. Descartes agrees, but when Seneca goes on to "elaborate on his teaching, he is not always exact enough in the expression of his thought." In chapter 2 Seneca repeats himself and then when "after having already used so many superfluous words," he finally gives his opinion on the sovereign good, what he says about following what is natural is "very obscure." In the fourth and fifth chapters Seneca gives more definitions of the highest good but does not make clear their relation to his previous definitions, which makes Descartes think that "Seneca did not clearly understand what he meant" because "the more one conceives better a thing, the more one is determined to explain it only in one fashion." Even when Seneca does say something of which Descartes approves—"happiness is in neither desiring nor fearing"— Seneca does not "give any reasons."

Again Descartes turns to his own view of the sovereign good, making distinctions with characteristic precision. You have to differentiate between three things: happiness, the highest good, and the final end at which our actions should aim. Happiness is not the highest good, but it presupposes the highest good; happiness is the satisfaction that comes from knowing that we have obtained the highest good. The result is that the final end of all our actions should be both the highest good and the contentment that is its attraction for us. To illustrate the difference, Descartes uses an analogy:

> It is like the way in some places there is a prize for shooting at a target, and you give people the desire to shoot by showing them that prize, but still they cannot get the prize unless they also see the target, but those who see the target are not just for that reason alone induced to shoot if they do not also know there is a prize to win. In the same way, virtue, which is the target, is not so much desired when one sees it alone, and contentment, which is the prize, cannot be gotten if the target is not what one is aiming at.
>
> Both are necessary, both a knowledge of virtue and the reward of self-satisfaction that comes from the practice of virtue.

Next Descartes performs an impressive feat of interpretation. Actually when their views are made clear and precise, all the sages of antiquity—Epicurus, Zeno, Aristotle—agree with him. Epicurus says the highest good is pleasure, Zeno that it is virtue, Aristotle that it is perfections of body and spirit. But Aristotle is thinking of human nature in general and that is why he encompasses all perfections, so that what he says does not conflict with Descartes's own view about the good for an individual. As for Zeno, although he goes too far in that he rules out all pleasures, even those that are licit, like Descartes he considers what each man can achieve himself, and he agrees with Descartes that this is virtue because any man can be virtuous by his own will. But Epicurus is right, too, because by pleasure he does not mean only sensuous pleasure but also contentment of the spirit, agreeing with Descartes's argument that pleasure in doing good is necessary because being virtuous alone, without a reward, would not make us happy.

When properly clarified, Descartes concludes, they are all really saying the same thing, and that same thing is the ethics he prescribes. Happiness is contentment, contentment comes from being virtuous, and virtue is nothing but a firm will to carry out whatever one understands is best as long as one has used one's reason to try to discover what is best.

To this, Elisabeth answers in a few days.

August 1645

Monsieur Descartes,

I think you must have seen, in my last of the 16th, that yours of the 4th was sent to me. And I did not have any need to add there that it shed more light on the subject it treats than anything that I have been able to read or think. You understand too much what you are doing, what I am capable of, and have too well examined what others have done, to be able to doubt that which, by an excess of generosity, you want to ignore, the extreme obligation that I owe you for having given me an occupation so useful and agreeable as that of reading and considering your letters.

Without them, I would not have been so able to understand what Seneca judges to be happiness as I believe I am now.

But I attributed the obscurity, which is found in Seneca as in most of the ancients, to the way he explains himself, which is very different from our own. The same things which are problematic with us pass for hypotheses with them, and the lack of logical connection and order Seneca observes is with the aim of acquiring admirers by surprising the imagination rather than of acquiring disciples by inform-ing the judgment. Seneca uses bons mots as others use poetry and fables to attract young people to adopt his opinions. The way he refutes Epicurus seems to support this opinion. He quotes that philosopher: "quam nos virtuti legem dicimus, eam ille dicit voluptati." And a little further on, he says in the name of his followers, "ego enim nego quemquam posse iucunde vivere, nisi simul & honeste vivat." From which it appears clearly that they give the name pleasure to joy and satisfaction of the spirit, to what Epicurus calls "consequentia summum bonum." But, neverthe-less, in all the rest of the book, Seneca speaks of this Epicurean pleasure more in the guise of satyr than philosopher, as if it were purely sensual.

But I charge much good to this, since it caused you to take the trouble of explain-ing their opinions and reconciling their differences better than they had done, and to show by a powerful objection against the search for this sovereign good, that not one of the great spirits was able to define it, and this against the authority of human reason since reason had not illuminated for these excellent personages the knowl-edge of what for them was the most necessary and the closest to heart. I hope you will continue, from what Seneca has said, or what he should have said, to teach me the means of fortifying the understanding, in order to judge the best in all the actions of life, which seems to be the only difficulty, since it seems impossible not to follow the best road when it is known. Have again, I beg you, the frankness to tell me if I abuse your kindness in demanding too much of your leisure, for the satisfac-tion of

your very affectionate friend at your service,
Elisabeth

Elisabeth, as always grateful for the gift of companionship, was now more iso-lated than ever. Her mother, with Charles-Louis out of favor for siding with Cromwell, celebrated Rupert's growing popularity with royalist troops, insensitive to the danger he was in. The queen laughed at the stories of Rupert's scarlet cloak and his constant companions, a small white lapdog and a monkey in a green coat, affectations that made him a subject of ridicule for Cromwell's men, who out-numbered and defeated the forces he commanded in the beginning of July, killing four thousand Englishmen. Defeat after defeat followed, leading to a quarrel with Charles and Rupert's dismissal as commander. In the meantime, the queen con-tinued to complain bitterly of the behavior of Charles-Louis, who was busy mak-ing prudent peace with the king's enemies in Parliament.

As the humiliation of owing more and more money took its toll and the queen sold the last of the crown jewels for pocket money, Descartes's letters must have been a breath of sanity for Elisabeth. How welcome it must have been to communicate on a higher level, to reflect without private interest or vendettas or prejudice, to reach for the objectivity and judgment so lacking in her family, except perhaps for the lost grandmother and aunt in distant Germany.

But how different still are these correspondents. Descartes analyzes like the mathematician he is, calculating mistakes, defining terms, pointing out contradictions, establishing the orthodoxy that will become Cartesianism, a doctrine that will eventually result in its own schisms, expulsions, rivalries. In contrast, Elisabeth pauses, reflects, notes beauty in language, beauty that is not only pleasurable but that also serves a purpose of "surprising the imagination." She is attuned to rhetoric, to motives and purposes behind words that serve to instruct but that can also delight, seduce, transform. How astute she is with some of these motives, with the rivalry that energizes Seneca's attack on Epicurus, with the designs that make him depict Epicurean pleasure as the pleasure of satyrs when he is well aware that this is not what Epicurus meant. Inconsistency, when noted by Elisabeth, is no simple logical blunder but a result of tangled motivations and intentions.

Above all, she hopes Descartes will not stop writing, that he will not forget her as he did after the trip to France when she lay sick that long, cold winter and spring. Because more important than the often pedantic style of Descartes's diversionary letters is their declared motive, affection and concern for her. Another man might have written love letters; Descartes sends the gift he has, the gift of thought.

On the first of September Descartes answers some of the points made in the princess's letter of 16 August, uncertain whether the princess is at The Hague or at the family's country property at Rhenen. He chooses to find a compliment in Elisabeth's response to his reading: "How I am glorified in finding that my judgment on the book that you have taken the trouble to read is not different from your own, and that my way of reasoning seems to you to be so natural." But some of the undertones in his letter suggest that he is not unaffected by her criticisms.

> I am assured that if you had the leisure to think, as much as I have, of the things treated of there, I would not be able to write anything of the matter that you would not have noticed better than myself. But because the age, the birth, the occupations of Y.H. do not permit that, perhaps what I write could serve to spare her some time, and that even my mistakes might give her occasions for remarking the truth.

Descartes follows this not-so-subtle allusion to his own ability to "spare her some time," given the incompatibility of study with her lifestyle, with another lengthy dissertation on virtue and the highest good.

Yes, illness can rob one of reason, and then happiness becomes impossible, but in no other case need the body disrupt spiritual contentment. We cannot will our dreams, but even there Descartes has found that because he is in the habit of controlling his sad thoughts during the day, he himself is never troubled by bad dreams. Indispositions that affect moods can make us prone to sadness and anger. Again the key is control, and the more excessive the emotion, the more satisfaction we are able to take in that control.

As for exterior impediments to happiness like accidents of birth, court intrigue, or adversity of fortune, these can make the spirit even stronger by getting it used to disappointment. In fact, prosperity itself can be seen as a disability and its loss an advantage.

> For when one has all things to hope for, one forgets to think of oneself, and then afterwards when fortune changes, one finds that one is that much more surprised as before one had faith in one's fortune. In the end, one can say generally that there is not anything that can take entirely from us the means to make ourselves happy, provided it does not trouble our reason. It is not the people who seem to anger us most who do the most harm.

There is one point on which Descartes remains adamant: true contentment depends on "witnessing that we have some inner perfection." Pleasures of the body, since the body constantly changes, are necessarily transitory. They will always appear greater than they will turn out to be in reality, and in our disappointment inevitably we suffer from the most serious impediment to happiness: repentance and regret. Descartes chooses examples that have special relevance to academic rivalry but that also foreshadow events soon to shatter any calm left in Elisabeth's family.

> Thus, for example, anger can sometimes excite in us desires for revenge so violent that they make us imagine there is more pleasure in punishing an enemy than in saving our honor or our life, and can make us expose imprudently both one and the other to this end. If instead reason examines on what good or perfection the pleasure one takes from vengeance is founded, it will find there no other good (at least when that vengeance does not serve to guard against someone offending us further) than that it makes us imagine that we have some sort of superiority and some advantage beyond that for which we are taking revenge. But this is often no more than a vain imagination which does not merit to be valued in comparison with honor or with life, or even in comparison to the satisfaction which one has in seeing oneself master of one's anger and abstaining from vengeance.

Some will risk their life or reputation for vengeance, and for what profit? One man slanders another on the mistaken view that diminishing the esteem of another will increase his. Was Descartes thinking of the hated Voetius? In fact, the only certain reliable pleasure, Descartes insists, is the mastery of passion, and the more violent the passion, the more pleasure one can take in that mastery.

It was a familiar teaching. Elisabeth, learned in the classics, had studied her Plato and was familiar with the Socratic dictum that mind should rule over body.

But here is a party to the discussion not present at debates
young woman involved in politics and family matters, a woma
cannot, accept the removal from involvement in affairs that is
tonism as well as the moral flowering of Descartes's philosophy. C
Descartes's own life a passion for revenge had played a not always
causing him to escalate the war of words with Voetius to the point of ,
the Utrecht magistrates on his head.

He catches himself midstream in his condemnation of passion. It is not that a
person should have no feelings: "I am not, however, of the opinion that one must
entirely distrust the [perfections of the body], nor that one must keep oneself from
having feelings; it is enough that one render them subject to reason." But only the
intelligent passions should be fostered, the passions of the soul. A passion to hunt
down error? Yes, but not just any hunting-down is conducive to virtue, not a passion for refutation, based on a false idea of one's own worth. How quickly waves
of (dare we say?) passion modulate this "rational" discourse, as righteous indignation and resentment of Voetius's "outrageous" indignation must have flickered in
Descartes's memory. No, a false idea of one's own worth, no matter how comforting, cannot be virtue, not in a man whose idea of his merits is so inflated. But
always the body and the passions of the body must be controlled, bent to the will
of the mind. Always, body is the culprit: the irrational physical wanting of a thing,
whether sex, drink, or food—pleasures that, once achieved, all too often sour in
the mouth. All this in contrast to the solid passions of the intellect, perpetual,
unchanging, reliable.

So Descartes warmed to the role of sage undertaken for Elisabeth's diversion.
Deep-lying differences of inclination, sex, and temperament enliven the discussion. Take the body. How should we think of it? As necessary encumbrance,
mechanism of survival, transitory site of unreliable pleasures, as Descartes does?
Or as a registrar of reality, site of involvement with others, as the body painfully
and pleasurably was for Elisabeth? Is the body a tool to be controlled and used as
it is for Descartes? Or is it a source of sympathetic knowledge of others, as it is for
Elisabeth? Should we live as masters in control of an alien animal nature, putting
at a distance all bodily feeling and devoting ourselves to abstract formulas of the
mathematical science by which our corporeal bodies can be controlled and
manipulated? Or should we attempt integration of mind and body, in which emotions become intelligent and the mind sensitive?

In the middle of September, Elisabeth and Descartes having found a fertile vein
of disagreement, the letters fly back and forth between The Hague and Egmond
so fast that they are crossing in the mail.

10

The Burdens of Civility

∽

To Descartes's letter of 1 September, Elisabeth replies from Riswyck, where she and her family are staying while their disheveled mansion in The Hague is being refurbished.

13 September 1645

Monsieur Descartes

If my conscience were as satisfied with the excuses that you give for my ignorance as I am with the remedies you give for that ignorance, I would be very obliged. And I would be exempt from repentance for having so badly used the time I do have for the use of my reason, which for me is longer than that of others of my age. Birth and fortune force me to use my judgment promptly in order to lead a life sufficiently difficult and free of prosperity to prevent me from thinking of myself, just as if I were forced to trust to the rule of a stern governess.

It isn't always prosperity, nor the flattery which accompanies it, which I believe can decisively keep fortitude of spirit from well-born souls and prevent them from bearing changes of fortune philosophically. I am persuaded that the accidents which surprise people governing the public, and who are without the time to find the most expedient means, carry them (no matter what virtue they have) into actions which afterwards cause the repentance which you say is one of the principal obstacles to happiness. It is true that a habit of valuing goods according to how they contribute to contentment and measuring that contentment according to the perfections which cause pleasure, and judging without passion those perfections and pleasures, can protect from many faults. But to evaluate goods, it is necessary to be completely acquainted with them and to be acquainted with all those among which we must choose in an active life would require an infinite science. You say that one must be content when one's conscience witnesses that one has used all possible precautions. But this never happens, because one does not simply find one's story; one always revises things which remain to consider. To measure contentment according to the perfection that causes it, it is necessary to see clearly the value of each thing, to see if those that only serve ourselves or those that make us more useful to others are preferable. The latter seem to be valued more by persons in whom there is an excess of spirit which torments itself for others, the former in persons in whom there is an excess of spirit which only lives for itself. And nevertheless, each inclination can be supported with reasons strong enough to make them continue all our lives. It is the same with other perfections of the body and the spirit—unspoken sentiment makes reason approve, a sentiment which you ought not to call passion but rather approval by something innate. Tell me then, if you please, to what point we should follow such a sentiment (being a gift of nature), and how to correct it.

I would like to see you define the passions, in order to know them better, because those who call them disturbances of the soul would persuade me that their force only consists in shattering and subjecting the reason if my reason didn't also show me that there are some that lead to rational actions. But I am assured that you will shed more light on this when you explain how the force of passion renders it any more useful when it is subject to reason.

I will receive this favor at Riswyck, where we are going to stay with the Prince of Orange until this house is cleaned, but you do not need to change the address of your letters for that reason to

your very affectionate friend at your service,
Elisabeth

Something has rankled. Again she feels maligned, misunderstood. First Descartes condescends, excusing her because of her age, birth, and occupations, from the burden of having to think. Making it worse, later in his letter he downplays the effects of high birth, the stupidity of court life, the adversity of fortune, implying that she should count her blessings because others are worse off. Prosperity might be even worse than misfortune. When one has good fortune, wealth, and status, bad fortune can surprise and hurt even more. So in all her trouble, she should count herself lucky?

But Elisabeth cannot accept this account of her situation from a man living at ease in the countryside, troubled by intellectual disputes and not by war, homelessness, or the misery of loved ones. For the first time, there is a note of exasperation with her friend and teacher. It is not so much that what he says is false, but that it does not capture her experience—certainly not her experience at the prince of Orange's court in Riswyck. There, exercising diplomatic restraint on her mother and younger brothers and sisters is a full-time occupation requiring her to attend to events with a concentration that she once owed only to her stern governess, Madame Plessen. Certainly both governesses and affairs of state have means of punishment at their disposal that cannot be ignored. And then there is the implied identification of her state of mind with the puffed-up egos of court toadies. Indeed, she is in a position to know those whose egos are in such an inflated state that they have a great distance to fall. But how could Descartes have so mistaken her? It is not that high birth has made her inordinately sensitive to changes in fortune that those less fortunate might take in stride, as he implies. Unlike others in her family, her main concern is not a royal status that seems laughable for a family stripped of the hereditary rule of a small German principality and a mother whose title of queen is the result of a disastrous one-year reign as the conscripted monarch of Bohemia. Even the family's Stuart blood is as much stain as honor, given events in England. No, this is not the point at all.

What he cannot understand is how debilitating is the pain she feels at the plight of her brothers, forced to become soldiers of fortune with no steadying influence and little future, and of her sisters, all but unmarriageable because of a mother too obsessed with her own pleasures and her sons' exploits to interest herself in their prospects. The mounting debt of the household, the disorder and abandon of daily life with undisciplined servants, thefts by retainers, furtive trips to sell more of the family treasures for foolhardy schemes, lies to satisfy importunate tradespeople—all are trying and require constant negotiation.

But with all this, she does not complain, only tries again to make clear what virtue is as she sees it. Virtue is not rational distance from emotion, not a stoic attitude of indifference toward events. It is the proper handling of life. Events surprise. No matter how ready we try to be for what will happen, infinite knowledge is impossible. We must act, and so repentance is inevitable. Should we reassure ourselves that we did the best we could, the best we could see to do at the time? The conjecture is contrary to fact. If the future is not laid out for us to know, neither is the past. The past is a story we tell to ourselves and others, and the story changes as we reflect, revise, think about what has happened.

Indeed, Descartes in his dealings with Voetius might have learned to revise his story, amend his position so that reconciliation, or at least coexistence, was possible. The magistrates had no more interest in church censorship than Descartes. Their concern was that the university not be torn apart, an interest that Descartes might have shared. Elisabeth's intelligent body might have been more sensitive to motives, feeling out solutions in muscles and nerves, soothing disagreements, restoring balance. Her substantial, passionate mind might have offered not superficial ratiocination but a sense of the nuances of the situation. For Elisabeth, mind and body are one; there is no dividing line. Can the dispassionate mind weigh correctly the value of emotions? Can it decide on a purely rational basis whether to act out of regard for itself or concern for other people's interests? No, she says, the very weighing of interests is in part a matter of temperament inborn in the body, temperament that makes some people aware of and sympathetic to others and makes others suffer blindness and deafness to motives and intentions. A classic difference, a difference between women and men, or between women and some men whose sovereign reason is—could it be true even of Descartes?—a servant to power and ambition, ruled by inclination and all too ready to find "reasons" for whatever temperament dictates.

When she was ill, Descartes had not made the trip into town. Why? He explained that he thought that if there had been any serious problem with her health he would have heard from Pollot. Or was his own tranquility worth more to him than the comforting of a friend? As always, Elisabeth is gentle. She allows the testimony of these long letters of 1645, written for her pleasure and diversion as she recuperates, to show that he cares even without his physical presence.

11

A Discourse on Prudence

~

hen Descartes answers Elisabeth's letter of 2 August on 15 September, he promises that there will be no more chapter-by-chapter reading of Seneca. Instead, he will respond directly to her question: how specifically do we know what it is "best" to do? Descartes, true to his ethics, is resolute in his answer. Two things are necessary: knowledge of the truth and never forgetting that truth so that you follow it in all things. Knowing his correspondent by now, Descartes does not stop there. Since we can't know everything, what exactly is it important to know so that we can have a happy life and avoid regret?

Again his answer is clear and distinct. First, we must know that there is an infinite and infallible God so we can see whatever happens as good and even take joy in our afflictions. Second, we must know that the soul is separate from the body. This means that we will not care much about what happens in this life. Third, we must see the grandeur of the universe as he laid it out in his *Principles*. We must know that "all the heavens are made only for the service of the earth, and the earth only for the service of man, which will make us inclined to think that this earth is our principal home, and this life of ours the best of lives." This knowledge must be put in the place of any ill-founded reforming consciousness. To think one can reform human life is an impious mistake.

> In place of understanding the perfections which are truly in us, [man] attributes to other creatures imperfections which they do not have and puts himself above them, and so enters on an impertinent presumption: he wishes to be of the council of God, and to take on with God the charge of running the world, which causes an infinity of vain iniquities and falsehoods.

Instead, we should draw the proper conclusion from the knowledge of the necessary goodness of things on earth for man and see how God arranges things for the best. Even in relations with others, one can trust to God's "invisible hand."

> Even though each one of us is a person separate from others and our interests in consequence are in one way distinct from the interests of others, a person must

always realize that he cannot survive alone, and that he is, in effect, only one part of the universe, and most particularly one part of this earth, one part of this state, this society, and this family, to which he is joined by domicile, by pledges, or by birth. Therefore, we must prefer the interests of all those entities of which we are part to the interest of ourself in particular, but do so always with measure and discretion. One would be wrong to expose oneself to a great evil in order to procure only a small good for one's relatives or one's country. And if a man is more valuable in himself alone than all the rest of his town, he would have no reason to wish to lose anything by saving that town.

Descartes tempers what might seem the selfish consequences of such an ethics. This does not mean that altruistic acts are not beneficial or that we should not involve ourselves with others.

If a person relates only to himself alone, he will not be so afraid to harm other men as he will be when he believes he can get back from them some small convenience, and in that case one would have no true friendship, or any fidelity, or generally any virtue. Considering oneself part of the public, one takes pleasure in doing good to all the world, and even may not fear to risk one's own life in the service of others when the occasion calls for it—indeed some would even lose their soul, if they could, to save others. This consideration is the source and the origin of all the most heroic actions which men do.

Nevertheless, Descartes continues, self-sacrificial, heroic acts must be looked at with a fair amount of suspicion.

But those who expose themselves to death by vanity, because they hope to be praised, or by stupidity in that they don't understand the danger, I believe that they are more to be complained of than to prize. When someone risks himself because he believes that it is his duty, or because he suffers some other evil and wants to return good to others, even though he perhaps does not consider with reflection whether what he does he does more for what he owes to the public of which he is a part or for himself in particular, still he does it always because of the consideration that he is part of a whole, however confusedly that is in his thought. And then he will love God as he should, for abandoning himself in all to God's will, he detaches himself from his own interests and has no other passion than to do what he believes to be agreeable to God. As a result of which he has satisfactions of spirit and contentments which are incomparably more valuable than all the little passing joys which depend on sense.

Descartes goes on to reiterate at some length many of his previous points. The pleasures of the body are fleeting, We should be resolute even when we cannot be certain of what is the best thing to do. Again, he presses on Elisabeth his conviction that "irresolution" is the greatest of evils, causing us the pain of "regrets and repentances."

All this to reassure a princess whose health is in danger, to provide diversion, to ease her troubled spirit. Or does this resolutely apolitical man protest too much in defending his own removal from politics and his native country for an expatriate life without civic responsibilities? One must forgive Elisabeth some frustration with her correspondent. Can he grasp her conception of a different kind of nobility consisting of wise rule, good marriages, well-run households, polity, and careful stewardship, virtues hard won and not a matter of fortuitous prearrangement? Still in Riswyck, Elisabeth answers the second of Descartes's letters.

30 September 1645

Monsieur Descartes

Although your observations on the ideas Seneca has on the sovereign good make reading for me more profitable than if I were doing it on my own, I have no difficulty exchanging them for truths as necessary as those which include the means of strengthening the understanding so as to discern what is the best in all the actions of life. But this is only on the condition that you add the explication of which my stupidity has need: the utility of what you propose.

That the existence of God and his attributes can console us for the misfortune which comes to us in the ordinary course of nature and in the order established there, as in the loss of goods in a storm, or health by infection in the air, or friends in death, yes, I agree. But those misfortunes which are imposed on us by men, for which the decision seems to us to be entirely free, for these the existence of God would only console us if we had a faith that could persuade us that God takes the care to regulate the wills of men and that he has determined the fate of each person before the creation of the world.

Furthermore, the immortality of the soul, along with the knowledge that it is much more beautiful than the body, is capable of making us seek death as well as fear it, since one cannot doubt that one would live more happily exempt from the sicknesses and passions of the body. And I am astonished that those who are persuaded of this truth and live without any revealed law on the subject would prefer a painful life to an advantageous death.

The great extent of the universe that you have shown in the third book of your *Principles* serves to detach our affections from what we experience in it; but it also separates us from that individual Providence which is the foundation of theology and which is the idea we have of God.

The consideration that we are a part of a whole, whose advantage we ought to seek, is really the force behind all generous actions, but I find much difficulty in the conditions that you prescribe. How measure the evils which one gives oneself for the public against the good which would come of it, without them appearing more grand, inasmuch as their idea is more distinct. And what rule would we have for the comparison of things which are not equally known to us, such as our own merit against that of those with whom we live? A natural arrogance would make us always tip the balance our own way; a natural modesty would esteem itself at less than its real value.

To profit from the particular truths of which you speak, it is necessary to know exactly all the passions and all the predispositions, the majority of which are insensible. Also, in observing the customs of the countries where we live, we find in them sometimes much that is irrational but that is nevertheless necessary to observe to avoid even greater inconvenience.

Since I have been here, I have very angering proof of this, for I hoped to profit from a stay in the country by having more time to use for study, and I find here, without comparison, less leisure than I had at The Hague because of distractions from those who do not know what to do with themselves. And although it is for me very dysfunctional to deprive myself of real goods to give them imaginary ones, I am constrained to cede to pressing and established laws of civility so as not to make enemies. Since I have been writing here, I have been interrupted more than seven times by these inconvenient visits. It is excessive kindness which protects your letters from a similar predicament on your end, and which obliges you to wish to add to your usual investigations, in communicating them to such an indocile person as

Your very affectionate, at your service,

Elisabeth

Again the subtle, or not so subtle, comparison of their situations. Elisabeth is constantly interrupted as she tries to write and think. What are the "interruptions" from which Descartes needs protection? The call to dinner, a visit from a friend wanting to talk philosophy? Indeed, "kindness" to her might protect him against such interruptions as these, allow him to finish a letter to a friend instead. In her situation it is dangerous to refuse to gratify "requests" that constantly take her from study and writing.

Elisabeth goes to the heart of the matter: the relation between self and others. Yes, perhaps we might think that God has made the world so that human interests converge. Yes, she might reassure herself by thinking that what is good for her is also good for others. But the problem of virtue in practice remains. How is it possible to judge our own interests against those of others? How is it possible to say that a desire for study is any more important than an obsession with wealth and status, or honesty any more important than the courtier's convenient lie? Descartes himself—Elisabeth did not say it but she might have thought it—may be sure of his merit, but can he see the situation from the Utrecht magistrates' point of view? Can he see their need to protect the university from controversy? Or does he only see that the professors at Utrecht are ignoramuses and that his merit and intellect outshine them all? How, questions Elisabeth, can we be so sure? If we are of a temperament that is naturally modest, we downplay our own worth; if we are naturally arrogant, we exaggerate it. And those customary rules of civility and politesse—can he know how irritating they are for someone in public life who must observe them constantly? How is one to judge when it is better to observe them to avoid greater harm? Habit for Elisabeth means the stress of court life. Habit for Descartes is the self-indulgent pursuit of knowledge.

She is still in Riswyck. The house in The Hague is not yet finished. Looking out the window at the formal gardens below as she writes, she watches dignitaries, flunkies, favor-seekers come and go. More and more, the stadtholder's wife,

Amalia, is recreating a Stuart pomp not at all to Dutch taste. Elisabeth might have cringed as she watched, remembering the time not so long ago when on that very patch of lawn a distant female cousin slapped her for a remark considered impertinent. Her mother holds court on the grass, dressed in her habitual black velvet and lavish strings of pearls. A constant parade of visitors arrives, departs. Soon Elisabeth will again be forced into civilities and festivities for which she has only contempt.

She is well aware of the necessity of not giving offense. Even as she sits and writes, they knock at her door. Again she is interrupted in her letter writing. Will she come and wait on Amalia? Will she see to Sophie, who is bothering their mother? Will she compose a letter in French? "All she is good for," her mother might have murmured disparagingly to one of her admirers. Can Descartes really think that he is equally pressed in his country retreat?

Still faithful to his promise, he replies at length, covering page after page with close writing. The discussion is no longer only diversionary; he himself is energized, even exercised, by the questions she raises. Before he receives her letter of 30 September, on 6 October he responds to hers of 13 September. Finding the issues urgent enough to omit any greeting, he proposes a surprising question.

> I have sometimes asked myself a question: is it better to be gay and content in thinking that the goods that one possesses are greater and more worthy of esteem than they really are and in ignoring or not stopping to consider those which are lacking, or is it better to take more consideration and to understand the real value of both one and the other and become more sad? If I think that the highest good is joy, I do not doubt that one must try to make oneself happy at whatever price, and I must approve the brutality of those who drown their displeasures in wine, or deaden them with smoking.

But of course, it is not so simple. Descartes understands how untenable this seemingly necessary consequence of his teaching must seem. Yes, virtue and the satisfaction one takes from it must be the highest good. But yes also, he cannot mean that one should deceive oneself. The pleasure from such a self-deception can only "reach the superficiality of the soul," he concedes, leaving an interior bitterness in the heart, where we know our actual worth.

Still, muses Descartes, any event can be looked at from a bias that is positive to oneself, including Elisabeth's lack of time for philosophy.

> So, when your Highness notes the circumstances which gave her more leisure to cultivate her reason, than many others of her age, if it pleases her to also consider how much more she has profited than those others, I am assured that she will have what she needs to be content. And I do not see why she prefers to compare herself to those in respect to which she has cause to complain rather than to those who can give her satisfaction. For the constitution of our nature being such that our spirit needs relaxation, so that we can use profitably only a few moments to research the truth, and that instead of perfecting oneself, one only suffers if one applies oneself

to too much study, we must not measure the time which we can employ in instruct-ing ourselves by the number of hours that we have had to ourselves but rather, it seems to me, by the example of what we see usually happens to others as being a sign of the general deportment of the human spirit.

So much for Elisabeth's complaints about distraction. Others, says Descartes, are worse off. As for the regret and worry that make her ill, "It seems to me also that one has no reason to repent, as long as one has done what one judged to be best at the time at which one was forced to make a decision, even though afterwards, when we rethink at more leisure, we judge we have erred." We must forgive our-selves. It is human nature not to think well "in the field." And even though van-ity is a mark of souls that are "feeble and low," stronger ones should do justice to themselves. "No one can know perfectly all the goods that we must choose between in the encounters of life." Mistakes are inevitable.

After this barrage of positive thinking, Descartes turns back to the relation between self and other, the question on which he and Elisabeth are so much at odds. If we stay only by ourselves, we will not share the goods of society, but for evil the same is not the case. We should not let the sorrows of others affect our happiness. Evil is only privation; it cannot be shared. If we feel some sadness when a friend suffers, "it is not so great as the interior satisfaction that always accompanies good actions, and especially those that come from pure affection for others and are not regarding oneself." Again Descartes resorts to analogy. We can take pleasure in sad plays, and we can take pleasure in the painful and fatiguing exercise of the body as in games. This is because in each case we see some per-fection in ourselves—in the case of games, in bodily strength or agility; in the case of drama, in our ability to feel for others' suffering and be moved by com-passion.

Are all passions then subjects of self-congratulation? Realizing that this cannot be the case, Descartes admits that the proper regulation of passion takes work. He concludes by acknowledging that he has omitted an essential part of that work.As Elisabeth reminded him: "To profit from the particular truths of which you speak, it is necessary to know exactly all the passions and all the predispositions, the majority of which are insensible."

Passion was a subject with which Descartes could hardly claim much experi-ence. His mother died when he was a year old, before any passionate attachment could form. He showed no signs of grief at his father's or sister's deaths, having been alienated from both of them for some time. His one known sexual relation-ship inspired little emotion. Although Hélène Jans, a servant woman working in a house where Descartes boarded, bore him a daughter in 1635, the two were soon separated, with Descartes accepting a financial arrangement until the daughter died at four. What few mentions Descartes makes of either of them in his letters are brief, cryptic, and have to do with the logistics of providing for their maintenance. In the only recorded conversational reference to the affair, he mentioned a "dangerous entanglement" from which he escaped by the "grace of God," a grace he prayed would continue.[1] There was even conjecture that not even casual lust precipitated the affair but rather a research project. At the time of the child's conception, duly noted on the dust jacket of one of Descartes's books, Descartes was at work on a treatise on the formation of the fetus. A few days after the child's death, Descartes was calmly discoursing in his letters on metaphysics and science as if nothing of note had happened.

There were those who reported a certain magnanimity in Descartes. There were stories about his kindness to a poor villager with an interest in mathematics and his intercession for a neighbor accused of murdering an abusive father. But these charitable involvements were transitory and superficial beside Elisabeth's unshakable and passionate commitment to family and country. Is this pleasant benevolence she is supposed to cultivate no more than her mother's fond indulgence for lapdogs and monkeys, or Queen Henrietta of England's trading of favors for favors?

Still, Descartes takes on with some initial confidence the job Elisabeth has assigned him of defining the passions. If an ethics of prudence is to be "of use," he agrees, they must be denumerated. From the very beginning, as he makes his first efforts at this daunting task, his approach is physiological. Elisabeth has read his account of the animal body in general and his mechanistic account of perception in particular, he says, so it will easy for him to explain to her.

> You know already how I conceive that different impressions are formed in the brain, some by exterior objects that move the senses, others by internal dispositions of the body or by vestiges of earlier impressions which remain in the memory or by the agitation of spirits which come from the heart. And in man, impressions are also formed by the action of the soul, which has some power to change impressions which are in the brain, just as reciprocally, impressions have the power to excite in the soul thoughts which are not dependent on will.

Once this foundation is laid, Descartes goes on, passions can be understood as thoughts that are caused by a particular "agitation of spirits" that one feels in one's soul, as opposed to sensory or bodily sensations.

> For example, when someone says in a town that enemies are going to attack, the first judgment which the inhabitants make on the evil which may happen to them is an action of their mind, not a passion. . . . Before their mind receives the emotion, in which alone consists passion, it is necessary that it face this judgment, or rather without judging, that at least the mind conceives the danger and imprints an image of it on the brain (that is done by another action that one calls imagining). In the same way, the mind determines spirits which go out from the brain by the nerves in the muscles to merge with those which serve to close up the openings of the heart, which in turn slows the circulation of blood after which the body

becomes pale, cold, and trembling, and now spirits which come from the heart towards the brain are agitated in such a way that they can serve to form there other images which excite in the soul the passion of fear; all of which follows so quickly one after another, that it seems that this is only one operation. And so it is with all the other passions: there is some particular agitation in the spirits which come from the heart.

For Descartes passion is a function of neural circuitry. In the brain there are images, real or imagined, of a thing that is dangerous. An image causes an agitation in the nerves that travels to the heart and lungs, resulting in physiological changes, pallor, trembling, and quickened heartbeat. These bodily "agitations" in turn go to the brain and register on the mind a particular passion distinguished by various physiological effects.

After this confident beginning, Descartes stops short. He cannot go on. The job is harder than he thought. He lets the post go without his letter. Then in the incoming post he receives her letter of 30 September with a new set of questions about the existence of God and the immortality of the soul. Perhaps with some relief, he turns from the difficult problem of emotion to these new questions. He closes with some last affectionate words: she will never be of use to others if she neglects herself, and please, be careful of her health.

Elisabeth replies immediately.

28 October 1645

Monsieur Descartes,

After having given so many good reasons why it is better to know the truth to our disadvantage rather than to fool oneself agreeably, and having shown that nevertheless, given that all things admit different considerations that are equally true, you should stop at the one which gives you most contentment, I am astonished that you want me to compare myself to those of my time in respect to what is unknown to me rather than what I cannot ignore even though the former might be more to my advantage. There is nothing that could tell me if I would have profited more in cultivating my reason than in what others do with the things that they care about, but I cannot doubt that with the time to relax that my body requires, nothing more would be needed for me to advance beyond what I have been able to up to now. If you measure the deportment of the human spirit by the example of the ordinary man, it would find itself of very little extension, because most people use thought only with regard to sense. Even with those who do apply themselves to study, there are few which use any more than their memory, or who have truth as the aim of their labor. If there is a vice in not pleasing myself by considering whether or not I have gained more than these persons, I do not think it is an excess of humility which is "as harmful a presumption if not quite as ordinary." We are more inclined to mistake our faults than our perfections. And in fleeing repentance for faults we have committed as an enemy to our happiness, we run the risk of losing the concern to correct them, especially when some passion has produced them, since we naturally like to be emotionally moved and to follow that movement. There is only inconvenience that comes from this flight which teaches us that recognition of faults can be harmful. And this, to my judgment, is what makes tragedies please the more, in that they excite more sadness, because we recognize that it will not be so violent as to carry us to extravagances, nor durable enough to corrupt our health.

And it does not really suffice to support the doctrine contained in one of your preceding letters, that the passions are the more useful when they tend toward excess if they are submitted to reason, because it does not seem that they really can be both excessive and submissive. I believe that you would clarify this doubt if you would take the trouble to describe how this agitation of spirits you refer to serves to form all the passions that we experience and in what way it corrupts the reason. I would not dare to ask you, if I did not know that you would not leave work uncompleted, and that in undertaking to teach a stupid person, like me, you will be better prepared for the inconveniences that unfinished work can bring you.

Still irritated at Descartes's condescension, Elisabeth protests that if certainty is a good thing, as he has argued, she is certain that with the time for study she would make progress in thought. Why should she waste time comparing herself to others? This feminine soul is no longer so timid, judging from the confident voice of her letter. Even as family troubles drag on, even as she endures the constant hustle of court life, these long philosophical letters must have seemed to her only the beginning of what might yet be a serious life of scholarship in close collaboration with a man she respected and admired.

Adroitly she turns his argument against him. If it is better to give to a situation the interpretation most advantageous to oneself, then why would she prefer a comparison of herself with others "of her age" that might turn out to be disadvantageous to her when it is so very clear to her now that if she had the leisure she would be able to advance in her studies far beyond what she has already accomplished, perhaps even emulating Descartes in her achievements. Why should she reduce herself by comparing herself to an ordinary person who hardly uses her mind?

Has Descartes not quite gotten over his dismissal of her as an aristocratic amateur who might be "able to get something out of his philosophy"? And why does he fail to credit the constant stress that keeps her from her studies? Certainly Descartes was no stranger to the importance of relaxation and leisure. It was his habit to stay in bed until noon so he could meditate without the interruption of having to get dressed. After a noon dinner, he regularly took time to walk or converse with visitors until late in the afternoon, when he would work again until a late supper. Hardly a schedule that Elisabeth could have duplicated at the prince of Orange's court.

And this celebration of prudence—was it prudent of him to have written the calumnious *Letter to Voetius,* the letter that got him summoned to the magistrates? Was it prudent of him to have left Paris, where he might have ingratiated himself at the French court? But Elisabeth is too loyal to say such things. It is not the word "prudence" that she contests, it is Descartes's failure to understand what prudence for her involves and the difficulty of achieving a balance between one's own needs and the needs of family, community, and friends. Yes, you must do what is best, do justice to others. But to do that you have to overcome your temperament. And it is all too easy for the naturally self-absorbed to forget what he might owe to his country or to family, or for the naturally timid to refrain from sacrificing herself for others. No, she will not take the proffered congratulation on insignificant achievements.

Many have commented on the gender neutrality of Descartes's concept of reason, on his apparent conviction that anyone, even a woman, can reason and gain knowledge. At the same time, he has trouble seeing Elisabeth's situation, trouble understanding the constant demands to give comfort and aid as well as the demands she makes on herself to be wise in affairs that it takes astute diplomacy to negotiate. What is important, as she sees it, is not the happy state of her soul but her impotence in the face of the suffering of others. The problem is not whether she should sacrifice her pleasure to others, it is her inability to help those she loves. Why would she, as he claims, be suffering from an "excess of humility" when, like anyone else, she is less inclined to mistake her virtues than her faults?

Never, no matter what arguments Descartes marshals or how much pain on her part is involved, will Elisabeth weaken on this point. There is moral danger in repressing passions, especially passions of remorse and repentance. Without painful hindsight, one may not have the will to correct one's faults, especially when the source is emotional. When we watch a tragedy, pleasure comes not from self-satisfaction but from knowing that the events depicted are not painfully real and the sadness caused will not drive us to extreme action or compromise our health as it does in real life. The fictional enjoyment of tragedy should never be confused with the pain of real life.

Not prudence but passion is the key for Elisabeth. One must understand passion, explain exactly how "agitations" in the nerves result in the vast varieties of loves, hates, fears, remorses. Is Descartes going to leave his—their—work "unfinished"? Is he going to be content with only the groundwork of scientific method, leaving its flowering in morals and medicine unexplained and running the risk that science wilts in the bud?

Immediately the answer comes back from Egmond (3 November 1645). No gallant pleasantries now, no effusive comparison with angel bodies or virtuous souls, only praise for her intelligence. "It happens so seldom that I encounter good reasoning, not only in the discourse of those I see in this desert of mine, but also in the books I consult, that I cannot read the arguments in the letters of your Highness without feeling extraordinary joy, and I find them so strong that I like better admitting defeat than undertaking to refute them."

He cedes her points. Yes, more care must be taken with the emotions. Yes, repentance is a "Christian virtue" and necessary for the correction of faults, whether committed knowingly or in ignorance. And yes, tragedies are pleasing because we know that they will not really upset us like events do in real life. And he did not mean to talk of pleasure in the mastery of excessive emotion; only an excess of the kind of passion that is submissive to reason is useful, not passion beyond the bounds of reason. How easy it is to admit defeat gracefully when, as he puts, it, "reasoning is fused with generosity of spirit and favorable judgments on others." He is, he promises her, back at work on the test she has assigned: "I have been thinking these days of the number and the order of all these passions, so that I can more particularly examine their nature, but I have not still sufficiently directed my opinions, touching this subject, to dare to write them to Y.H. and I will not fail to make up for this as soon as I can."

12

The Consolations of Theology

~

*D*escartes had been diverted from his study of the passions by Elisabeth's objections to his theological points. In the rest of his letter of 6 October, Descartes continues to bolster his defense of prudence with religious arguments. If we know God exists and is infinite in power, then we must accept that everything happens by God's will. There can be no distinction between contingent and necessary events; all events, no matter how "particular," must be by God's will. Yes, the separability of the soul proves its immortality, but this alone cannot be a pretext for suicide. That requires an argument for why this life is bad, which cannot be proven. Therefore we should accept with joy whatever happens. All must be by God's will. In consequence, this life must be seen as good. When we pray, it is wrong to think we can teach God what to do. We can only pray that we will obtain what God willed from eternity. As for obligation to others, God has arranged society in such a way that the interests of self mesh with the interests of others. The prudence that dictates that you cannot promote your own interest without also attending to the interests of others is by divine arrangement.

Descartes strengthens his case with scholastic arguments. One cannot prove the existence of God without considering God perfect, and he would not be perfect if there were something in the world that did not come from him. It is illogical to believe that any thought could possibly enter into a man's mind without being willed by God. Therefore if there is evil, it is only privation and not a positive presence. By necessity, God is the universal and the total cause of all that happens.

Elisabeth, with an unsettled childhood spent in the midst of war and a family who had lost its home and lands, who every day suffered from the bad judgment of those close to her, has trouble accepting such arguments. Perhaps the will of God might be invoked for comfort in cases of natural disaster or physical illness, but one could hardly do the same in cases where misfortune is caused by the negligence or evil of men, she argues. What use is the consolation of knowing God exists and has created the world when we are wronged by men? Are we really to think that God directs everyone's will? And if the physical body is so unworthy of interest, why then do we not commit suicide and rid ourselves of it? As for the vastness of the universe revealed by Descartes's science, does it bring us closer to God or does it do the opposite, prevent a personal and feeling relation with God? In the remainder of her letter of 28 October, Elisabeth makes it very clear that Descartes has not satisfied her on these points:

It is this which makes me continue to say to you, that I am not persuaded by arguments that prove the existence of God that God is both the immovable cause of all effects which do not depend on the free will of man and also the cause of effects that do depend on the free will of man. From his sovereign perfection, it follows necessarily that he could be the cause of our will—that is to say, that he might not have given free will to men—but since we feel that we have free will, it seems to me repugnant to common sense to believe it is as dependent on God's operations as he is on his own being.

If one is really persuaded of the immortality of the soul, it is impossible to doubt that the soul would not be happier after the separation of the body (which is the origin of all the displeasures in life, as the soul is of the great contentments)—that is, unless you adopt an opinion like Mr. Digby's. His teacher—whose writings you have seen—made him believe in the necessity of purgatory by persuading him that the passions which are dominated by reason during the life of man leave vestiges in the soul after the decease of the body which torment the soul because they find no way to be satisfied in such a pure substance. I do not see how that accords with the soul's immateriality. But I do not doubt at all that provided a life is not poor in faith, it would be abandoned for a condition that one knows to be better.

By that individual Providence which is the foundation of theology, I understand the Providence by which God has from all eternity—by means as strange as his incarnation—prescribed for a part of all of creation, and a part so inconsiderable beside all the rest, as you have represented this universe for us in your Physics. And that he has done it so as to be glorified by that part, which seems an end very unworthy of a creator of this great universe. But I present to you with this last the objections of our theologians rather than my own, having always believed it to be a thing very impertinent for finite persons to judge the final cause of the actions of an infinite being.

You say that you do not believe that one needs an exact cognizance how far reason ordains that we interest ourselves for the public because when each one relates only to himself, he also works for others if he is prudent. This prudence is the whole of which I demand only a part. For, in possessing it, one would not fail to do justice to others as to oneself and if it is a fault that a brave spirit loses sometimes the means to serve his country in abandoning himself too easily to his own interest, it is also a fault if a timid spirit loses himself in his country, to the fault of risking his own good and fortune for its preservation.

I have always been in a condition which makes my life very useless to those I love; but I seek my own conservation with much more devotion since I have had the happiness to know you, because you have shown me the way to live more happily that I did before. All that is lacking for me is the satisfaction in being able to witness how much this obligation is felt by

Your affectionate friend at your service,
Elisabeth

Abstract argument with conclusions contrary to experience would never satisfy Elisabeth. Yes, from God's perfection it may follow logically that God could have mapped out the will of men, which would mean that he did not give free will to men. But the conclusion is against common sense, given that it is a matter of experience that we feel we are free to act as we choose. Even more crucial for Elisabeth is the relation between believer and God, a relationship that in her view Descartes puts into jeopardy. How in the vast universe revealed by Descartes's science and ruled by natural law is there room for humans to be God's people, for the sense that God has "prescribed for them" and wants to receive their devotion?

Descartes responds to these objections in his November letter, deferring to some of her points. Certainly he "would not dare to contradict" the Christian teaching that repentance is a virtue, or that it helps to make us correct our faults, even those we commit in ignorance. As for suicide, no, by the light of natural reason we can know nothing sure about the afterlife, and so the "goods" of this life must be preferable. On the other hand, if the vast expanse of the universe were to count against the "mysteries of religion," then astronomers in all times would have been considered enemies of the faith.

He continues to struggle to explain the apparent contradiction between free will and the dependence of all events on God's will.

> It implies a contradiction to say that God has created men of such a nature that the actions of their will do not depend on his, because this is the same as to say that his power is at once finite and infinite, finite because there is some thing which does not depend on it, and infinite because he has been able to create this independent thing. But, as knowledge of the existence of God must not keep us from being assured of our free will in that we experience it and feel it ourselves, so also the knowledge of our free will must not make us doubt the existence of God. Because the independence that we experience and feel in ourselves, which is enough to make our action blamable, is not incompatible with a dependence which is of another nature, according to which all things are subject to God.

In thinking of God as infinite and perfect, we must think that all is dependent on his will. In thinking of ourselves, we think of ourselves with free will. But this contradiction doesn't have to make us either doubt the existence of God or reject the commonsense conviction that our actions depend on free will and so are blamable. This is because the dependencies are of "a different nature." Even Descartes could not have been happy with this sophistry borrowed from the Jesuits.

From the vantage point of the twenty-first century, it may be hard to understand the energy with which this question of the relation between God's omnipotence and men's freedom was debated in the seventeenth century. New conceptions of the vast extent of the universe, the random swarming of atoms, physical laws that govern events with no purpose or aim required a massive shift in orientation. How did humans fit in the new world of physical force? The logical puzzle of reconciling God's foreknowledge with human responsibility, long debated in the Schools, took on new urgency, separating intellectual rivals like Descartes and Gassendi and also marking political and theological divisions. Calvinists, believing in predestination, were against church government, whereas Arminians emphasized choice and clerical intervention. Catholic Jansenists turned their heads away from the unredeemable evil of human will; Dominicans taught that God's will determines future actions; Jesuits, with a commitment to the training of the will in church education, supported order and obedience to authority. For Descartes, however, not politics but the knowability of the universe was at stake.

His career in science began with a mystical vision of a world unified in mathematical structure. In his *Meditations* he argued that a science that can discover this vast, ordered cosmos is not in conflict with religion but complementary to it. No miraculous Providence can survive in such a world, but there is a divine plan, and that plan is the very object of science. In fact, science would not be possible without determinism. If there is to be a definitive map of the heavens, a map of the physiology of a man's passionate life so that he can keep his emotions in order, a map of the functional mechanisms of his body so he can maintain bodily function,there must be fixed configurations of past, present, and future to which science refers. For Descartes, science, the representation of a perfect and immutable order governed by natural law, is a secular theogony. Freedom of human will fits as best it can.

What keeps Elisabeth coming back to the problem of freedom of the will, however, is neither science nor logic, but morality. How, if all is determined, can we make sense of moral deliberation and moral responsibility? Her divine Providence is the experience of contingency Descartes denies, the pull of possibility and aspiration against quietism or resignation, and the indeterminacy that supports both remorse and hope. The God of Elisabeth's morality is no dictator with the iron hand of natural law but a guarantor of forgiveness, inspiration, and grace.

Descartes in his well-provisioned country "desert" strains and stretches to offer rational theological consolation for Elisabeth's ethical anxiety. Given her involvement in affairs, for Elisabeth to "get to the end of what she wants to accomplish" would require, he writes, either that all men be wise or that she be able to predict their God-determined irrational choices. Since neither is part of God's plan, she should accept her limitations. In such a situation, less intelligent minds than hers may actually do better, being more adept at predicting the actions of others on the basis of what they themselves would do.

What lesson is there in this for Elisabeth? Her family might be destroyed, but she should relax and realize that her own inability to save it shows that she is a superior person unable to predict the choices of stupid men? In the wake of the new crisis that will now break—a crisis that will cause the first serious rift in their friendship—nothing is further from Elisabeth's mind than self-serving hindsight. Soon after she received Descartes's letter of 6 October urging on her the consolation that lesser minds might be better at devising policy than her own, she heard some shattering news from Paris.[1] Her brother Edward had married a Catholic.

13

Traitor to the Cause

~

Anne de Gonzague was eight years Edward's senior and of loose reputation, notorious for a long-standing liaison with the duke of Guise. What was much worse, as part of the marriage agreement, Edward had abjured Protestantism and converted to Catholicism. He had made a choice, some might even say a prudent one, but a choice that in Elisabeth's judgment should not have been made and would not have been made if Edward had been virtuous. Edward's marriage and conversion trivialized generations of religious and political commitment. Was she to console herself that the choice was predetermined? Should she reassure herself that it was her own superiority that kept her from seeing the danger and being able to prevent it?

The seriousness of the situation was rooted in the past. The marriage of Elisabeth's father, Frederick, the Palatine elector, to Elisabeth's mother, daughter of James, the Stuart king of England, united the two wings of Protestant reform. The union was hailed as "a wedding for religion" that symbolized a new era of liberal thought and freedom from Catholic domination in Europe. The Palatine court, converted to Calvinism and fortified by activist emigrants, had been the first to warn of the danger of an international alliance of the Hapsburg empire, the papacy, and Spain that might entrench doctrinaire Catholicism in Europe. To counter this threat the Palatines proposed an international Protestant league to unite rebels in Holland, French Huguenots, the English monarchy, and France. When their international movement met with mixed success, they persisted, concentrating on Germany and establishing a mutual defense league against Bavaria, the center of Catholic repression. The Heidelberg Catechism, developed in the Palatine, could be repressive, but Catholicism, for Protestants like Elisabeth, represented the evil of autocracy and imperialism. Catholicism was the dictatorial regime of Philip of Spain, financed with gold plundered from the Americas. It was the Inquisition in Spain that burnt heretics at the stake. It was excesses of aristocratic luxury at the expense of common people. It was Jesuits who drove Protestants out of Catholic territories, imperial troops who attacked and razed the Palatine, brutish soldiers who took the papers and books of Palatine intellectuals and trampled them under their horses' hooves. At Frederick's death, the mantle of leadership in this Protestant cause passed to his sons. Edward's conversion to Catholicism was no simple personal choice; it was an affair of state.

The Dutch papers, never very respectful of the Palatines, had a heyday. The queen of Bohemia was beside herself. The household in The Hague was in an uproar. Edward's brother Philip was hastily recalled from his studies in Paris in fear that the Catholic contagion would spread. Elisabeth, whose religious sentiments went considerably deeper than her mother's, was devastated. When the Polish Diet refused to give permission for her to marry Wladislaw and remain Protestant, she had steadfastly refused to marry. If some part of the family's fortune and territories were to be restored, family honor, respectability, and suitable alliances were essential. The Protestant cause in the Holy Roman Empire could not be defended by a family that did not take its morals or its religion seriously. As one onlooker described the scandal of her brother's wedding:

> I forgot to tell you that the Prince Palatine, Edward, who married the sister of the queen of Poland [ironically, Anne of Gonzague's oldest sister Marie married Wladislaw, Elisabeth's old suitor], then made public abjuration of our religion, and swore faith in the Roman to the great scandal of the name which he carries being descended from so many brave men who have won fame by their piety and by their constancy in protecting the purity of the Testament of our Lord.[1]

If the inconveniences of court life had kept Elisabeth from accomplishing all that she wished in philosophy, Edward's perfidy, especially now that peace talks were under way, along with the hope that the Palatine territories might be recovered, brought to a temporary halt her intellectual life and any hope she had of emulating Descartes's prudence. Edward's marriage greatly embarrassed the Palatine envoys at Westphalia, already at a considerable disadvantage because of lack of funds for entertainment and display. Sweden, an ally, was outraged. France, an enemy, now expected concessions. Descartes would have to wait until the end of November for a response to his arguments for the dependence of all things on God's will.

The Hague
30 November 1645

Monsieur Descartes,

You would have reason to be amazed that after witnessing that my reasoning seems to you not ridiculous, I waited so long to take the advantage offered by your letters. And it is with some shame that I confess the cause, because it has overturned all that your lessons seemed to have established for my spirit. I believe that a strong resolution to find happiness in things that depend on my own will might make me less sensitive to things from outside, that is, I believed it until the fault of one of my brothers made me see my weakness. It has more troubled my health and tranquility of soul than all the troubles which have yet happened to me. If you bother yourself to read the papers, you will see that he has fallen into the hands of certain sorts of people who have more hate than affection for our house and religion, and has let himself be caught in their traps to the point of changing his religion to make himself Catholic without giving the slightest indication that he was following his conscience. I must see a person whom I love with as much tenderness as I have for anyone, abandoned to the bad opinion of the world and the loss of his soul (according to my faith). If you had less charity than bigotry, it would be an impertinence to talk to you of this. And I wouldn't do it, if I were not in the habit of telling you my faults, as to the person most capable of correcting them.

I confess that, given that I still cannot understand how the independence of a free will is more repugnant to the idea we have of God than its dependence is to the will's liberty, it is impossible for me to make the two consistent, being as much impossible for the will to be at the same time free and attached to the decrees of Providence as it is for the divine power to be both infinite and limited. I do not see this compatibility of which you speak, nor how the dependence of the will could be of another nature than its liberty, if you would take the trouble to teach me this.

In regard to contentment, I admit that the present possession of it is much more assured than its attainment in the future, on whatever good reason it may be founded. But I have trouble persuading myself that we have always more good in life than evil. More is necessary to constitute good than evil: man has more places in which to receive displeasure than pleasure, there are an infinite number of errors for one truth, there are so many ways to lose one's way for one which leads down the right path, there are so many persons with the design and power to do harm for a few who have either the design or the power to serve. In the end, all which depends on the will and the heart of the rest of the world is capable of inconveniencing one, and according to your own opinion, there is nothing which depends only on our own will and heart that is sufficient to give a real and confident satisfaction.

As for prudence in that which concerns human society, I do not expect infallible rules, but I would be much eased to see those which you would give to someone who, in living only for oneself, in whatever profession he has, does not neglect to work for others, that is, if I dare to ask you for more light, after having so badly used that which you have already given to

Your very affectionate friend at your service,

Elisabeth

As always with Elisabeth, theology and ethics must pass the test of experience. So many people with the design to harm. So few willing to help. The family held up to ridicule, the Protestant cause a joke. There is no chance that Elisabeth will be able to console herself that Edward's choice was the will of God. Weeks later as she writes this letter she is still shaken. Good so hard to obtain, evil so easy. More pain than pleasure, more ways to go wrong than right. Was Elisabeth really convinced for a time of Descartes's ethics of prudence, convinced that if she restricted her desires to what was within the reach of her will, she would no longer be troubled in mind and body? Convinced, that is, until this family crisis, one with such personal resonance? She had given up the only marriage likely to be offered to her, and a royal one at that. Married and a queen, she would have had status and an opportunity for good works; she could have advanced the intellectual life of a country and helped her family. She would also have experienced some portion of the sexual affection that she had a right to expect. Yes, she had passed Descartes's geometry "test" with flying colors; now she had to admit to her "shame" the "weakness" that had made her utterly fail the test of virtue as he set it. Again she is ill both in mind and in body.

What are we to think of her account of the main event, the account that Descartes would now read as a mark of moral retrogression and as an insult to his faith? "A certain kind of person." Is this a tactless reference to Descartes's old teachers, the Jesuits, for whom he has so much admiration? Was she simply mouthing Protestant bigotry that painted the Jesuits as devils willing to engage in endless machinations to tempt the weak back to Papism? The Jesuits were Descartes's heroes; he respected them even as he disagreed with them. He still very much hoped for their approval of his new philosophy. Or were these people the frivolous précieuses of the salons of Paris among whom Anne was a familiar figure, with their promiscuity, superficiality, and appetite for the novelty of Cartesianism? Did Elisabeth have actual knowledge of the plots of political enemies on the Catholic side, eyeing Palatine territories for their own, plotting to restore a dogmatic Catholicism in all of Germany, eager to use any means to discredit her family? Perhaps. But in the letter, what seems to be foremost on her mind is Edward himself. He converted without the least indication of a crisis of conscience, as if religious faith was a convenience to be exchanged when circumstance or desire demands.

How could she think it anything but a travesty, with the family once again subject to scorn? Certainly that was nothing new. The high jinks of the young fatherless princes, the extravagance of the household, the lack of management of servants, the eccentricities of the queen of Bohemia with her lapdogs, low-cut gowns, and extravagant strings of pearls hardly went unnoticed. And hadn't she added the disclaimer, "according to my faith"? Certainly to either Catholic or Protestant, Edward's bandying about of religious commitments must represent a loss of soul, a loss of integrity and honor, and all to become the plaything of a worldly woman and her friends. Is Elisabeth complacently to think that Edward's actions were planned out in advance by God, that there was nothing that he or she, or their mother with closer surveillance of her children or a clearer sense of their situation, could have done to prevent the marriage? She refuses such a cure for unhappiness and remorse. If philosophy is a device to achieve peace of mind at all costs, yes; if philosophy is inquiry into truth, truth must be allowed to hurt to the point of injury.

Twice now Descartes has warned her off metaphysics. Establish the most basic of truths, lay a foundation, and then leave it alone, he tells her. Never has she been willing to take that advice, advice that we must think Descartes meant quite seriously both for her and for himself. For Descartes philosophy is a building up of foundations, a buttressing and shoring up of conviction, to be done once and left alone. Elisabeth asks philosophy to do more, to serve as continuing reflection on surprising experience, no matter how contradictory or painful. Descartes says, detach your emotions, leave it alone, all has been planned out in advance, this is the best of all possible worlds, restrict your will to what depends only on you. For Elisabeth it is precisely such an ethics that leads to transgressions of duty such as Edward's. She challenges Descartes. Would he please explain to her how it is possible to live only for oneself and still work for others? Just as freedom of the will is inconsistent with the will's dependence on God's will, living only for oneself, as Edward appears to do, is incompatible with duty to the public.

Much as Elisabeth condemned Voetius and the zealots of Utrecht for saying that Descartes was an atheist, she might have suspected something opportunist in his "proofs" of God,[2] something suspect in the facility with which God becomes a token guaranteeing that everything that happens will be for the best, making ethical struggle unnecessary. Elisabeth's faith is more skeptical, more accepting of the puzzles of theology, more willing to leave the question open as to how Providence is possible, how evil is explained, how freedom of choice and moral responsibility are compatible with God's sovereign power. It is harder and harder for her to accept Descartes's stoicism, all very well for a scholar in his garden whose worst fear is that the ban on discussing his work at the universities will not be lifted. But Edward's marriage, coming as it did without warning, was a contingency that exhibited no plan, only sheer unpredictable event, mishap after mishap. So many errors for one truth, so many vices for one virtue, so many persons ready to hurt rather than help. And, as Descartes himself observed, it is impossible to live without those others, given one's dependence on them, given one's place in a social fabric.

By 27 December there was still no answer to her letter. From Descartes came only ominous silence. No comment on her troubles, no consolation or sympathy from her friend.

Then, out of the blue, a young man appears at the door of the Palatine town house with a short note from Descartes, a brief request that Elisabeth talk to the young man and agree not to hurt his chances for a post at the university. Nervous, tongue-tied, he stays only for a few minutes. The next day, Elisabeth writes the following:

The Hague
27 December 1645

Monsieur Descartes,

    The son of your Professor Schooten brought me yesterday the letter which you wrote on his behalf to keep me from engaging to favor his rival for the post. When I told him that I was not only without any design of harming his chances but rather obliged to serve him, as much as I can, since you have asked me to like him and to be responsible for him, he then asked me to recommend him to the Curators. Only having the acquaintance with two of them, Messieurs de Wimenom and Bewen, the latter being out of town, I began by talking to the first, who promised me to work for the same Monsieur Schooten, even though there is some plan to abolish this professorship as superfluous. This seems to be really the only difficulty he has to deal with, his competitor not being really in the running next to him, other than that some scrupulous persons may fear that he would introduce Arminian errors of religion with his mathematics lessons. If he had given me time to ask him to call again to learn the success of my recommendations, I would have had the chance to tell him about things which I believe would help him in his ambitions, but he was in so much haste to get away, I had to chase him to the door to ask to whom I should address my offices for him. I know that if he had only thought of me as your friend, without thinking of titles, which embarrass those who are not accustomed to them, he would have made use of our acquaintance differently, judging that I would never act, in any business which I know you are interested, with only ordinary care. And I pray you to believe that I would never lose the occasion to witness, in effect, that I am truly,

Your very affectionate, at your service,
Elisabeth

P.S. I am afraid that you have not received my last letter of the 30th of November because you have made no mention of it. I would be upset if it got into the hands of one of those critics who condemn as heresy any doubts one has about received opinions.

A certain bewilderment. Why has there been no response of condolence, no sage philosophical advice, not even a correction of errors after her letter confessing her pain at Edward's marriage? Then, after all those days of silence, suddenly this gauche young man appears at her door with a curt note. He is obviously bright, capable, embarrassed to be in the presence of royalty, and so unsure of her friendship with Descartes that he cannot even speak properly. And what is she to think of the suggestion that she is now potentially an enemy, someone who would work against a protege of Descartes's, try to hurt his chances, prevent him from teaching at the university? And the note, so cold and businesslike, with none of the pleasantries she was used to, none of the leisurely disputation of theology nor the detailed respect for her arguments. Only a wounded or angry plea: please, at least, do not hurt the chances of this poor young man, my old friend's son. As if she would.

Hadn't Descartes read the papers, seen the things that were said about her family? And most important, how could he have failed to understand what she was suffering? In her letter Elisabeth says none of this. Nothing personal or philosophical, only business. The professorship, a university chair in mathematics at Leyden, a university where Descartes's work was somewhat less controversial than at Utrecht, had been held by the young man's father, now deceased, but because there was another chair of mathematics at Leyden, there was some talk of eliminating this one. Only this, she reports, seems to be the cause for delay. She is familiar with the university; its officials speak frankly to her of university policy. They reassure her that this young man is the leading candidate for the post and faces only the ridiculous possibility that some zealot might fear that he might slip a lack of conviction about predestination into his sums.

Still nothing comes from Descartes, nothing after that long, leisurely summer of letters crossing back and forth, nothing after the growing intellectual intimacy and fruitful discussion, nothing to advance their shared intellectual life. Only frosty silence. Now, when she needs a friend the most.

Elisabeth adds a postscript: has Descartes gotten her letter? Could it have fallen into unfriendly hands to be read by those who might take her doubts about the goodness of life for heresy?

Then a few days later, the letter she has waited for finally arrives.

14

A Silence between Friends

~

Egmond
January 1646

Madame,

    I cannot deny that I was surprised to learn that your Highness had been angry, to the point of being inconvenienced in her health, by a thing that most of the world would find good and which several strong reasons would make excusable to the remainder. For everyone of my Religion (which makes up, without doubt, the greatest number of people in Europe) are obliged to approve it, even though they may see circumstances and motives that are blamable. For we believe that God uses diverse means to attract souls to the faith, the way someone might take monastic vows with a bad intention, which leads him, afterward, to lead a very saintly life. As for those of any other faith, if they speak badly of it, one could excuse their judgment, for as in other affairs, in which there are diverse parties, it is impossible to please some without displeasing others. If they considered that they would not be of the religion they are unless they or their fathers, or other relatives, had left the Roman, they would not have any reason to mock or name inconstant those who quit theirs.

As was her habit, she would have taken the letter to her room to read quietly and pleasurably by herself, expecting to find that events in Descartes's own life excused his silence. With those first chilly words, she would have known that she had offended. As she read, did her hand shake, tears come to her eyes? Did she experience again the rush of remorse now habitual with her? In one impulsive gesture, could she have alienated someone so important, and perhaps irrevocably? She might have laid down the thin sheet of paper, tried to remember exactly what it was she had written, going over each sentence in her mind. What had she said? Should she, could she, have put it differently? Edward may have lost his soul, she said. But she added, "according to my faith" to show that she respected other opinions. She said that she wrote so freely of the subject out of confidence that her friend was less "bigoted" than "charitable." A hot flush comes over her face. Thinking it through. Had she, in effect, called him a bigot? Should she have known that he would be offended at her harsh judgment on the Catholic marriage and so earn the epithet she hurled at her family's enemies? She had written the letter in good faith, with no thought for the consequences;

she had written to a friend in a reflex of honesty and trust built up over two years of letters and visits, of sharing thoughts, troubles, doubts, worries, faults, arguments, without fear of hostility or ridicule, without fear, above all, of silence or disinterest.

Strange, after all the theology, all the metaphysics, after pages of arguments back and forth, that the rational Descartes would have taken her pain at her brother's marriage as such an insult. Strange that even as she unhesitatingly helped his old friend's son, faithfully championing his philosophy at the university, he is angry at her still. It cannot be from political conviction. As a young soldier of fortune, out to see the world, Descartes signed on first to the army of the Protestant prince Maurice of Nassau and then to the army of the Catholic duke of Bavaria, who was preparing to oust Frederick from Bohemia, without seeming to care or know much about either cause. Since these adventures, his interest in politics had diminished rather than evolved. Politics was something to stay clear of so one could get on with intellectual work.

The letter goes on:

> As for what regards the prudence of the times, what is true is that those who have Fortune with them have some reason to keep to themselves and to close ranks to keep it from escaping, but those members of a house from which Fortune has fled are not wrong, it seems to me, to agree to follow different roads, so that, if they do not all find Fortune, there will be at least one who will encounter it. Meanwhile, because each one believes that each of them has several resources, having friends in different camps, this makes them more considerable than if they were all engaged in only one. Which prevents me from being able to imagine that those who were the authors of that counsel wished to harm your house.

And with that curt advice, Descartes coldly slams the door on further discussion of the matter.

> I do not pretend to think that my reasoning could prevent your Highnesses her bad feeling, I hope only that time will have diminished it before you get this letter, and I would fear to refresh it, if I say any more on the subject.

She might have put the rest of that long letter down unread, to finish reading later when she is calmer, when the pain of what she could not have helped but feel as a blow—even if she could never be sure whether she caused it herself— would have begun to heal. It might have been days before she could bring herself to come back to the remaining pages that sit on her desk like an open wound.

On and on the letter goes, page after page of argument, Descartes defending his theology against the claim of free will. Again he proposes an analogy that strangely foreshadows a tragedy that would further darken the reputation of Elisabeth's family.

If a King who had forbidden duels, and who knows very assuredly that two gentle-men of his Kingdom, living in different towns, are quarreling and are so angry at each other that nothing can keep them from fighting if they come together, if, I say, this King gives one of them some commission to go on a certain day to the town where the other is and then he gives also a commission to this other to go on the same day to the place where the first is, he knows assuredly that they cannot help but meet each other and fight and thus contradict his orders, but he does not con-strain them for all of that. His knowledge, and even his will that would have to have determined their action in this fashion, does not prevent it being voluntarily and freely that they fight when they come to meet, as they would have done if he did not know anything about it and it was on some other occasion that they met. And they can also justly be punished for disobeying his order. What a King can do in this, in regard to free actions of his subjects, God, who has foreknowledge and power that is infinite, can do infallibly in regard to men.

"Theologians" understand this, Descartes admonishes Elisabeth. "They distin-guish in God the absolute and independent will by which he wishes that all things are as they are, and the other will which is relative, and which relates to the merit or demerit of men, by which he wishes that they obey his Laws."

As for her statement that life holds more evils than good, again proper dis-tinctions are the answer. Good as a "rule for our actions" must be a unique stan-dard by which to judge. On the other hand, if one is considering the good in life or in a situation, then "one takes as good anything that can be found there from which one could have any convenience, and one calls bad that from which one receives an inconvenience." In other words, one makes a relative judgment, just as in considering a job one weighs the honor and profit it might bring against the pain of the work and the loss of time. We can make it so that "all the evils which come from outside us, as great as they can be, only appear before our soul as sad-ness which actors excite in us, when they represent before us tragic actions."

But he has said all this to her before, and a sigh of frustration is almost audi-ble. "I confess that it is necessary to be very philosophical to get to this point." And then in a more spiteful tone, "Anyway, I believe also that even those who let themselves be carried away most by their passions, judge always, inside them, that there are more goods than evils in this life, even though they don't realize it them-selves, because even if they call death to their aid when they feel the greatest griefs, it is only in order to help them bear their burden as if it is in a story, and they do not really want to lose their lives." Anyway, even if they do kill them-selves, he concludes, it is not by a "well-reasoned judgment."

Nor—he must be weary by now of repetition—does this mean that the prudent man will do no good deeds. In fact,

it ordinarily happens that those who are thought to be diligent and prompt to please receive also many good offices from others, even from those whom they have never obliged, offices which they never would have received if those others believed them to be of another humor. The trouble they must take to please is not so great as the conveniences which the friendship of those who know them give to them.

All this is very well arranged, he explains. What costs little to one man may be very valuable to another, so that it is always possible to make a good bargain. And even if sometimes one gains by doing evil and loses by doing good, this is the exception and cannot change the "rule of prudence."

As for me, the maxim that I have most observed in all the conduct of my life has been to follow the high road and to believe that the principal finesse is not to want to have to use finesse. The common laws of society, which tend always to make one do good to others, or at least to not do bad, are, it seems to me, so well established that whoever follows them faithfully, without any dissimulation or artifice, leads a life much more happy and more assured then those who find their utility in other ways, which, in truth, succeed sometimes by the ignorance of other men and by the favor of Fortune but very often happen to fail. In thinking that they are so establishing themselves they are ruined. It is with this simplicity and this frankness that I profess to observe in all my actions, that I profess to be also . . .

With this curt summary, Descartes closes, omitting his usual affectionate compliments. Five months go by before Elisabeth brings herself to answer this letter.

Affairs of state might have been an excuse. Now there was concern for Philip. Recalled from his studies in the aftermath of the Edward affair, he was up to no good. With no serious employment, he roamed the streets with dissolute bands of aristocratic young men fond of hard riding and destructive pranks. There was a plan afoot that Philip would be sent to raise troops in Hamburg and transport them to Venice by way of Holland, and Elisabeth was much taken up with the negotiations.

It was no time for more scandal. The Swedes who had invaded the Hapsburg empire were gaining the upper hand, and the Catholic emperor had begun to make concessions. In August, the emperor agreed to give the right to vote on war and peace to independent Protestant territorial rulers. This was the condition, long pressed by Elisabeth's cousin Frederick William of Brandenburg, that stood in the way of serious peace negotiations. Talks, it seemed, could now begin in earnest. With Philip honorably occupied, there was hope that the Palatine cause would get a hearing. As always with the Palatines, nothing was easy. The queen had washed her hands of the scheme to send Philip to Venice, having grander, less realistic ambitions for him. Elisabeth—and other members of the family with a clearer view of Philip's temperament—urged it as a good way to keep him out of trouble. Given her mother's disapproval, it fell to Elisabeth to conduct matters, which she did with her usual diligence and finesse, answering dispatches, deciding on terms, weighing pros and cons. In the meantime, Philip's departure was continually delayed, keeping him restless and without occupation in The Hague.

But affairs of state had never before kept Elisabeth away from philosophy. What could she have said in answer to Descartes's letter? An abyss had opened between them, more unbridgeable than a resolvable intellectual disagreement. To find virtue in doing favors for those in high places, making friends in all camps? To play the shallow game of patronage and politics that she so hated, to play it without commitment or moral involvement? To argue the point was impossible, not when this advice went against her very sense of what was right and good. Was she, as Descartes asked, to measure out benevolence in self-interested thimble-fuls? If no one could think such a demeanor "noble," could dishonor be cured by a satisfying inner conviction that she had "magnanimously" done all that she could?

15

Master of Passion

~

*M*eanwhile, regardless of wounded feelings, Descartes was hard at work on Elisabeth's topic: the passions, those same passions that had precipitated Edward's disloyalty and Elisabeth's lack of "prudence." What are emotions? Are all of them to be repressed? If not, how is it possible to choose which are healthy and to be encouraged and which are "not conducive to virtue"? Elisabeth had convinced him of one thing at least. Without a theory of passion to support his ethics, the new science was vulnerable to attack.

The manuscript *The Passions of the Soul* that Descartes brought to Elisabeth in early March of 1646 was a map of the soul, both the human soul and the soul of a man, René Descartes. Descartes's other writings—technical treatises on geometry and optics, discourses on method, meditations on metaphysics—were objective and reasoned in the style of the new rational science. The treatise on passion was a description of man, or a new man, or a certain man, of his joys and sorrows, agitation and equilibrium, loves and hates. Written as a systematic defense of the moral and medical advice that he pressed on Elisabeth without success, inspirited with a genuine desire to have her and others partake of the contentment he believed himself to enjoy, *Passions* is a diary, a confession, a credo that lays bare the interior motivation of one man's rational philosophy.

In *Passions*, the theoretical separation between mind and body that Elisabeth had questioned in her first letter to Descartes becomes a way of life. The key to the achievement, as Descartes presents it, is in the scientific understanding of passion as a variety of bodily "mechanisms." In great detail, he elaborates the physiology he had only sketched out before. A stimulus is registered first on the brain and then on the soul, which, purely active, purely willful in rational thought, "suffers" a passion that can disrupt and distort rational thought. The source of that passion is "animal spirits," a circuitry of mechanical energy—blood circulation, heartbeat, muscle tension—whose purpose is not to inform but to protect the body from harm. Although the circuitry operates automatically in animals, in men bodily energies also register on the soul so as to "incite the soul to correct and contribute to the actions which may serve to maintain the body."[1] But—and this is the main lesson to be learned from studying the passions scientifically—in man, or in a man like Descartes who has achieved philosophical detachment, the separation between body and soul holds. The rational soul is only "indirectly" affected by emotion, and the passions are only indirectly affected by the mind. The key to removing any possible deleterious effect of passions on the soul, therefore, is the fostering of mental separation and the proper understanding and regulation of passion, so that the soul suffers only those passions that are pleasurable and healthful. Admittedly this is difficult. The agitation of bodily spirits, as Elisabeth continually pointed out, can last well after any precipitating cause. The purpose of a treatise on the passions, then, is moral as well as scientific: to set out in more detail the attitudes and practices that make possible the emotional hygiene and discipline that can help a man overcome weakness and achieve virtue and happiness.

The first task is a properly scientific understanding of passion. As protective bodily mechanisms, Descartes argues, passions are not distinguished by any real diversity in the objects that cause them but only by elements in objects that can harm or help the body. On that basis he lays out the causes and physiological effects of six "primitive passions": wonder, love, hate, desire, joy, and sadness. All have their source in wonder at a potentially interesting event or object and have distinguishable physiological effects depending on whether the remarkable object is seen as good or bad for the body, attainable or attained, and possessed or not possessed by others. As Descartes explains it, love results in a steady, strong pulse beat, a gentle heat in the chest, and the easy digestion of food. Hate is distinguished by uneven and feeble pulse beat, fits of chills, a biting, severe heat in the chest, and nausea. When desire is added to love or hate, other physiological effects prepare the body for action.

The problem for a man with a "strong" rather than "weak" soul who is not carried away by his emotions—a man like Descartes—is not only that the passions give "exaggerated" messages about what is harmful or helpful to the body but also that many passions are painful and disturb one's happiness. The key to a good and happy life is to learn to conquer passion. One must substitute for unthinking passionate action "determinate judgment" as to what is good or evil, along with the will to carry out what is in one's power. As he writes in his dedicatory preface to Elisabeth, reason and will, and not conflicting emotions, are the "proper arms" of the soul, the weapons with which it fights against destructive and disturbing passion. Torn between confrontation and flight, a man may waver ineffectively. Wavering between a declaration of love and reticence, he may suffer a kind of stasis. Using the weapons of the soul, he decides rationally whether he should fight or retreat, declare himself or not. Not all souls, Descartes acknowledges, are born so strong, but even if one has from birth a "weak" soul—like Elisabeth's?—it is possible, with the proper training of judgment and will, to regulate the passions and the mind so that unhealthy or painful emotions do not trouble rational thought.

Under the guise of a catalog of passions and their effects, Descartes describes how a man or a woman can win the battle against depression and mental malaise and achieve virtue. Morality, he wrote, is just this: the regulation of desire. Once passion is under control, a man can live virtuously, knowing the good, desiring and willing only the good, never desiring anything that does not depend on his own will. To help achieve this goal, one can reflect diligently on the truth that everything outside of one's own power is determined for all eternity by God.

Immediately, Descartes is back to the tangled question of free will and determinism. To cease to care about everything not in his own power, a man needs the consolation of believing that what happens is God's will. But for him to get moral satisfaction from doing what is best, he requires free will. Straddling the contradiction that Elisabeth refused to pass over, Descartes maps out the way to forestall regret, anger, and grief. What is not within the compass of a man's own will must be accepted stoically because it is God's will. What he does himself in a properly studied way is to his credit. Should you be angry at what other men do? Not really. Although a man who has mastered his emotions may assume that others also feel free, from his own God's-eye view, their freedom need not be acknowledged. A man can live from the center of his own mind as a "noble" soul, sure that "nothing pertains to him but his own will," thinking that he cannot be blamed for anything if he uses that will correctly. At most he "generously" assumes that others can manage to maintain the same kind of life for themselves.[2]

Descartes's "generosity" is not the common, altruistic variety. It begins with self-esteem, the satisfaction that comes when you undertake nothing for which you do not feel capable, when you are secure in your own mind and confident that you have acted according to your own determinate judgment. A man is "generous" in Descartes's sense because he can afford to be affable, courteous, obliging; he can afford it, because he is invulnerable. He is never fearful, because he is confident of his virtue; he is never angry because he expects nothing from others.[3] The alternative is pride, a vice based on no inner merit, pride that can be puffed up by flattery. In contrast, the generous man assumes that others are as capable of self-esteem and invulnerability as he is.

Of all the beneficial passions, "generosity" is the one Descartes most praises. The generous man is not bothered by pity, a painful emotion that for Descartes is evidence of weakness and error and to be avoided. People prone to pity imagine, when they see someone in pain, that the misfortune could happen to them. Pity therefore comes from self-love and not love of others. The generous man may feel a kind of pity, but his sadness for others has no "bitterness." Descartes repeats his theater analogy: The generous man feels pity the way he feels pity at a theatrical production, as a passion that does not touch the interior of his soul. Inside himself he feels only pleasurable satisfaction at his ability to feel concerned for others. Although an "ordinary" man may feel more pity the more a victim cries out, the noble generous man pities only the weakness of someone who would give in to passion.[4] These are not new insights for Descartes but elaborations of the many points he made in his letters to, and conversations with, Elisabeth. They are insights that Descartes himself lived by and by which he regulated his relations with friends.

Take, for example, a letter written nine years before to his grief-stricken friend Huygens on the occasion of the death of Huygen's wife.

> If I were to measure you by the standard of vulgar souls, the sadness which you have expressed from the beginning of the illness of [your wife] would make me fear that her death would be completely unbearable for you. But, not doubting but that you govern yourself entirely according to reason, I am persuaded that it is much easier to console yourself and to recover your accustomed tranquility of spirit now that there is no longer any remedy which before gave occasion for fear and hope. For it is certain that once hope is gone, desire ceases or at least weakens and is relieved. And when there is little or no point of desiring to recover what one has lost, regret cannot be very strong. . . . But a soul that is strong and generous, like yours, knows too well to what condition God has made us born into to wish by any ineffectual wishes to resist the necessity of his law. And even if one cannot submit without some pain, I esteem so highly friendship that I believe that all which one suffers for its sake is agreeable, so that even those who go to their death for the good of persons they love seem happy at the last moment of their life.[5]

These are the attitudes, long characteristic of Descartes's responses to painful events, that *Passions* elaborated and systematized.

To achieve stoic equanimity, Descartes acknowledges, takes work, especially for those born with less aptitude for "nobility." But, he concludes optimistically, anyone with instruction and self-training can to some extent correct native deficiencies. If one reflects on free will, if one constantly reminds oneself that the passions exaggerate, if one constantly diverts oneself from unpleasant emotions and fosters agreeable thoughts, if one reasons out the best action in any situation and does it without regret, he—or even she—can become a master of passion. "The principal use of prudence or self-control is that it teaches us to be masters of our passions, and to so control and guide them that the evils they cause are quite bearable."[6]

Of course, one should not extinguish all feeling, he repeats. The soul has its own safe pleasures: the pleasure of the rational contemplation of abstract ideas, the pleasure of logical argument. The key to the "good life" is to experience those reliable pleasures without contaminating them with any bitterness or pain. Then one can experience "the sweetest of all joys, because its cause depends only on ourselves."[7] In one of the most rhapsodic passages of the treatise, Descartes praises the great virtue of a "secret" inner joy. Even though outwardly we may feel grief—say, at a loved one's death—inside we can take satisfaction in our invulnerability as well as in a sense of our own virtuous magnanimity. Drawing on his old advice to his friend Huygens and, perhaps, his own furtive experience with the servant woman, Hélène, Descartes uses once more the example of the death of a wife.

> For example, when a husband laments his dead wife whom (as sometimes happens) he would be sorry to see brought to life again, it may be that his heart is oppressed by the sadness that the appurtenances of woe and the absence of one to whose conversation he was accustomed excite in him; and it may be that some remnants of love or pity which present themselves to his imagination draw sincere tears from his eyes, notwithstanding that he yet feels a secret joy in the inmost parts of his heart, the emotion of which possesses so much power that the sadness and the tears which accompany it can do nothing to diminish its force.[8]

In such cases if we pleasurably view a sad event as if we were in a theater, we can actually take pleasure in the emotions it excites. With self-satisfaction to content us "inwardly," we accomplish a kind of emotional alchemy, and grief transforms to pleasure; calm within, we happily observe grief's righteous manifestations in our outward tears. In other words, the rational soul has its own colder heart, an impregnable inner core of self-satisfaction, barricaded against disappointment, sensible only of its own perfection, and providing a satisfaction "so powerful in rendering a man happy that the most violent efforts of the passions never have sufficient power to disturb the tranquility of his soul."[9] What philosopher has bared his soul more intimately to a lover than Descartes did to his friend Elisabeth in this treatise?

It is a month and a half before she responds, pleading that she has been busy with Philip's mission.

25 April 1646
The Hague

Monsieur Descartes,

The treaty which my brother Philip has signed with the Republic of Venice, since your departure gave me an occupation much less agreeable than the one you left me, occupation beyond my experience and to which I would not have been called except to make up for the impatience of the young man whom it concerned. This prevented me until now from taking advantage of the permission you gave me to present to you the obscurities my stupidity makes me find in your Treatise on the passions. They are of small number, since it must be impossible to ignore that the order, the definition, and the distinctions which you give to the passions, and therefore to all the moral part of the treatise, go beyond what anyone has yet said on the subject.

But since the physics part may not be so clear to the ignorant: I do not see how one can know the diverse movements of the blood, which cause the five primitive passions, since they are never alone. For example, love is always accompanied by desire and joy, or desire and sadness, and to the measure that it is strong, others think also [here there is a break in the manuscript]. How is it then possible to tell the different beating of the pulse, the different digestion of meats, and other changes of the body, which serve to reveal the nature of these movements? Also, as you note, none of these passions is the same in all temperaments: mine is such that sadness takes away the appetite, that is, as long as it is not mixed with any dislike, such as comes only from the death of a friend.

When you speak of the exterior signs of passion, you say that admiration, joined to joy, makes the lungs fill up with many jolts to cause laughing. To which I ask you to add in what way admiration (which, according to your description, seems to only operate on the brain) could open up so promptly the orifices of the heart to create this effect.

The passion that you note as the cause of sighs does not seem to be the cause, since dress and the fullness of the stomach can also produce sighs.

But I find less difficulty in understanding all that you say about the passions than I do in practicing the remedies that you prescribe for their excess. For how can one foresee all the accidents which can take place in life, when they are impossible to count? And how can we prevent desiring with ardor things which tend necessarily to survival (like health, and the means to live) which nevertheless do not in fact depend on free will? The desire for knowledge of the truth is so just that it is naturally in all men; but an infinite knowledge would be needed to know the real value of goods and evils which customarily move us, since there are many more than a single person could imagine, and it would be necessary to know perfectly all the things which are in the world.

Since you have already told me the principles of a life on one's own, I would still like to know your maxims in regard to a civil life, a life that makes us dependent on persons who are not very rational. In such a life, up to now, I have always found that experience serves me better than reason. I have been so often interrupted in writing to you that I am constrained to send you this fragment and to take advantage of the messenger from Alcmar, having forgotten the name of the friend to whom you wanted me to address my letters, and because of that I do not dare to send back your manuscript, insofar as I have knowledge of this messenger, not being able to decide to risk to the hands of a drunkard a piece of such great value, which has given so much satisfaction to

Your very affectionate friend at your service,

Elisabeth

The pain of the rift lingers. There is still a lack of warmth, of admiring compliment. Immediately Elisabeth turns to what she sees as the deficiencies in Descartes's account of emotion. Nor does she hesitate to continue to confess to some of the emotions that Descartes advises against. She feels inadequate, pushed beyond her expertise in the Venice matter that had been thrust upon her by default. She confesses "stupidity" in that she cannot see that Descartes is right about the passions.

Her remarks on Descartes's physiological account of the passions are devastating. No matter what she says, these are not a few details to be cleared up so that those ignorant of physics can understand. Can passions be identified in a laboratory, the way one might isolate chemical compounds? No, because passions are never experienced alone. Along with love always comes desire or sadness. And even if love were detachable from desire, isn't the physiological manifestation of passion different in different individuals, to say nothing of the fact that the supposed physical effects of passion that he notes could be due to a tightly laced bodice or a too-full stomach? Is it possible physiologically to know what one is feeling? Is the gentle heat in the breast and regular pulse Descartes describes love or satisfaction at an admirer's attention? Is that upset in the bowels hate or indigestion? To Elisabeth, always reflecting, always revising the "story" of what happened, what one feels is an open question, not a matter of fact to be decided by taking the pulse or measuring blood pressure.

But more important to Elisabeth than the inadequacy of a physiological definition of different passions is the irrelevance of such an account to morality. Yes, let us say we can identify the physiological effects of each passion, make a correlation between reports of anger and muscle tension or heat in the chest. But what can this have to do with the remedy for painful passion? Descartes's remedy for passion is a rational psychology that lays out the utility and disutility of emotions, along with the resolve to do as science dictates. But how is that crucial passage from the fact of passion to the "best" thing to do accomplished? If everything is ordained by God for the best, there is no room for will at all. If space is left for free action, then to be in control of emotion one would have to have complete hindsight and foresight, which is impossible. Even if the facts are clear, how is one to know the relative value of goods and evils, or foresee all that might be in store for us? And what about desire for those things that are necessary to life, like health and the means of subsistence? They are not always in our power, but is there any way to stop wanting them?

Elisabeth closes with the question she has pressed all along. Descartes's philosophy might work for an isolated scholar, but what about a morality for life with others, the life that she and most people must, and want to, live?

16

A Certain Languor

~

*D*escartes answered promptly in May, prudently choosing to take pleasure in her "favorable judgment" rather than offense at her criticisms. He is not surprised, he confesses, that he committed mistakes, given that he had not examined the passions before. What he sent to her was only a preliminary sketch; it will need work to make it ready even for "eyes less clear-sighted than hers." As for the physiological part, yes, he did not map it all out—"That is a thing so difficult that I did not think it would be understood, even though I myself am satisfied of the truth of the principles which I presupposed in this writing." For Elisabeth's sophisticated understanding, he gives more detail, on the workings of kidneys, lungs, heart. Then one by one he attempts to answer her doubts about his method. Yes, the passions are typically mixed, but they are not always mixed in the same way, so that it is possible to separate out the physiological effects of one from another. Yes, there are variable physiological effects of emotion, but this can be laid at the door of past associations. Even if some emotions, like admiration, do not arise from bodily excitement but from an idea, admiration, like other passions, can cause physiological effects such as those associated with surprise. That similar physiological effects have purely physical causes does not mean that they cannot also be caused by passion. Yes, his method cannot really cure the body but only make the soul less troubled by it, and yes, only bad passions need to be so closely monitored.

So the master of rational argument expertly—if somewhat wearily—parried Elisabeth's concerns about the mental contentment that he has urged on her. His examples are revealing. For his account of the variability of emotional response, his example is sadness, which takes away the appetite of some people and augments that of others. Again he draws on his motherless infancy. Someone—like him?— at the beginning of life might not get enough nourishment, and so forever sadness for him will be connected with hunger. Another might be given harmful food, causing him to associate eating with sadness. Again the absent mother surfaces, dead when he was just past one year old, leaving him alone with a stern father and a hunger for affection that will never be satisfied or even expressed—so much so that he refuses to think that his mother cared for him at all but rather says that she died at his birth instead of in the process of giving birth to another son.

On distinguishing mixed emotions, he chooses the example of love and desire.

> If love was always joined to joy, I would not know to which of the two to attribute the heat and the dilation that they make felt around the heart, but since love is also sometimes joined to sadness and then one feels again this heat but not that dilation, I judged that the heat pertained to love and the dilation to joy. And even though desire is almost always found with love, they are not nevertheless always together in the same degree, for even when one loves very much, one still desires little when one does not conceive any hope. And because one does not have then the diligence and the promptitude that one would have, if the desire was greater, one can judge that it is from desire that it comes and not from love.

Great love, little hope. Great love but desire smoldering rather than aflame. Purely a subject of objective research? As for the perfect knowledge that Elisabeth charges would be necessary for his ethics to be useful, yes, it might have seemed that he excuses "a certain languor" in those situations in which perfect knowledge of the outcome is impossible. But he still admires those who are resolute, who do their duty even though it does not seem as if much will come of it. He ends the letter with compliments.

But this languor business festers. Immediately Descartes has second thoughts, and he writes another letter. He has been thinking. Yes, perhaps he did make a mistake in the draft of the treatise when he included among the "excusable" passions a certain languor. Especially he is upset because it was a point that she had expressly mentioned to him. Of course irresolution cannot be defended.

It is not clear when and where Elisabeth noted this "languor" that causes in Descartes such a flutter. It might have been at one of their meetings in The Hague.[1] Or it might have been in the deleted part of her letter, one of very few faults in the copies of the letters found by Foucher de Careil. Descartes ends his second note, "I assure myself that your Highness understands very well my thought, even when I explain it badly, and she will pardon the extreme zeal that obliges me to write this, for I am as much as I can be, René Des . . ."[2]

It is a bit of a mystery, this tremor over a languorous lack of passion in uncertain circumstances. "I am as much as I can be, your René Des . . ." But not . . . what? Not your lover, not even a very faithful friend? I love, but of course having no conceivable hope, I must be excused for failing in the "diligence and promptitude" that ordinarily accompany desire? But no, of course Descartes does not say this. He does not have to, as he says, because he knows that she will understand his thought better than he can explain it.

Odd, too, that the offending passage as it finally appears in the published version of the treatise also concerns love.

Languor is a tendency to relax and be motionless . . . and the passion which most usually causes this effect is love joined to the desire for a thing whose acquisition is not imagined to be at the time possible; for love so occupies the soul in considering the object loved that it employs all the spirits which are in the brain in representing to it its image, and it checks all the movements of the glands which do not contribute to this result.[3]

Unrequited love accompanied by a languor that prevents one from thinking about anything else? Excusable? That is a question that these two, given what is between them, might have had to face. Elisabeth and her middle-aged philosopher, locked together in an affection that can never be consummated, but that, at moments, as when she offers him her sympathy and concern when he is unfairly attacked or when he lays at her feet a new manuscript on a subject she has initiated, reignites and distracts them, causing a kind of paralysis, an excusable lack of energy for anything else.

Certainly, for Elisabeth, with the Philip affair on her hands, it was no time to be "languorous." Descartes reassures her that, yes, she is right, irresolution can be dangerous even when the results of action are not at all sure. It is understandable that in the Venice affair Elisabeth might have hesitated, wondering if Philip, young and headstrong, was capable of such a commission. Would it make him a mercenary, a soldier of fortune, as her mother insisted? As usual Elisabeth, immersed in changing events, exercises all her tact and resolution. Of course, Descartes advises, forgetting his claim of inexpertise in the affairs of the world, you must take time to deliberate about an action. But then, once the matter has begun, you must be resolute and not hesitate to proceed. Either the action is going to succeed and delay over details will cause more harm than good or, if one fails, delay only signals to the world one's failure. It is better to get on with it. If one delays, the chance may escape. Above all, one should not worry unduly about things that might happen, because even if they do, they might not be so bad. Given that other men are not rational, as they would have to be if one were to map out a sure course, it is best to take a gamble and trust to divine providence.

It is a safe enough explanation of the energy Descartes gives to this question of languor, but somehow a question remains. Had Elisabeth taken the remarks about languor too literally, referred indiscreetly to the passage in the treatise that deals with the languor of unrequited love, the languor that makes a man, or a woman, in love listless, unable to marshal his or her energy? Is this why whoever copied the letters carefully smudged out certain phrases? Is the prudent Descartes suddenly worried that in his treatise he might have encouraged in Elisabeth a romantic but unhygienic paralysis? Had he made it seem excusable to be made dysfunctional by love?

17

Murder in the Streets

~

*I*n early July of 1646, Descartes received the following letter from Elisabeth.

Since your trip is set for the third to the thirteenth of this month, it is necessary for me to call in the promise which you made of leaving your agreeable solitude to give me the happiness of seeing you, before my leaving here prevents it for six or seven months, which is the longest term that the queen, my mother, and my brother and the sentiment of the friends of our family have prescribed for my absence. It will seem too long, if I do not assure myself that you will continue to allow me to profit from your Meditations by letter, since without their assistance, the cold of the North and the caliber of people with whom I will be able to confer there will extinguish that little ray of common sense which I have by nature and which I have recovered by your method. I am permitted in Germany enough leisure and tranquility to be able to study, and from that I draw the greatest treasure, of which the most satisfaction will come from your writings. I hope that you will permit me to take with me the Passions, even though your book has not been able to calm those which our latest misfortune excited. It is necessary that your presence bring the cure that neither your maxims nor my reason have been able to apply. The preparations for my trip and the affairs of my brother Philip, joined to a charitable concern for the pleasures of my Aunt, have prevented me up to now from giving you the thanks I owe you for the helpfulness of your visit; I beg you to receive them now from

Your very affectionate friend at your service,
Elisabeth

P.S. I was obliged to send this by messenger, because promptness is more necessary to me at this moment then security.

So Elisabeth announces to Descartes the forced exile that would now take her away from The Hague and his company. The "latest misfortune" was a sad and gruesome affair. Monsieur Espinay was a French captain stationed at The Hague. He had an unsavory past. A protégé of a French nobleman, he had seduced his patron's mistress and been forced to flee France. In Holland, he continued his adventures as a ladies' man, boasting that he "played with" only princesses or mistresses of princes. Regardless of his reputation, he was welcomed by the queen of Bohemia into her court and allowed intimate access to her and her daughter, Louise. Charming, skilled in flattery, always dressed elaborately in the latest court fashion, he amused and titillated the two women, taking liberties with them in private and public that were watched with growing anger by the queen's sons.

Louise's temperament was very different from her sister's. A minor artist of some talent, she was addicted to romantic adventure, heedless of convention, and volatile in emotion. Whether or not Espinay managed to "play with" the queen, he certainly seems to have succeeded with Louise. It was common gossip that she had an illegitimate child by him at Leyden. But Espinay's worst fault was his tongue. When he began to boast that he had succeeded with both the queen and her daughter, Elisabeth's brother Philip, restless and delayed in his departure for Venice, lost his head.

There are several versions of the story. This much is clear. One night Philip either challenged Espinay to a duel that was aborted by police intervention or he and several comrades attacked Espinay. In any case, Espinay managed to escape. Perhaps because he had little respect for Philip's swordsmanship, he refused the advice of friends to lie low. On the afternoon of 20 June 1646, as Espinay was leaving the house of the French ambassador where he had lunched, he was set on by Philip and a band of men and assassinated in the street in broad daylight. What the odds were against Espinay, whether he was armed or not, whether the attack was premeditated or an impetuous act of the moment, whether it was Philip, certainly present physically, who actually struck the fatal blow—all this remains unclear. The French took one side in the matter and the Dutch press the other. A great outcry went up at the murder. So threatening were angry crowds around the queen's house that the magistrates dispatched a guard to protect the princesses. A warrant went out for Philip's arrest, and he fled the country. Amid much muttering about the shocking privilege of the nobility, he was not seriously pursued beyond the borders of Holland.

The queen was beside herself with fury. Gossip said that she saw nothing wrong with Louise "amusing herself" and was only furious at the loss of a favorite courtier. Certainly much damage had been done to the family reputation, and just when there was some chance that the Palatine might be recovered. With Philip gone, Elisabeth, as usual, was the scapegoat. She had always disapproved of the frivolous behavior of both her mother and sister; she was certainly vocal with Louise in her disapproval of the disreputable Espinay and the freedoms he took; she was in agreement with Charles-Louis and Philip that Espinay's behavior was an insult. As a result, she was accused by her mother of inciting Philip to commit murder or, at the very least, of having an intolerable degree of sympathy with the criminal. Refusing to live any longer with her daughter, the queen banished her from The Hague, sending her back to Germany to the relatives who had brought her up.

One can only imagine the bruising scenes that went on between mother and daughter. Elisabeth senior was known for outspokenness and harsh language. Years of resentment of her daughter's silent criticism, years of impatience with her refusal to play seriously the game of court politics must have come to the surface. Steadfastly, the mother defended Louise, whom she proclaimed innocent, a claim hardly borne out by Louise's subsequent history of elopement and sexual adventure. According to Elisabeth's optimistic estimate, she would be gone from The Hague for a period of six months. In fact she would never see her mother again. On the few subsequent occasions when Elisabeth senior referred to her daughter in letters, she did so with suspicion and resentment. For all intents and purposes Elisabeth had been disowned.

This time Descartes rose to the occasion. As soon as the crime became known, he made the trip into the city to see Elisabeth. Even in the best of all possible worlds, it is hard to view murder with equanimity. In her letter Elisabeth expresses gratitude for his helpfulness and for the promises he gave to visit her again before he his departure for France.

The references to philosophy in this sad, constricted little note, written with care in case it should fall into the wrong hands, are poignant. Neither philosophical maxims nor reason nor Descartes's moral treatise have brought this princess happiness or protected her from harm. She is now caught up in a painful flurry of activity, trying to ameliorate her brother's fate, pacifying the aunt who will accompany her in exile, trying to keep out of the way of her furious mother. All the time she sadly prepares to leave for the "cold of the North." She cannot look forward to the prosperous rolling hills and fertile vineyards of her Palatine homeland, which have been destroyed by imperial armies. She goes to a region devastated by war and numbed by backwardness. How will she confer with scholars and intellectuals there? With whom will she discuss philosophy? Where will she find the thriving intellectual life of Holland? As if she were going to prison, she reviews what she will be "allowed." She will be "permitted" books, and so she wants to take his *Passions*. And she hopes that she will still have the benefit of Descartes's reflections, if only by letter. She cannot think that the term of their separation will be for very long. She looks forward to a visit before she leaves.

What must have those visits in The Hague been like? Elisabeth, shaken and pale, Descartes, awkward and at a loss, realizing that even his "prudence" must fail in such extreme circumstances, trying to console, something at which he had very little practice. All around her is enmity. Her brother Charles, out of the line of fire in England, is happy enough that she bears the brunt of it. Descartes is her only friend. He offers her what he can. They will continue their work together, he reassures her. They will read together, as they did when she was ill. This time—might he have leant closer to her, all the intimacy their situation allows?—the book will be of her choosing.

18

The Prince

The text Elisabeth chose for their joint study at one of those last meetings in The Hague before her departure for Germany was Machiavelli's classic work of practical politics, *The Prince*. It was a relevant choice, considering her situation. What had she and the rest of the family done wrong in the management of Philip and his affairs? How should she have conducted herself differently? If she had acted more deliberately in the Venice negotiations, with less care to detail, might Philip have been safely away from The Hague in Venice? Should she have been less open in talking to him about her disapproval of her mother's and sister's behavior, less descriptive of the offensive behavior of this prancing seducer with his foppish manners and feather-plumed hats? Clear, straightforward honesty, her instinct in such matters, might in hindsight have been a mistake. When dealing with people who are not rational, perhaps dishonesty, manipulation, and subterfuge are more effective policies, just as Machiavelli insisted, just as Descartes also had intimated.

As soon as Elisabeth left, Descartes made good on his promise, dutifully completing his reading assignment. In September 1646, he writes a long letter of comment to her in Germany. He finds little to approve of in Machiavelli. Machiavelli's strategies are too tyrannical, he complains. Perhaps duplicity can be defended with one's enemies but not with one's own people, to say nothing of one's friends. Friendship is holy; no one should pretend it. And certainly a prince should keep his promises, guard the faith, and enforce customary laws. Only if "good" means backward superstition or intolerance in religion should a prince be evil. As he glosses Machiavelli's position in one passage:

> he supports precepts that are very tyrannical, such as to want to "ruin a whole country in order to remain the master of it, to exercise great cruelties provided that it is done quickly and all at one time, to try to appear a man of good but not be one in fact, to keep one's word only so long as it is useful, to lie, to betray, and then, in order to rule, to strip oneself of all humanity and become the fiercest of all the animals."

But it is a very bad thing to write books in order to undertake to give in them advice that, in the end, cannot even give any assurance to those to whom one gives it, for as he admits himself, "They cannot protect themselves from the first person who is willing to give up his life to get vengeance on them."

As he did with Seneca, he went on to say what he thinks Machiavelli should have said, expressing a surprising degree of complacency about the means by which power is achieved.

> Instead, to instruct a good Prince, someone newly installed in a State, it seems to me that one must propose to him completely different maxims and suppose that the means with which he has established himself have been just, as in effect, I believe that the means Princes have used practically all have been whenever the Princes who practiced them judged them to be so. For justice between Sovereigns has other limits than between individuals, and it seems that in these encounters God gives the right to those to whom he gives the power.

Might makes right? If an autocratic prince wins, he must be good because God has willed it? Certainly it was an attitude that Elisabeth, with her family driven from their lands by imperial troops, would not have approved. But regardless of his lengthy, line-by-line critique of the *The Prince* and long passages in which he details his own view of proper policymaking, Descartes continues to plead political reserve. One should not presume to interfere in the affairs of princes. He, for one, is not of the opinion of Machiavelli "that just as it is necessary to be down in the plain, to better see the shape of mountain when one wants to draw them, just so one ought to be in private life to better understand the office of a Prince." Drawing pictures is one thing, says Descartes, the motives of princes are another. One has to be a prince oneself or close to princes to understand them. As a private citizen, he defers to Elisabeth. He has no wish, he says, to be her teacher in such matters but only writes to her in his old role, to divert and amuse her at a difficult time.

> This is why I deserve to be mocked if I think I might be able to teach something to your Highness on this matter, nor is that my design, but only to have my letters give her some diversion different from those which I imagine she had on her journey, which I hope was perfectly happy, as without doubt it would be if your Highness resolves to practice the maxims which teach us that the felicity of each person depends on himself. It is necessary to be so out of the Empire of Fortune that even though one loses no occasion to retain the advantages that she can give, one does not think oneself to be unhappy each time she refuses. In all the affairs of the world there are a quantity of reasons pro and con; one should stop at considering those which serve to make one approve the things one sees happen.

Descartes cannot resist anxiously rehearsing once more the maxims of his old Stoic ethic. A person's happiness should depend on himself, he should expect nothing from Fortune. She should think positively.

Either because he understood that there might be restrictions on her correspondence and that he might be suspected of having influenced her in her supposed murderous intent, or because he simply wants her to be able to write freely about her circumstances in Germany, he adds a postscript. They should have a code, a numerical cipher so that their correspondence can be kept secret.

Having arrived in Berlin after a long journey, Elisabeth answers.

Berlin

10 October 1646

Monsieur Descartes:

You are right to think that the diversions that your letters bring me are different from those which I had on the journey, since they give me a satisfaction much greater and more durable. Even though I have found in taking this trip all that the friendship and embraces of my relatives can give to me, I consider them as things which can change, unlike the truths which your letters bring, which leave impressions on my spirit which will contribute always to the contentment of my life.

I have a thousand regrets in not having carried the book overland which you took the trouble to examine to give me your opinion, letting myself be persuaded that the baggage which I sent by ship at Hamburg would be here sooner than us, and it is not here yet, even though we arrived the 17th of September. This is why I cannot represent the maxims of that author otherwise than a very bad memory can furnish of a book which I have not looked at in 6 years. But I remember that some of his maxims I approved, not because they were in good faith but because they caused less evil than those which many impudent and ambitious rulers go by, who I know only tend to stir things up and then leave the rest to Fate. Those of Machiavelli all tend to stability.

It also seems to me that to teach the governing of the state, he takes the state most difficult to govern—where the prince is a usurper, at least in the opinion of his people. In this case, any opinion he might have himself, even as to the justice of his cause, might serve to put to rest his own conscience but not his affairs, when the laws restrict his authority, or the powerful undermine it, or the people speak against it. And when the state is so disposed, great violence is less evil than little, since the latter offends as much and gives pretext for a long war. The former takes away the courage and the means available from the powerful. Similarly, when violent acts come quickly and all at once, they anger less then they surprise, and are more bearable for the people than the long train of misery that civil wars bring.

It seems to me that he also adds, or rather teaches, by the example of Alexander, the Pope's nephew, whom he proposes as a perfect politician, that the Prince must use for his cruelties a minister whom he can afterward sacrifice to the hatred of the people. And if it appears unjust for the Prince to destroy a man who has obeyed him, I think that persons so barbarous and unnatural that they want to serve as hangmen for a whole people, for whatever consideration that might be, are not worthy of better treatment. As for me, I prefer the condition of the poorest Dutch peasant to that of a Minister who would obey such orders, or to that of the Prince who is constrained to give them.

When the same author speaks of allies, he supposes, similarly, that they are as wicked as they could be and affairs in such an extremity that it would be necessary to either lose the whole Republic or break his word with those who would not protect the Republic any longer than it is useful to them.

But if he is wrong to make general maxims out of what ought only to be practiced on very few occasions, he sins equally with almost all the sacred Fathers and ancient philosophers, who do the same thing. I think it is from pleasure that they take to declaiming paradoxes that they can later explain to their students. When this philosopher here says that a Prince will ruin himself if he wishes always to be a good man, I believe that he means not only that to be a good man one must follow the laws of superstition, but also that one must follow the common law—that one should do to each what one would wish done to himself. But Princes can almost never practice this rule with their individual subjects; it must be broken almost every time that public utility requires it. And since, before you, no one has said that virtue consists in following right reason, but have prescribed some more particular laws or rules, one should not be very surprised that they have failed to define virtue very well.

I too find that the rule which you note in his preface is false, but only because it does not apply to someone with clear thinking in anything that is proposed to him, as you are, and someone who by consequence, from a private retreat far from the press of the world, is able to teach to princes how they should govern, as it appears in what you have written on the subject.

For me, who have only a title, I work to make use of the rule that you put at the end of your letter, trying to make the present circumstances as agreeable as I can. Here I do not encounter much difficulty. I am in a house where I have been loved since my infancy and where everyone conspires to give me embraces. Even though these sometimes turn me away from more useful occupations, I easily support this inconvenience for the pleasure there is in being loved by one's relatives. Here is the reason, Monsieur, why I have not had any sooner the leisure to give you an account of the happy success of my voyage with the promptness with which I corresponded before and to tell you of the miraculous spring that you told me about at The Hague.

I have been only a little distance away, at Cheuningen, where we meet with all the family who come from here. M. the Elector wanted to take me to see the spring, but since the rest of our company opted for another diversion I did not dare to contradict them and was satisfied to see and taste the water, of which there are several sources of different taste, but only two are used principally. The first is clear and salty and a strong purge; the other is a little whitened, with a taste like water mixed with milk and, they say, refreshing. One speaks of how many miraculous cures there are, but I do not hear that from anyone worthy of trust. They say that the place is full of poor people who claim to have been born deaf, blind, lame, or hunchbacked and to have been cured in this fountain. But because these are mercenary people, and they encounter here a nation pretty credulous about miracles, I do not believe that this should persuade a rational person. Of all the court of my cousin, M. the Elector, there is only his grand Escuyer who felt better from it. He had a wound under his right eye, from which he lost his sight on one side because of a little membrane which had come over the eye, and the salted water of the spring, being applied on the eye, dissolved that membrane, so that he could then discern people when he closed the left eye. Otherwise, being a man of strong complexion and bad diet, a good purge could not harm him as it has many others.

I examined the number code you sent me and find it very good, but too prolix for writing all the meaning, and if one only writes a few words, one can find them by the quantity of the letters. It would be better to make a key of words by the alphabet, and then mark some distinction between the numbers which signify letters and the ones which signify words.

I have here so little leisure to write that I am constrained to send you this scribbling in which you can note, from the difference of pen, all the times I have been interrupted. But I prefer to appear before you in all my faults than give you reason to think that I have a vice so far from my usual as to forget friends in my absence, principally a person toward whom I do not cease to feel affection without ceasing also to be reasonable, as you are Monsieur, to whom I will be all my life,

your very affectionate friend at your service,
Elisabeth

Reunited in Berlin with her relatives, who have a sincere affection for her and admire her talents, Elisabeth for once is willingly distracted from philosophy. Her grandmother Juliana is dead but her Aunt Charlotte, now dowager electress of Brandenburg, is with her, along with her childhood friend and cousin, Charlotte's son Frederick-William, now elector of Brandenburg, and Frederick's young daughter Hedwige-Sophie, who becomes Elisabeth's student. The family greets her warmly, in sharp contrast to the cold reception she was used to with her mother. Instead of having to withstand suspicion and constant critical scrutiny, Elisabeth basks in care and sympathy, quickly recovering some of her old good nature.

She is still the careful and skeptical observer of physical fact, tasting and analyzing the waters from the Fountain of Hornhausen, touted for its miracle cures throughout the long, maiming years of the war. She observes closely, as a prince should, the pitiful condition of the people in the aftermath of the war. One-third of the population was dead. The territory was full of the poor, crippled, and blind, at the mercy of unscrupulous merchants waiting to steal their last pennies by puffing up the virtues of spa water. Compared to The Hague, Berlin, the second town of the region, was a primitive backwater. There was no bookstore; the printers put out no serious works; the name of Descartes was unknown.

Remarkable in this letter are Elisabeth's revived spirits. In closing, she reminds Descartes that she feels deep affection for him but, she playfully reassures him, only within the bounds of reason, perhaps referring again to that inexcusable languor. She pays homage to his moral advice, if not as maxims she can follow then as marks of his affection. Indeed, his long letter and his prompt reading of *The Prince* must have warmed her heart as much as the embraces of her relatives. She is attuned to that now with him: affection expressed as mutual interest and mutual exploration of ideas.

On the subject of Machiavelli, of course, there is much disagreement. Elisabeth had read *The Prince* six years before at age twenty-two, the impetus probably an Italian treatise that appeared in the same year defending the Palatine cause by drawing on Machiavellian principles. Not having her copy of The Prince yet, she shows a retentive memory in her recall of points that impressed her at that first reading. She is not going to excuse Descartes from having opinions on politics. Although she agrees with him that persons in private life may not be able to understand the motives of rulers, someone as clear-thinking as he ought to be able to. And she does not hesitate to correct what she sees as naive reactions. Descartes's "good faith"—seeing rationally what is best and doing it regardless of the consequences, looking to the state of one's own conscience rather than to the state of one's affairs—is not adequate as a civic morality, she tells him. Whatever the value of such an ethic for a person who lives "only to himself," it can be disastrous in a ruler. After all, wasn't it just such simple-minded policy that brought on the disaster in Bohemia?

Again, Elisabeth and Descartes approach texts differently. Descartes pays little attention to context or motives; he looks for a match with truth as he sees it. As with Seneca, Elisabeth does not read Machiavelli for a map of reality so much as for understanding of the intention of what is written. Machiavelli is referring not to ideal republics but to real territories like the medieval Italian principalities or territorial enclaves in central Europe where the development of nation-states was retarded and a succession of violent take-overs made civic life impossible. How is a stable government to be found and maintained in such situations, a question certainly pressing now that the Thirty Years' War was coming to a close?

Machiavelli, she says, takes the hardest situation that a ruler can face—where he is a usurper, where there is much opposition and allies are not to be trusted. How in this hardest case can a ruler achieve "stability"? Having seen the effects of war, Elisabeth has no problem in promoting stability at the cost of moral compromise. As for taking the hardest case and drawing general maxims from it, again her revived spirits allow her some wit. Isn't this what all you great philosophers do to get attention, shock people?

More seriously, she continues, in extreme political situations, universal maxims like "Do unto others as you would have them do unto you" are useless. When you are responsible for the public good, you cannot treat one of your subjects as you would like to be treated yourself, not if the public good demands something different. A ruler and a subject are not on an equal basis. Nor can a life of responsibility for others be lived without remorse and compromise. Unlike philosophers, on their deathbeds prince and captain have necessarily much to regret.

Descartes's ethics require an interior self-satisfaction and trust in Providence to arrange things. It is an ideal that is all too close to the irresponsible ruler Elisabeth cites, a ruler who follows his own maxims, satisfies his own conscience, and then leaves the rest to Fate. If it could be said that this was the sad result of Descartes's intellectual campaigns at Utrecht, of course Elisabeth is too tactful to mention it. What she does make clear is her opinion that the good and noble ruler, who follows customary law, sincerely supports the faith, never lies or breaks his promises, is at best a dupe who will be usurped and at worse a villain who can bring down ruin on his country. Or his university? Poor Descartes. First the passions, a subject with which he had little experience, and now politics, a subject in which he is equally untested.

19

Magic Powers

~

*D*escartes answers in November, genuinely relieved to hear about Elisabeth's happiness, even if his observation that "it seems to me that
[you] now have as much good as one could wish for rationally in this
life" might be somewhat overstated. Poor Elisabeth. Yes, finally she is with those
who love and admire her, but she is paying a heavy cost in terms of social obligations. She has no library, no source of books. Family fortunes are not much
improved. Still she finds Descartes's maxims hard to follow. If there are no present
objects that offend a person's sense and if he follows reason, he should be content,
he continues to remind her. Not that you forget affairs that are far away, he adds,
but if you have no passion for them, you will be able to make even better judgments than when you are actively suffering from them. There is a new urgency in
Descartes's prudent advice now that Elisabeth seems to have a chance of happiness. "Just as bodily health and the presence of agreeable objects serve well the
spirit by chasing away all passions which participate in sadness and giving entry to
all those that participate in joy, thus reciprocally, when the spirit is full of joy, this
also serves to make the body healthy and present objects appear more agreeable."

In a rush of relief at her happiness, Descartes confesses unreservedly some of
the stranger characteristics of *The Passions of the Soul*'s "interior joy," as he continues to try to convince her of the power of positive thinking.

And also I even take the risk of thinking that this interior joy has some secret force
that makes Fortune more favorable. I would not write this to anyone with a weak
spirit, for fear of leading them into superstition: but as for your Highness, I only fear
that she will make fun of me that I am so credulous. Nevertheless, I have an infinity of experience, and in addition the authority of Socrates to confirm my opinion.
The experience is that I have often remarked how the things I have done with a gay
heart and without any interior repugnance tend to work out for me happily. Even in
games of chance, where it is only fortune that rules, I have always found the outcome to be more favorable when I have reason to be happy than when I am sad. And
that thing which is commonly called the "genie" of Socrates, without doubt it is not
anything else but that Socrates was accustomed to follow his interior inclinations,
and thought that things that he undertook would work out happily when he had this

secret sentiment of gaiety, and unhappily when he was sad. It is true that it would be superstitious to believe in this as much as he did, because Plato reports of him that he would even stay home anytime that his genie did not tell him to go out. But in regard to the important actions of life, when they are so doubtful that prudence cannot tell one what one ought to do, it seems to me that there is good reason to follow the counsel of one's genie, and that it is useful to have a strong persuasion that things that we undertake without repugnance, and with the freedom that ordinarily accompanies joy, will not fail to succeed for us.[1]

So, he pleads with her, take this opportunity to be happy. Being happy will make good things happen. It is better that she has no books, so she doesn't worry herself with reading. And she should never think of politics except when the courier is ready to leave. Especially she should stop reading Machiavelli, so full of depressing difficulties and cruelties. He passes on to lighter topics, to the fountain at Horn, its chemical makeup, its medical benefits, ending on the same cheery note with which he began: be happy, because just being happy makes things work out.

It is hard to know what to make of the odd little passage about the genie. Alchemy, astrology, divination, even psychokinesis were part of the lore of the day, taught by various secret societies. At one point, Descartes himself was accused of consorting with the Rosicrucians, although he denied it, quipping that although Rosicrucians say they are invisible, he was very visible. He did, however, confess that he had looked for a member of that mystic brotherhood to talk with on his travels in Germany. And why not? To control nature, to decipher its secrets, to use magic numerical formulas to change the world to suit our desire— these claims from the Rosicrucian manifesto, *Fama Fraternitatis*, echoed those of the new science. In Descartes's *Discourse on Method* he explained how his method would make man "lord and master of the universe." Scientists were men, as the Rosicrucian *Fama* put it, "imbued with great wisdom, who might partly renew and reduce all arts (in this our age spotted and imperfect) to perfection; so that finally man might thereby understand his own nobleness and worth, and why he is called Microcosmus, and how far his knowledge extendeth into Nature."[2]

But Descartes's intimation that Elisabeth might not like this talk of secret powers and magic genies was well founded. She replied.

Berlin
29 November 1646

Monsieur Descartes

I am not so much accustomed to the favors of fortune that I would wait for anything extraordinary in that regard; it is enough for me that it does not send me very often these accidents which would give cause for sadness to even the greatest philosopher of the world. And since nothing like that has happened since my stay here, and present objects are all agreeable to me and the air of the country suits me, I find myself in a condition to be able to practice your lessons in regard to gaiety, even though I do not hope for any such effect in the conduct of my affairs as you have had in games of chance. The success which you have encountered there when you were otherwise disposed to joy proceeds, apparently, from the fact that you con-duct yourself more freely, which ordinarily means that one wins.

If I had the opportunity to dispose of my person, I would not depend so easily on an effect of chance to be in a place where I could find subjects for contentment, in contrast to where I came from. As for the interests of our House, for a long time I have abandoned them to destiny, seeing that prudence alone, if it is not helped by other means left to us, is not worth the trouble. It would require a "genie" stronger than Socrates' to work there with success. Since that genie did not help him avoid prison or death, it has not much to boast of. I also have observed that times when I follow my own inclinations, I have succeeded better then those in which I let myself be led by the advice of those supposedly wiser than me. But this I do not attribute so much to the felicity of any genie as to the fact that having more affection for what touches me than anyone else does, I am better able to examine what might harm or be advantageous than are others on whose judgment I might rely. If you still want me to give some role to an occult quality of my imagination, I think you must be doing that to accustom me to the humors of the people of this country, particularly the doctors, who are more pedantic and superstitious than any I have known in Hol-land. As a result, all the people here are so poor that no one studies or reasons but to survive.

I have had all the trouble in the world to escape the hands of the doctors, so as not to suffer their ignorance, not that I have been ill, but only that the change of air and diet has given me in the place of gall some pustules on my fingers. From which these Monsieurs judge that there is still some bad matter hidden, which is too big to be evacuated and to which it is necessary to put purges and bleeding; but since I feel otherwise so well disposed that I fatten in the wink of an eye, I make a value of stub-bornness where reason is useless, and have managed to take nothing to date. I understand more than the doctors here, because everyone here takes chemical extracts, of which the effects are swift and dangerous.

Those who have researched the ingredients of the Spring at Hornhaufen believe that the salty source contains only ordinary salt; to the other they accord nothing. Also they attribute (this is principally the Lutherans) the effect more to a miracle than to the composition of the water. For me, I will take the surer part, according to your advice, and not use any.

I, myself, hope never to be in a state to have to follow the advice of the "doctor of Princes" [Machiavelli], since violence and suspicion are things contrary to my nature even though I only blame the tyrant for his first design of usurpation and his first enterprise. This is because afterwards the route which serves to establish that enterprise, however rude it may be, always does less evil to the public than a rule contested with arms.

But this study does not occupy me enough to make me morose, since I use the lit-tle time left to me after the letters I have to write, and the necessary accommodations I must make for my relatives, to reread your works, where I profit more in an hour for cultivating my reason than I would all my life in other reading. But there is not any-one here rational enough to understand them. Although I did promise to the old Duke of Brunswick, who is at Wolfenbuttel, to let him have them to decorate his library, I do not believe that they will serve to decorate his brain, which is already completely occupied with pedanticism. I let myself go here for the pleasure of entertaining you, without thinking that, without sinning against the human race, I could work to make you waste your time (which you use for your profit) in reading the nonsense of

Your very affectionate friend at your service,

Elisabeth

The master of reason advises her to trust to a magic genie that things will work out? Be happy in one's heart and trust to fate? Elisabeth had never been willing to take that advice, and it would have been surprising that she would start when it turns out that fate is not the ordinance of a divine commander of souls but a genie to be evoked with light spirits. Unlike Descartes, she expects no magical intervention. She asks only of fortune that it not deal her out catastrophe that not even the "greatest philosopher in the world" could face with equanimity.

Yes, things are calm for the moment and she is happy. But even if she were free, like Descartes, she would not believe or trust to any genie for well-being. A lot of good Socrates' genie did him, she observes wryly, since he was executed by the state of Athens for impiety. With all this, there is a lovely lightness in this letter. Peace for once, leisure for pleasantries, wit, irony—all this is permissible with someone she knows well and trusts.

Characteristically, Elisabeth is less interested in secret inner joys than she is in observing what is going on around her. Always she is attentive: to poverty in Germany, to the despair that makes the people rush to have recourse to the magic of spa water. Carefully she assesses prevailing medical practice in Germany and the degree to which it is based on reason rather than superstition. She shows herself well taught by Descartes, able to prescribe her own cure, or at least avoid harmful ones pressed on her by ignorant doctors. In a few months she has blossomed. She is in the cold north, in backward Berlin, but she is with cheerful, loving people who bring back her native wit and spirits. By the end of the letter she is telling jokes. With all her poking fun at the stuffy baron and the backward doctors, she was creating quite a sensation in Berlin. The Berliners were not used to seeing a handsome, educated, outspoken woman who did not busy herself with social calls and needlework but who was intent on introducing medical men and professors to the new scientific philosophy of her friend René Descartes.

Descartes's answer in December is almost ebullient with relief that she is happy, happier than he has ever seen her, he says. He reassures her about the pustules on her fingers. It is nothing, he says, common among young people, so common he doesn't even count it as an illness. Better just wait until spring. and if the affliction is not gone by then she can easily cure it by eating no salted or spiced meat and taking some gentle purgatives or broth. Bleeding might help, but he advises against it because there are risks in this remedy. Above all no drugs, which must be used with great care; one small mistake and they can be damaging. The same thing is true for science, he complains.

> It is almost the same in Science when it is in the hands of those who borrow from it without knowing it well. Because, in thinking of correcting or adding something to what they have learned, they change it into error. It seems to me that I can see the proof of this in Rhegius's book, which has finally appeared.

He doesn't send the book on. She can see it when she gets back. There is a note of bitterness.

> I am not surprised that your Highness does not find any doctors in the country where she is who are not entirely preoccupied with the opinions of the Schools, for I see that, even in Paris and in all the rest of Europe, there are so few that, if I had known before, I would not perhaps ever have bothered to publish anything.

Somewhat feebly, Descartes tries to resurrect his own positive thinking.

> Anyway, I have this consolation that, even though I am assured that many have not lacked the will to attack me, still there has always been someone willing to enter the lists for me, and I have even received compliments from the Jesuit fathers whom I have always believed to be among those who feel themselves to be the most interested in the publication of a new philosophy, and who would pardon me the most, if they thought they were able to blame me for anything with good reason.

20

An Ungrateful Disciple

~

*I*n his December letter, Descartes refers to an affair that was causing him much teeth gnashing. Another storm was brewing over his work. A long, sardonic letter of explanation that he sent to the Utrecht magistrates in May of 1645 had gotten no response, perhaps because no one understood the French in which it was written. In any case, Descartes's letter was given out for translation and forgotten. Clearing up the issue was clearly more important to Descartes than it was to the magistrates, who must have wished only that the quarrel between Descartes and Voetius would die a natural death.

Now in addition, his follower Rhegius at Utrecht was increasingly an embarrassment. A frequent visitor at Endegeest, Rhegius began as a faithful if not very gifted student, but increasingly his sharp tongue and impolitic excesses were harming as much as helping Descartes's reputation. Certainly he helped to make Voetius, the acknowledged theological authority of the city and rector at the university, into an implacable enemy of Cartesianism. After the Voetius affair, Rhegius, afraid of losing his position at the university, began to tailor Descartes's philosophy to suit the authorities, omitting any controversial metaphysics and concentrating only on physics, making what Descartes considered to be a mess of the whole thing. Descartes read Rhegius's manuscript *Fundamental Physics* with dismay. As he saw it, it was nothing but a confused mishmash of his own ideas. He pleaded with Rhegius "as a brother" not to publish. When Rhegius, increasingly intractable, ignored this advice and published anyway, Descartes was in a fury. Rhegius was making Cartesianism look ridiculous.

In the meantime Elisabeth was having her own difficulties. Her youngest sister, the sweet, gentle Henriette, who would die tragically a few years later, was seriously ill. As usual it was Elisabeth's job to nurse the patient and supervise her treatment. In addition, the queen mother of Sweden was visiting in Berlin. Because she was the sister of Elisabeth's aunt, Elisabeth was obliged to follow in her train.

Most depressing of all, whatever was to have been her original term of exile, her mother showed no signs of wanting her back in The Hague. Increasingly it was clear that her banishment was to be for an indefinite period, along with her separation from Descartes.

Berlin
21 February 1647

Monsieur Descartes

I esteem joy and health as much as you do, but I like your friendship as well as virtue, since it is principally from that which I take both joy and virtue, joined with a satisfaction of spirit which surpasses even joy, you having taught me the means to achieve it. I can no longer lack resolution to take any remedy for the little inconvenience which remains to me, since this has met with your approval. I am at this moment so well cured of my skin problem that I do not think I have any need to take medicines for purging the blood in the spring, having enough discharged the bad humors and exempt, I would think, from the fluctuations which cold and stoves would have given otherwise.

My sister Henriette has been so sick that we thought her lost. It is her illness which prevented me from answering sooner to your last, requiring me to be always near to her. Then, just when she is doing better, we were obliged to follow the train of the Queen Mother of Sweden, every day and at night at dances and balls, diversions very inconvenient for those who could do better, but which inconvenience the less when one does them for and with persons whom one has no reason to mistrust. This is why I have more accommodation for these things here than I did at The Hague.

Always I would be happier to be able to use my time in reading Rhegius's book and your opinions on it. If I do not return to The Hague the coming summer—which I cannot answer for, not that I have changed my plan, but because this depends in part on the will of others and public affairs—I will try to get this letter to come by the ships which go from Amsterdam to Hamburg, and I hope that you will do me the favor of sending yours by the usual channel. All the time when I read your writings, I cannot imagine that you might, in effect, repent to have published them, since then it would be impossible that they would be received and be useful to the public.

I have been encountering here for a little while one man who sees something in your work. This is a doctor of medicine, named Weis and very learned. He has told me that Bacon first made him suspect the philosophy of Aristotle, and that your method made him entirely reject it and convinced him of the circulation of the blood, which destroys all the ancient principles of medicine, which is why he confesses to have consented to your thesis with some regret. I have just pressed on him your *Principles*; he promises to give me his objections. If he finds any, and if they merit the trouble, I will send them to you, so that you can judge of the capacity of someone I find to be the most reasonable among the doctors of this place, since he is capable of digesting your reasoning. But I assure myself that no one would know how to estimate you at such a high level as does

Your very affectionate friend at your service,
Elisabeth

What a contrast between Descartes's two followers. Rhegius ineptly copied and borrowed from Descartes's ideas; visiting at Egmond, he looked at unpublished manuscripts and then voiced Descartes's findings as if they were his own, publishing a unauthorized, garbled version of his *Physics* without the metaphysics that supports it and makes it intelligible, all in deference to the hated Voetius, who couldn't care less about speculation in physical science as long as theological dogma stays intact. So different from Elisabeth the faithful friend and critic. Would that Elisabeth had been a professor and could have supported Descartes at the university as diplomatically as she handled the appointment of M. Schooten.

Elisabeth is no sycophant; she continues to work subtle transformations in the maxims that she professes out of gratitude to accept. Descartes's prudence, and the joy and inner satisfaction that come from it, are to be valued, but more for their deep source, the friendship that keeps her friend writing and talking to her. This is the real root of happiness, as she sees it. As for the medical advice, again she is an intelligent patient, contributing her own interpretation of disease not as simple physical disfunction or the failure of the rational mind to rule the body but as organic reaction to physical circumstances, in this case to "fluctuations in heat" in poorly heated houses and a damp and cold climate.

She apologizes for having so little time to read Rhegius's book and Descartes's comments. She deplores the fact that she will not return soon to The Hague so she can consult with him in person and console him in his disappointment that his main supporter at Utrecht is a false friend. He should send his letters to her by the "usual channel," her sister Sophie, who will enclose them in her own letters so they will not be intercepted and he can speak freely. For his friendship and support, she offers hers in return. Never think of not publishing, the world needs your work, she reassures him. She is promoting his ideas, not in faculties of theology, where they will not be well received, nor at universities where vested academic interests block acceptance, but where such ideas are needed most, with practicing, intelligent doctors who are open-minded about the new science.

In his answer in March, Descartes shows his gratitude by more than words. Because she does not seem likely to return that summer, his plan is to make a trip to France to handle his affairs, but he will delay his departure for two months while he waits to hear definitely about her plans. Again he shows concern for her health.

> I praise God that you are now in perfect health, but I ask you to pardon me if I dare to contradict your opinion, in regard to not using any remedies, because the problem you had with your hands is gone, but there is still a danger, for your Highness as well as for Madame your sister. Even though the humors which are purged in this way have been arrested by the cold of the season, in the spring they may bring back the same problem, or put you in danger of some other sickness, if you do not remedy it by a good diet, using only meats and beverages which refresh the blood, and which purge it without effort. As for drugs, whether the Apothecaries' or the Empyrique's, I hold them in such low esteem that I would not dare to advise anyone to use them.

About the ungrateful Rhegius he is scathing; he cannot see what he possibly could have said that made her think that his opinion on Rhegius's book would be very interesting, except that he said nothing about it, thinking that she could come to her own opinion. Since she has not read it, he will tell her quite frankly to forget it, because there is nothing in it worth reading. It contains only Descartes's own "assertions in bad order and without their proper proofs." It contains nothing new, and almost everything in it had already been published by Descartes. Worse, Rhegius has included some findings on physiology that Descartes had not wanted to make public and that Rhegius copied surreptitiously and inaccurately, so that what he wrote had no value and might even be dangerous. And now Descartes has heard that Rhegius plans to publish a second book on medicine along the same lines, no doubt with the same distortions and plagiarisms. Nothing this man could write will ever be any good, rails Descartes, nor can he be relied on to oblige Descartes in anything.

Nevertheless, since Elisabeth has asked, he will send Rhegius's *Physics* by way of Sophie but will send with it a book he approves of by Hogeland, who does not copy but follows his own line of thought and comes to the same sound principles without, perhaps, ever having read Descartes's writings. Descartes also promises Elisabeth to send on the French version of his *Meditations*, which he thinks he will have before his departure for France.

Elisabeth receives the books and answers in April.

Berlin
11 April 1647

Monsieur Descartes,

I had not really regretted my absence from The Hague until you summoned me to be there and I felt deprived of the satisfaction which I would have had in your conversation while you are there. It seems to me that I would leave any such talk more rational. Even though the repose which I find here, among people who care for me and value me so much more than I merit, surpasses all the goods which I could have elsewhere, it does not approach that pleasure, which I nevertheless cannot promise myself in a few months, nor even predict how long, since I do not see that Madame the Elector, my Aunt, is in a humor to permit my return, and I do not have any pretext to press her with it before M. her son is with her, and even that, if he asks it himself, would not be until the month of September, and it may be that his affairs will oblige him to come sooner or to stay away longer. Thus I can hope, but not assure myself, that I will have the happiness to see you again at the time you have proposed for your return from France. I hope that you encounter on this voyage the success which you ask for. If I had not had experience of the constancy of your resolutions, I would fear that your friends would make you stay there. I beg you meanwhile to give an address to my sister Sophie, so that I can have your news sometimes, which is always agreeable to me, no matter how long it is on the road.

After Easter, we will go to Krossen, which is the estate of Madame my Aunt, on the frontier of Silesia, to stay there three weeks or a month, where the solitude will give me more leisure for reading and I will busy myself with all the books you have had the kindness to send me, for which I ask you here to accept my thanks. I have had more trouble in reading the book of Rhegius for what I know that he has put in it of your work than for what is in it of his own. Other than that he goes a bit fast; he has profited from the assistance of Doctor Johnson, as he himself has told me, who was able to trip him up even more, having a spirit sufficiently confused by faith. And there, too, he does not take the patience to understand things which he has read or heard. But even though I excuse all the other faults of this Rhegius, I do not know how to pardon him for the ingratitude which he shows toward you, and I judge him to be simply lazy, because your conversations have not been able to give him other sentiments.

M. Hogeland has been assuredly successful in what he has printed, since he has followed your principles, which I have not been able to make understood by one of the doctors in Berlin, preoccupied as they are with the Schools. And that one which I named in my last letter has not visited me, since I gave him your Physics, which is a sure sign that everyone here is doing well, since he is the house doctor.

When I told you that I did not want to use remedies for the pustules that I had last autumn, I meant those that come from the apothecary, since herbs that are stimulating and purge the blood are food for me in spring, not having ordinarily any appetite in that season for anything else. I also let myself be bled a few days, since I have gotten into a bad habit of it that I cannot change right now without being afflicted with a headache. I would be afraid of giving you this angering story of myself, if your care for my health had not reached me. It would give me even more vanity, if I could find in it other cause than the extreme kindness that you have for

Your very affectionate friend at your service,

Elisabeth

Regardless of Descartes's assurance that there is nothing in it, Elisabeth has read the faithless Rhegius's book, although she waits for a quiet stay in her old childhood home at Krossen to read the rest of the books Descartes sent. Her reading of Rhegius, though not flattering, is considerably more indulgent than Descartes's. She knows Rhegius personally, in fact knew him before she knew Descartes. Her diagnosis is that he lacks care, is a bit lazy, and has been led astray by her old chaplain. Faith and science make a confusing mix. Has Descartes really managed to clear it up? No, she does not say it. But she does have a willingness to listen to Rhegius's explanations, to attend to the context in which he writes and the influences on him. And she has a certain sympathy with any attempt, however failed, to cast the new science in terms consistent with orthodox religion.

Nor is her concern for her own health so straight and narrow as Descartes might like. She has developed, she says, regardless of his warning, an addiction to being bled, which she originally resorted to as a cure for headache. She chides him a bit for telling her what she already knows. No, she is not about to sit down to large meals of spicy meat; she knows to eat salad and other vegetables to cleanse the system. But as always, the cure he provides is not so much the prescribed scientific remedy as it is his caring and inquiring about her health. Even in Berlin, in her cousin's house, much as she is loved, her maladies often go unnoticed. The source of the most potent medicine her doctor-philosopher provides is not science but those forbidden emotions: fear that she will become seriously ill, regret that they cannot see each other, a sense of loss that she is no longer near him.

21

An Accusation of Blasphemy

~

y Descartes's next letter, Rhegius and the bungled *Physics* are the least of his worries. Affairs at Leyden have now taken a turn for the worse. On 27 March, a Professor Triglandius, a supporter of Aristotle, argued the thesis that Cartesian philosophy was blasphemous. The offending text was Descartes's *Meditations*, in which Descartes temporarily, and for the purpose of refutation, supposed that God might be a deceiver creating a world of illusions in which there is no reality. When Heerebord, a supporter of Descartes, protested, a storm of controversy resulted and the meeting in which the thesis was considered broke up in disorder.

Descartes had known of Heereboord's unsolicited interest in his work as early as 1641, when Heerebord failed to sign the report of the decision of a university commission that teaching should conform to Aristotelianism. More of a diplomat than Descartes, however, Heereboord managed to present Cartesian ideas in a way that made them seem more or less consistent with Aristotelianism. He published a thesis, *Philosophical Freedom,* that argued that one should bring to the study of philosophy a virgin spirit and a lack of prejudice and preconceived ideas and named as pioneers in that endeavor both Aristotle and Descartes. The latter he praised in the hyperbolic rhetoric of the day as a "demi-god," adding the gratifying invocation, "Salute, oh most grand of the philosophers, guardian, savior and revenger of Truth, of Philosophy, and of the Liberty of thought."[1] Descartes chortles at Heereboord's success at pulling the wool over the Aristotelians' eyes in an 8 January 1644 letter to his friend Pollot. "These things hardly affect me at all, but they are coups d'état for my adversary [Voetius], who I think does not sleep so well at night as I do." Heereboord's support was all the more gratifying because it was on his own initiative; Descartes could not be accused of undue influence or behind-the-scenes coaching as he could with Rhegius.

Coming on the heels of his disappointment with Rhegius, the charge of blasphemy from a quarter where he counted on support took Descartes by surprise. That blasphemy was a terrible crime he did not deny; what seemed to him enormous was that he would be charged with it, especially on the basis of a work that he had undertaken expressly to prove that God exists and that God's existence is in no way inconsistent with rational thought. In a panic, he wrote to Heereboord for details of the situation. In May he mailed off another indignant and inflammatory letter to the curators of the university at Leyden.

In his letter to Elisabeth of 10 May, he complained bitterly of what he considered a conspiracy among the theologians at Leyden who are now, he thinks, trying to turn the magistrates there against him. "There is a troop of Theologians, Schoolmen, who seemed to have lined up together to try to oppress me by slanders, so that, while they are coming up with all that they can to try to do harm to me, if I do not take care to defend myself, it will be easy for them to commit offenses against me." Again his worry was that his enemies would bring the police down on him. "They say that the Theologians want to be the judges in the matter, that is to say to submit me to an inquisition more severe than ever there was in Spain." Bitterly he blames the democratic Dutch. "People here do not honor probity and virtue, but the beard, the voice, the eyebrow of the Theologians, so that those who have the most effrontery and who cry out the loudest have the most power, as is the case in all popular states." His friends have advised him to ask the French ambassador or Elisabeth's relatives in the House of Orange to get the hearing quashed. But no, he says in martyred tones, he demands full "satisfaction" at Leyden and also at Utrecht; he demands adjudication no matter what the outcome, "complete satisfaction for his injuries." Forgetful of his opening reassurances that reasons for staying in France could never be outweighed by reasons to return to see her in The Hague, he threatens that if he does not get justice, he will leave Holland for good. "I demand only justice, and if I cannot get it, it seems to me that the best thing will be that I make a quiet retreat."

Still he is careful to close with reassurances. "But, whatever I think or I do, and in whatever place in the world I go, there will never be anything that will be dearer to me than obeying your commands." The master of passion clearly has his hands full.

On 20 May at Leyden the matter was reheard. Again the decision went against Descartes. All teaching should be "within the perimeters" of Aristotelianism. A ban was imposed on discussing Descartes or mentioning his name. A letter was sent to Descartes announcing the decision, to which Descartes replied with yet another indignant letter. If only his loyal and influential royal friend were there to console him.

In a sympathetic answering letter from Krossen, Elisabeth, who had independently received the news of Triglandius's attack and the April meeting that ended in disorder, urges on Descartes a more reasoned approach.

Krossen
May 1647

Monsieur Descartes

It has been three weeks since someone sent me the impertinent thesis of Professor Triglandius, adding that those who argued for you there were not defeated by reason but were silenced by the tumult that resulted at the Academy, and that one Professor Stuart (a man of wide reading but of mediocre judgment) tried to refute your Metaphysical Meditations. I believe that this will give you the same pain as has the calumny of the school of Voetius, but not, I hope, the resolution to leave Holland, as you witnessed in your letter of the 10th of this month. It is unworthy of you to give ground to your enemies, and it would look like a kind of banishment, which would bring you more prejudice than anything that Messieurs the theologians could do against you. Slander is not so considerable in a place where those who govern cannot exempt themselves from it, nor punish those who do it. The people there pay a great price for that sole liberty of speech, and the speech of the theologians, being privileged everywhere, cannot receive restraint in a popular state. This is why it seems to me that you are right to be content if you obtain what your friends in Holland counsel you to demand, even though you need not follow their advice in demanding it, the resolution you ask for being more appropriate for a man free and assured of his work. But if you do go on with the plan of leaving the country, I also will abandon the plan I have to return there, if the interests of my house do not recall me, and will rather wait here until the result of the Treaty of Münster or some other happening returns me to my fatherland.

The land of Madame l'Electrice is in a situation which is good for my complexion, being two degrees closer to the sun than Berlin, surrounded by the river Oder. The land here is extremely fertile and the people have come out of the war better than elsewhere where the armies stayed a longer time and there was so much damage by fire. There is now in some of the villages a great quantity of flies that one calls "cousins," so that several men and animals suffocated or became deaf and blind. They come in the form of a cloud and go the same way. The inhabitants believe that it comes from fodder, but I attribute it to the extraordinary flood of the Oder, which this year continued up until the end of April, and also that it has been very hot.

I received, a few days ago, the books of M. Hogeland and of Roy, but dispatches here have prevented me from reading all but the beginning of the first, in which I would judge highly the proofs of the existence of God if you had not accustomed me to asking for the principles of knowledge. But the comparisons by which he shows how the soul is unified with the body and constrained to accommodate itself to its form and to take part in the good and the bad which happens to it still do not satisfy me; since the subtle matter, which he supposes to be enveloped in a grosser one by the heat of fire or fermentation, is nevertheless corporal and receives its pression or movement by the quantity and the superficies of its little parts, which the soul, which is immaterial, cannot do.

My brother Philip, who has brought me the two books, informed me that there are two more en route, and since I haven't ordered any, I believe that they are your *Meditations* and your *Principles of Philosophy* in French. I have the most impatience for the latter, since you have added there something that was not in the Latin, which I think must make a fourth book, since the three others appear to be as clear as it is possible to make them.

The doctor of whom I spoke to you before has told me that he has several objections touching minerals, but he does not dare to bother you with them until he has had a chance to examine your principles. His practice keeps him from it. People here have an extraordinary belief in his profession, and if it were not for the great dirtiness of both commoners and nobles, I believe that there would be less need of it than for any people of the world, since the air is very pure. I have had here more health than I ever had in Holland. But I would not wish to have been always here, since there is nothing but my books to prevent me from becoming stupid to the last degree. I would have complete satisfaction if I could witness to you the esteem which I have for the kindness that you continue to have for

Your very affectionate friend at your service,
Elisabeth

Elisabeth writes from her old childhood refuge, where she and her grandmother and aunt waited out the war. In lovely rolling countryside between two rivers, surrounded by birch and oak forests, away from the bustle of court life, relieved of having to dance attention on the queen mother of Sweden, Elisabeth has time to appreciate beauties of place, noting that Krossen is much less ravaged by fighting than other areas. As always she is an acute observer, reflecting with interest on the swarms of flies that harass the neighborhood and consulting the opinion of local farmers on the cause. In contrast to Descartes, who thinks of illness as the interior dysfunction of bodily mechanisms, Elisabeth relates health to environmental effects such as standing water, poor hygiene, damp, lack of exercise, and bad air, foreshadowing later public health approaches to disease.

But she has not lost her interest in metaphysics, as evidenced by her comments on Hogeland. No, she cannot agree with Hogeland that the soul is fused with the body and must partake in whatever bad or good happens to the body. The mind must have some degree of independence. One can only speculate as to how she might have developed such a thesis if she had stayed on at Krossen living the quiet country life, untroubled, like Descartes at Egmond, by state politics.

Perhaps most interesting are her comments on Dutch politics, for which she has considerably more sympathy than Descartes. Descartes was willing to profit from the privacy and amenities available in a prosperous democratic republic, but he had no particular love for, or interest in, the great bustling humanity of the Dutch cities. Full of diverse people, by necessity tolerant, with an unruly press, Dutch culture had many of the features of democracy today. Although the Dutch Reformed Church was the established church, other sects were free to worship discreetly. Although Protestantism was necessary for officeholders, the simple declaration of conformity required was little more than a formality. In all this Descartes took little interest. As one commentator described his attitude: "He walked out among the crowds not considering these men other than he would see trees or animals passing by in a forest."[2]

Always the private citizen, Descartes reacted to events as they affected him, often missing larger political dynamics. He has been insulted by the theologians. His work has been maligned. He will leave if he does not get satisfaction. Elisabeth, the princess, was more familiar with the intricate political balance in Holland between the House of Orange, the clergy, and the citizens who sat as magistrates.

This was the nonhierarchical popular government it was the Protestant revolution's aim to foster. Under such a government it is one thing to have one's views maligned, another to be arrested. In a country in which there is free speech, in a popular state like the Dutch Republic, no theologians, not even of the religion of science, are allowed to dictate, although they may speak their opinions. In a popular state one can speak against those in power or against those out of power. For this great good, Elisabeth reminds Descartes, there is a cost. Some slanders go unpunished. There is no way the magistrates can silence the theologians, any more than they can silence Descartes. Regardless of university moratoriums on debate, in Holland Descartes's books are not censored but are freely circulated.

Indeed the general consensus was that Descartes exaggerated the danger. True, university authorities exerted their power to regulate instruction. But Descartes's insistence on escalating conflict, his slanders of Voetius and others, were at least partly responsible for the ban on the discussion of his work at Utrecht and at Leyden. Whatever his lectures on "prudence," in this matter Descartes's emotions got the best of him, and his virtue of understanding what is best and acting on it failed. Raw passion, that same passion that was to be so carefully regulated in his treatise, seemed more in control than reason. Much more effective was the tactic of his wise supporter, Heereboord, whose reasonableness might have prevailed at Leyden if Descartes had not written indignant letters.

Similarly, Descartes's attempt to find a docile tool in Rhegius, through whom he could manipulate and escalate matters at Utrecht, also worked to his disadvantage when Rhegius proved equally malleable in the hands of the authorities who controlled university positions. Persuasion, rhetoric, sensitivity to other interests—these are the skills of politics in a popular state, skills that Elisabeth was developing as she advised her brother and cousins. Friends in positions of power, manipulations of stooges, and vindictive self-assertion were more effective in the retrograde bureaucratic states of the Catholic monarchies than in the Dutch Republic. They were not providing much help to the "prudent" theist Descartes.

22

A New Patroness

⤳

On 6 June 1647, just as he was to leave for another trip to France and before he could have received Elisabeth's May letter, Descartes wrote to her again from The Hague. He began with nostalgia and a reversion to courtly gallantry: "Passing through The Hague to go to France, since I cannot have the honor of receiving your commandments and paying my respects, it seems to me that I am obliged to write these lines to assure your Highness that my zeal and devotion will not change even as I change my location."

Unknown to Elisabeth as she read these lines was that the change in location on Descartes's mind was not a trip to France or even the eventual possibility that he might reside permanently in his native land. Descartes goes on to give his friend the first hints of a new influence in his life. He describes a correspondence with a friend, Chanut, recently posted to Sweden as a diplomatic representative of France.

I received two days ago a letter from Sweden from an envoy of France who is there, who proposed to me a question on the part of the Queen, who knew about me because he showed her my response to a letter he had sent to me. The way he describes this queen, with the conversations he reports with her, make me judge that it seems to me that intercourse between the two of you would be worthy of you. And since there are so few of the rest of the world who are worthy, it might not be a bad idea for your Highness to have a very close friendship with her. Other than the contentment that you would get from it, this would be desirable for other reasons.

So Descartes broaches the subject of Sweden, diplomatically casting his contacts there as a project undertaken for Elisabeth's benefit. He has found a friend for her, an aristocratic woman who, like her, is interested in intellectual matters, a friend who might be valuable "for other reasons," no doubt referring to the key role of Sweden in the peace negotiations that would soon decide the fate of Elisabeth's family. Awkwardly he continues:

I had written before to my friend in Sweden, responding to a letter in which he spoke of her, that I did not find it unbelievable what he said about her because the honor I have in knowing your Highness has made me understand how much persons

Fig. 22.1. The painter Dumesnil shows Christina of Sweden in all her glory, surrounded by learned men and scholars. Descartes stands at her table, pointing out pertinent passages.

of high birth can surpass others. But I do not remember if it is in the letter that he let her see, or in another earlier one. And since it is likely that he will show her from now on the letters that he gets from me, I will try always to put in them something which will make her wish for the friendship of your Highness, that is, if you do not forbid it.

So with this, his first mention of Christina to Elisabeth, Descartes gave the impression, accepted as sincere by most of his biographers, that his main motive in pursuing a relationship with the Swedish queen was the promotion of Elisabeth's interest.

The reassurance was somewhat disingenuous. In Holland controversy had died down, but not at all to Descartes's satisfaction. As he put it to Elisabeth, "they have made the Theologians who want to harm me be quiet, but by flattering them, and by being careful to not offend them as much as one could have—they attribute the thing mostly to time. But I am afraid that this 'time' will endure forever, and that they will let them take so much power they will be insupportable." Although Descartes made it sound as if Chanut had recently approached him, in fact Sweden had been on his mind as a possible refuge for some time. Chanut and Descartes had made friends on the latter's visit to Paris in 1645. When Chanut was assigned to Stockholm and left from Amsterdam with his family later that year, Descartes saw them off. In Descartes's first letter to Chanut at his new post in March of 1646, at the height of his troubles with Voetius, he makes what might be read as an overture to the Swedish queen. He complains bitterly to Chanut about the stupidity of those around him. No wonder, he says, he has chosen to live far away from the world, when in that world so many people are "impertinent and importune," and "most men judge so badly that I ought not to stop for their opinions." So, he says resentfully, he must work in solitude with no one to help him. Might there not be somewhere a community of scholars worthy of him? "I am afraid that the world is too large, because there are so few honest people to be found in it. I would wish that they were all assembled in one city, and then I would be happy to leave my hermitage, to go and live with them, if they would wish to receive me into their company."

Christina's plan to attract intellectuals to her kingdom was well known, as was the young queen's ambition to make Sweden a center of learning and culture. It is more than possible that Descartes had already discussed such a possibility and his part in it with his friend Chanut while they were together in Holland. He apologizes to Chanut that his *Principles,* which he has sent on to him, has so little in it about morality, which he knows is Chanut's—and no doubt Christina's—main interest as a diplomat and man of affairs. But in his *Physics,* he says, he has established a foundation for morality, the major tenet of which is not to fear death or any other misfortune. Also he is working on a related topic, he tells Chanut, one that might interest the queen: a treatise on passion, a work that he doubts he will publish but that is very much concerned with morality.

Chanut, by no means brilliant, a kind-hearted and busy man and a skillful diplomat, was no student of philosophy. He wrote back apologies to Descartes that he had not, unfortunately, had much time to read the *Principles,* gracefully professing himself a faithful admirer and believer whether he read the work or not. In November, Descartes's hints become broader. He has heard from another source that Chanut has presented a copy of the *Meditations* to the queen. In a passage no doubt meant for her eyes, Descartes disclaims any ambition of being read by someone of such high rank. He has heard such great things of the queen. Since the Schoolmen are always against him and trying to harm him, he is looking for supporters of "greater merit, whose power and virtue might protect him."

Poor Elisabeth. Her protection could hardly match that of a ruling monarch, but Descartes had not completely forgotten his old friend. On this one occasion, he does dutifully mention her to Chanut. "I would not believe," he writes, "that aristocrats could be interested in philosophy if I had not seen by experience, in the Princess to whom I dedicated my *Principles of Philosophy,* that persons of high birth, of whatever sex, do not have to be very old to be able to go very much beyond other men in erudition and virtue." But there is still the problem that Christina, like Elisabeth, is more interested in morality than in physics. He worries. Morality, after all, is something he always thought he should not get mixed up in. If they are going to call him a skeptic when he refutes skepticism and an atheist for proving the existence of God, what will they say if he tries to lay out the sources of value?

He closes with an answer to Chanut's conjecture that to write as he does about emotion, he must not have any himself. He does have emotions, he protests, and in fact could not live without them. Not anger, a man should be above anger, but anger should not be confused with indignation. He has that often enough, and rightly, against "the ignorance of those who wish to be taken for professors." Of course, this has to be distinguished from impermissible indignation, mixed with malice. Poor Descartes, back again in the whirlpool of passion. What a difficult business it is sorting out these emotions!

He and Chanut continued to correspond, Chanut writing with an intimacy unusual in Descartes's friends and suggesting topics that he knows will interest Christina. And there was good reason to hope, as Chanut knew, that Christina would be interested, if not in metaphysics, then at least in acquiring a famous thinker for her stable of scholars. Eccentric, hot-tempered, volatile, and clever, Christina was actively involved in recruiting intellectuals and artists. Those who were already expatriates in tolerant Holland were a special target, because they were already at least partly acclimated to the rigors of the Swedish winter.

Diplomatically Chanut broaches to Descartes a topic in which the young Christina was sure to be interested. "What is love?" he asks in December of 1646. Chanut confesses he does not understand it. It involves so many appetites and impulses directed at such bizarre objects. He, himself, has simply decided to love what he loves without thinking much about it. One thing that troubles him, though. Can we love God with passionate human love? Or is wonder and confusion more appropriate? He goes on to try to generate some love in Descartes for his queen. She has great force of spirit; she runs the country herself. She would understand Descartes's *Principles* as well as anyone could. When she has time off from affairs of state, she explores deep matters, and she has a sharp wit. "I assure you it is necessary to speak in front of her with great circumspection."

Always the diplomat, Chanut skirts the question of whether this queen has actually found the time to read Descartes's work. As evidence of her interest, however, he passes on one of her questions about love. Which is worse, excessive love or excessive hate? He could not satisfy her with his answer, he says. Perhaps Descartes, the philosopher, can.

Love was certainly a question on which a prospective courtier could reasonably expect to be tested, and on 1 February 1647, on his return from France, Descartes tackles the topic with gusto in a long letter to Chanut obviously meant for Christina's eyes. After disposing of Chanut's problem of whether we should love God—yes if it is intellectual love based on the judgment that an object is good, no if it is passionate, bodily love—Descartes turned to the problem of confusion in love. The main thing, he says, is to make a distinction between love that originates in the body and love that originates in the soul. Bodily attraction is a mechanism; a certain heat in the heart and blood in the lungs makes you want to open your arms and embrace something. The confusion comes because other bodily passions can intervene, other strings of nerves get pulled. Also the mind can say no. In yet another reference to his motherless infancy, Descartes cites early experiences as a possible source of confusion. The joy of being nourished as an infant or the hate that comes when nourishment is denied can stay with one to adulthood, causing confusion in love.

Having learned some lessons about flattery, Descartes cleverly transforms Chanut's question about God into a compliment to the queen. No we cannot say to someone so high as God or a queen that we love them. But we can love them, just as he can see that Chanut loves his queen:

> If I asked you in all good conscience if you did not love this Great Queen, with whom you are at present, you may well say that you have for her only respect, veneration, and wonder. I would dare judge that you have also a very ardent affection for her. For your style flows so well, when you speak of her, that, even though I believe all that you say, because I know that you are very truthful and I have also heard this from others, I nevertheless do not believe that you would be able to describe her as you do, if you did not have much zeal for her, nor that you could be near to such a great light without receiving some of the heat from it.

Heat in the breast, blood in the lungs, a thirst that makes you want to open your arms and embrace an object, and now the Snow Queen, source of illumination, warming the hearts of men in the cold of the north.

Descartes then turns to providing a long and labored answer to Christina's question. Love for a meritless object is bad, and also love is more likely to be excessive than hate, but any love has some good effects, no matter the object. He again recalls his absent mother. The first feelings of love come when there is heat in the infant's heart from sufficient food. If, on the other hand, there is something harmful in the food, the child feels hate. From birth the strings of the body's nerves are worked, until the mind can correct them.

Poor Chanut, it was all a bit much for him. After considerable time, he answers. He would have answered sooner, he says, if he had understood Descartes's letter better. Of course he has great faith in his friend, and understanding is not necessary for him to know that what the philosopher says must be true. Indeed it is the letter itself, rather than what it says, that is the medium of desire, says Chanut, echoing Elisabeth. Understanding or not, he is "ravished." He showed the letter to the queen's physician, who wanted to borrow it, but no, Chanut will not let it out of his sight.

Clever man. As soon as she hears of it, Christina demands to see the letter. Chanut continues to refuse. He plays Christina like a fish. He will read it to her, he promises, at a quiet time. Forbidden fruit. She makes time, sits down with him alone, represses her native restlessness to listen or seem to listen, this girl queen with her pale face and irrepressible energy.

Her response was positive, Chanut reports in triumph. Although she coquettishly insists that she cannot judge about love because she has never felt it and she has a quibble about Descartes's use of the infinite, she proclaims that "Descartes must be the most happy of men" and his "situation is to be envied."

Although these remarks might bear a number of interpretations, Chanut is more than happy. Careful as one has to be around this queen, she has approved his friend. Flushed with success, he brings up another love problem: what is it that makes us love one person rather than another before we have had any chance to judge a person's worth? Why that impulsive outpouring of affection he feels for Descartes? What should one do? Should one go with it or resist? And if one ignores this feeling because it is based on no rational judgment, then how does one tell love from "an exchange of offices among honest people" or a "trade of favors"? Oh, the master of passion has his hands full with these lover's questions.

Chanut ends with an apology: if Descartes is tired of all the questions, let him know, and he will be silent. He professes his devotion. "Ask me only if it is not true that, apart from the veneration I have for your virtue and beyond the obligations I owe you, I am still impelled to love and honor you by a secret movement, which I do not resist, and which makes me, more than to any other man, your very humble, very obedient, and affectionate servant."[1] Does this "secret" joy presage a more intimate personal pleasure than a win at the gambling table?

Descartes responded energetically and happily, with many reciprocal compliments. After discoursing on Christina's problem with infinity, he gives his answer to Chanut's question about the exclusiveness of love. Again it goes back to childhood, says Descartes. When we feel an affection for someone, it leaves a kind of fold in the brain that can be reactivated. Once when he was a young boy, he liked a girl who was cross-eyed; after that he was attracted to anyone he saw who had the same defect—that is, until he learned better.

But Chanut got more than this rather unromantic solution to his romantic difficulties. Descartes adds:

> we do have reason to prefer those to whom our secret inclinations join us, provided that we also see in them merit. And when the secret inclinations are caused in the spirit and not the body, I believe that they must always be followed, and the principal sign that allows you to know that an inclination comes from the spirit is that it is reciprocal, which does not often happen with the others.

He adds seductively that since Chanut reciprocates his friendship, it must be that way with them.

From success to success. In September, Christina has a new question for him. She has heard a lecture on the sovereign good from a Swedish professor and found it wanting. She has appealed for elucidation from Descartes through Chanut. In a considerable advance, this time she gives the philosopher leave to address her directly. Chanut writes to Descartes immediately on 21 September. So insistent is the queen and so important is it to act promptly once her attention has been gained that even though the mails could hardly have arrived so fast, he writes again renewing the question on 9 November.

So the Swedish affair had gained momentum, with Descartes finally realizing that something more explicit had to be said to Elisabeth than in his June letter. Indeed, he had no choice but to tell her more now, because he was about to take a step that affected her directly. He was writing his first letter directly to Christina, and he wanted to enclose with the accompanying letter to Chanut some of the letters on the passions and morality that he had written to Elisabeth.

23

The Purloined Letters

~

The twentieth of November was a big day of letter writing for Descartes, and difficult letters they were. First, he wrote a long letter to Christina giving her his views on the sovereign good. Then he wrote to Chanut, enclosing copies of six of the letters he had sent to Elisabeth and also a draft of the treatise on the passions that was the fruit of their correspondence. And then he wrote the hardest letter of all, to Elisabeth, explaining what he was doing.

His letter to the queen opens with the compliments he used to save for his old patroness. "I take [your] commandment for such a great favor, that the desire which I have to obey turns me away from all other thoughts." He then goes on to answer her question, reiterating the morality he had been urging on Elisabeth. The key to happiness is to have a "firm and constant resolution to do exactly all the things which one judges to be the best and to use all the forces of one's spirit to know them." Then, even if things turn out badly, one can take satisfaction in the fact that one has done one's best. Certainly on the basis of this morality there was nothing to resent or reproach in Descartes's behavior. He saw the good of Christina's interest, both for him and for Elisabeth. He resolutely does all in his power to foster the connection. So far so good. Next, the letter to Chanut.

Egmond
20 November

Monsieur

It is true that my custom is to refuse to write my thoughts regarding morals, and this is for two reasons: first, there is no point in bringing up a matter which the malicious can so easily take as a pretext for calumny; the other is that I believe that it is only for Sovereign rulers, or for those authorized by them, to get embroiled in regulating the morals of others. But these reasons do not apply to the opportunity which you have done the honor of giving me, in writing to me on the part of the incomparable Queen you are with at this time that it would please her if I write to you my opinion on the highest good. For this commandment gives me authority enough, and I hope that what I write will not be seen by anyone but you and her. It is because I wish with so much passion to obey her that, even though some reserve is necessary, I would wish to be able to cram into this letter all that I have ever thought on this subject. In effect, I wanted to put so much in the letter I have taken the liberty of writing to her that I fear I have not given sufficient explanations. To make up for that defect, I am sending you a collection of some other letters, in which I argue at greater length the same things. And I have added to them a little treatise on the Passions, which is not the least part of it. Because it is principally the passions that are necessary to try to know to obtain the sovereign good that I have described. If I had also dared to add there the responses that I had the honor to receive from the Princess to whom the letters are addressed, the collection would have been more complete, and I would have also been able to include two or three more of my letters which are not intelligible without them, but I would have had to ask her permission, and she is now far away from here.

For the rest, I do not ask you to present this collection to the Queen right away, for I would be afraid not to guard sufficiently the respect and veneration that I owe to Her Majesty if I sent her letters that I wrote to someone else, rather than writing to her herself what I judged was pleasing to her; but if you think it good to speak to her of it, saying that it is to you have I have sent the letters, and if after that she wants to see them, I would be free of this scruple. And I am persuaded that it will be more agreeable to her to see that I wrote to another what I addressed to her, so that she would be assured all the more that I had not changed or disguised anything out of consideration for her. But I ask you that these writings do not fall, if it is possible, into other hands.

Not easy, these royal negotiations. That done, he sat down to write the hardest of the letters, to Elisabeth. He omits the usual opening compliments and gets right to the point.

Egmond
20 November 1647

Madame

Since I have already taken the liberty of letting your Highness know about the correspondence I have begun to have with Sweden, I think I am obliged to continue, and to tell you that I have since received several letters from the friend that I have in that country, by which he has let me know that the Queen being at Uppsala, the seat of the University of the country, she heard a lecture by a Professor of rhetoric, who my friend thinks is the most able and reasonable of that University, and that she had given him for his topic a discourse on the Sovereign Good of this life. But after the lecture, she said that people there only confuse matters, and that it was necessary to get my opinion. To which my friend answered that he knew that I was very much taken up with writing on such matters, and that if it pleased her Majesty that he ask me, he did not think that I would fail to try to satisfy her. On which she expressly charged him with asking me, and he promised her that he would write with the next mail, and that he would counsel me to write and address my letter directly to the Queen, to whom he would present it with the likelihood that she would receive it well.

I thought that I should not miss this chance, and considering that, when he wrote me this, he could not have received a letter in which I spoke of those letters which I wrote to your Highness touching the same matters, I had thought that the plan I had in that regard was ill-conceived, and that it would be necessary to take another tack. This is why I wrote a letter to the Queen, where, after briefly putting my opinion, I added that I had omitted many things, because considering the number of affairs that are encountered in the running of a great Kingdom and which her Majesty had to take care of, I would not dare to ask of her a longer audience. But I said that I would send to Monsieur Chanut some writings, in which I had put down more fully my sentiments touching the same matter, so that, if it pleased her to see them, he could present them to her.

The writings which I sent to Monsieur Chanut are the letters that I had the honor to write to your Highness, touching the reading of Seneca's *De Vita Beata*, up to the midpoint of the sixth letter, where, after having defined the Passions in general, I said that I was having difficulty enumerating them. With this, I also sent to her the little *Treatise on the Passions*, which I took the trouble to have transcribed from confused notes which I kept. And I told him that I did not ask him right away to give these writings to the Queen, because I was afraid of not being respectful enough to her Majesty if I sent to her letters that I had written to someone else, rather than writing to her herself what I thought would be agreeable to her, but that if he found it all right to speak to her about them, saying that it was to him that I had sent them, and that after all she wanted to see them, I would be free of any scruple, and would be persuaded that it would be agreeable to her to see that what I had written to another was what I had addressed to her, because then she would be more assured that I had not changed or disguised anything for her benefit.

I had not judged it appropriate to put anything more about your Highness, not even to mention your name, which of course he was not ignorant of, given my earlier letters. But considering that he is a man who is very virtuous and a great judge of persons of merit and I hardly doubted that he would honor your Highness as much as he ought, and still he rarely referred to any of this in his letters, even though I mentioned something of it in all my letters, I thought that it would be necessary to be careful in speaking of it to the Queen, because he did not know if this would please or displease those who had sent it. But if from now on I have the occasion to write of you to her herself, I will not have need of an interpreter. The aim I have had this time, in sending the writings to him, is to try to get her to interest herself in these thoughts, and that if they please her in the way I have been persuaded to think they will, she will have occasion to confer with your Highness. To whom all my life, I will be . . .

Ah, what a tangle. The confusions in this letter are not due to translation. Have pity for this courtier with two mistresses. Given the situation, Descartes does the best he can. Not wishing to offend Elisabeth, not only because of her remaining influence with the House of Orange and the Dutch universities but also because of her affectionate and supportive loyalty, Descartes nevertheless has shifted the focus of his hopes. To his credit, there seems to be a genuine desire to have Elisabeth also profit if possible. Could they perhaps both find refuge, two philosophers, under the auspices of Queen Christina? If that is the best thing that he can see to have happen, whether Elisabeth can be part of it or not, should he not resolutely will it and try as best as he can to bring it about, at least for himself?

But as the convoluted excuses and explanations in his letter indicate, even Descartes must have had some scruples. Were his letters to Elisabeth public documents like the dedication to the *Principles*, there for all to see? Public documents that, even if unpublished like the treatise on the passions, could be shown to interested parties? Or were they personal, written in response to experiences that Elisabeth communicated to him in confidence at an unhappy time in her life? Did the letters express only ideas, hopefully not "confused" but rather "clear and distinct" and empty of passion, innocent of any address that would introduce passion or interest and blur the truth? Or had they been, or been taken as, letters of love and affection? Clearly Descartes is not completely confident of the proper response to these questions. Yes, sending the letters to Sweden could be justified on the grounds that if the queen became "interested" in Elisabeth's ideas, she might then show the interest in Elisabeth that had been lacking to date, at least as evidenced by Chanut's total silence on the subject. But on the other hand, to send one person's letters to another would seem a considerable breach of faith.

In the end, the message of the letter, the message that Elisabeth with her skills of understanding no doubt read, is that, much as Descartes has tried, her own interests in Sweden do not look good. Although she would certainly not want her friend to sacrifice himself and his own prospects, he will continue magnanimously, as he pursues his own interest, to do the best he can for her also.

If he had known or thought more about Christina, he might have rated the possibility rather small that any permanent good would have come of it either for Elisabeth or for himself. Christina, still very young, a monarch from childhood, used to having her own way and to center stage, used to treating people as royal playthings, was unlikely to want to share the limelight with a rival princess, especially a princess known as among the most learned women in Europe. Furthermore, there was considerable question whether Christina's interest in philosophy, or even her interest in ruling Sweden, would be sustained sufficiently to give Descartes a safe harbor for his old age.

In a letter Descartes received from Elisabeth in December, there is pointed silence on the subject of Sweden. Instead she acknowledges receipt of the long-awaited French version of his *Meditations*. If she had received the letter of 20 November telling her that Descartes's letters to her were to be recycled for use with another royal patroness, she does not mention it. Nor does she mention the reference to Sweden in Descartes's earlier letter, which she certainly has received. Instead she attempts to turn his mind to matters that might seem "less considerable" but that in her judgment are more important.

Berlin

5 December1647

Monsieur Descartes,

Since I have received, some days ago, the French translation of your Metaphys-ical Meditations that you sent me, I am obliged to render you thanks in these lines. I do so even though I do not now know how to express my sentiment of apprecia-tion for your kindness without asking for a new kindness, that is, to excuse the inconvenience that I give you in reading and responding to my letters which take you away so often from useful meditations to consider subjects which, without the partiality of friendship, would not seem important. But I have received so many proofs of the friendship which you have for me that I presume enough to not find it difficult to tell you that I have read the above translation with some satisfaction, since it makes your thoughts much more mine when I can read them well expressed in a language which I use ordinarily, even though I believe that I understood them before.

My admiration grows every time I reread the objections which people make to you, how it is possible that persons who have been employed so many years in med-itation and study do not comprehend things so simple and clear, and that most, in disputing the true and the false, seem not to understand how it is necessary to dis-tinguish them, and that Gasendus, who has the greatest reputation for his knowl-edge, has made, after the English, objections less reasonable than all the others.

This shows you how much the world has need of a Treatise on Erudition, that you on another occasion wanted to write. I know that you are too charitable to refuse a thing so useful to the public, and, for that, I have no need to make you remember the promise which you gave to

Your very affectionate friend at your service,

Elisabeth

What a complex range of emotion plays in these letters, an orchestra of tone and timbre, melody underlaid with bass notes, the very music of feeling. Descartes's indignation is not part of Elisabeth's range; here more gentle currents flow—of regret, worry, remonstrance, affection, and, yes, love. She will always be grateful that Descartes, one of the major minds of the day, has been so kind as to give her his attention. Reading his work in French, the language she speaks with her family, recreates for a moment their old marriage of minds. Not just rational understanding of ideas expressed in the dead idiom of Latin but moving with the rhythms and accents of the thought. She scolds his critics like an indulgent moth-er, recalling him to what she sees as his proper mission to the world. Will he now write the work she has been waiting for, that the world has been waiting for, the treatise on erudition? Will he now make clear how one might acquire knowledge, write a treatise on scholarship, on practical methods of reading and gaining wis-dom? This indeed might be of great use in promoting Cartesianism as an intellec-tual method.

Alas, Descartes's mind is elsewhere. He has been worried, he says in his letter of 31 January, to know what to say to her about the treatise on erudition because he would not want to seem lacking in zeal in obeying her commandments. The truth is he has given the project up. He will only make everyone mad at him again, he has already said most of what he wanted to say in the preface to the *Principles* that she already has, and he is working on another project on the physiological functions of animals because what he has written on the subject has been poorly translated and he needs to put it in better order. Furthermore, this may be the last peaceful winter he will have in Holland, and he does not want to take on anything too taxing.

The suggestion that Descartes's residency in Holland is drawing to a close had to do not only with ongoing prospects in Sweden but also with new prospects in France. There is word that the king there might be willing to give him a pension. The possibility of a sojourn in Sweden recedes temporarily before the possibility of honor in his native land.

> The reason that makes me think I will have less leisure from now on, is that I must return to France next summer, and spend there the rest of the winter; family affairs and many reasons make this necessary. They have also done me the honor to offer to me a pension from the King, without my asking for it. Which would not alone be able to keep me there, but many things could happen in a year.

Again he adds assurances. If it were possible for him to live near Elisabeth, he would prefer that place to anywhere else, including his native country. Since it is not possible, he may be moving on, if not to Sweden, then to France.

Ignoring her silence on Sweden, he brings her up to date on that situation. His letter to Chanut with the enclosure to Christina along with the diverted letters to Elisabeth has been delayed. His friends in Sweden are still waiting for delivery. Again Descartes praises the queen. He has heard further of her virtue and intelligence and that she is interested in his *Principles*. Queenly patronage aside, Descartes still relies on this friend who has taken such a close and concerned interest in his affairs. Turning to her for reassurance and praise, he tells her that in another packet he has sent on yet more of the insulting work of Monsieur Rhegius for her sympathetic review.

24

Affairs of State

~

*D*escartes made his trip to France with high hopes, but things did not go well for him there. Paris was in the throes of political upheavals in the aftermath of the war, and no one paid much attention to him. Nor was the pension forthcoming. So much for the return of the prodigal son. He poured out to Chanut his disappointment in May of 1648. "I see here [in Paris] so many persons who are mistaken in their opinion and their calculations that it seems to me to be a universal sickness. The innocence of the 'desert' from where I come pleases me much more and I do not think I can keep from returning in a very little time." In political conflicts between king and parliament he had little interest. Unrest might eventually lead to peace, but "while waiting I would better take myself to a country already at peace."

Meanwhile in Berlin, other plans were in the works. In June Elisabeth writes to Descartes in France about the possibility of a visit of her own to Sweden as a companion to the queen mother.

Krossen
30 June 1648

Monsieur Descartes.

The numbness which I had in my right arm because of the mistake of a surgeon who had cut part of a nerve in bleeding me has kept me from replying sooner to your letter of 7 May, the one which let me know the new effect of your perfect generosity in your regret in leaving Holland and in not being able to hope that you could give me the pleasure of your conversation there, which truly is the greatest good I could expect and the sole reason that made me dream of returning. For that, either the arrangement of things in England might have served or despair that anything could come of things in Germany.

In the meantime they are talking here of the trip that you proposed before, and the Mother of the person to whom your friend has given your letters has gotten an order to make it happen without anyone knowing in her country that it comes from any further away than her own proper efforts. One has badly chosen this "good woman" for keeping a secret, and she did not do it at all well. She did perform the rest of her commission with much passion and wishes that a third person go with her, which it is not really in the cards to do, but it is up to the will of her relatives, who will be without doubt in favor of the trip. If they send the money which is necessary, it is decided that it should be undertaken, since at this point there will be means perhaps to render service to those to whom it is owed and that he [the third person] could return with the "good woman" just mentioned, who does not pretend to stay there. There is nothing in this to change the reasons that have been written to you against this trip, and the death of this woman (who is quite sick), or that she be obliged to leave before the response of the relatives of the other arrive are the most evident that might prevent it. I have received, three weeks ago, a very obliging letter from the place in question, full of kindness and of protestations of friendship, but which did not make any mention of your letters, nor of what had been written on them. Also the command to the "good woman" was only by word of mouth.

I have still not given you an account of my reading of the French version of the *Principles of Philosophy*. Although there are some things in the preface for which I have need of your explanation, I will not add that here, because it would make my letter too long. But I will let you know them another time. Promise me that in changing your residence, you will keep always the same charity for,

your very affectionate friend at your service,
Elisabeth

It might have strained even Descartes's brilliant mind to decipher this letter, written in fear of spies and treachery. A plan is afoot for Elisabeth to visit Sweden in the summer of 1648 as companion to Christina's mother, who was related to Elisabeth's relatives and is now resident in Berlin. Whether or not this trip was encouraged by Christina or was in any way the fruit of Descartes's interventions is unclear. More likely the source of the invitation was closer to the Palatines. In any case, Elisabeth shows little enthusiasm for the visit. Mary Eleonore, Christina's mother, was a difficult woman. Notorious for her lack of good sense, emotional to the point of irrationality, obsessed with dress and cosmetics, totally uninterested in anything outside of her own feelings and her own body, she was so distrusted by her husband, Christina's father, that by the terms of his will he expressly excluded her from any influence on government or Christina's education. The prospect of an extended trip with her could not have been attractive. Elisabeth was already tired to death of being with her in Berlin.

However, there might be definite political advantages for the Palatines in such a trip. In pressing for the return of the Palatine, Sweden's help was crucial. Given that the Swedish royal family was related to the Palatines, there was hope that they would champion the Palatine cause at the peace table. No doubt this is why Elisabeth's mother and brother are in favor of the trip and are apparently willing to advance money for it. On the other hand, the trip could mean just another useless round of festivities. Given that the relation between Christina and her mother is hardly cordial, it might even be disadvantageous to arrive under the queen mother's wing. Elisabeth had not had an invitation from the queen herself or any indication directly from that quarter that she would be welcome; the letters from "friends" are from supporters of Palatine interests in Sweden. Nor is it likely that

Elisabeth, having ample informants who could tell her about Christina, could have been as sanguine about the queen's character and reliability as Descartes.

Before he received this letter, Descartes had written to Elisabeth to tell her that he is not so happy with his situation in France. The struggle played out between parliament and king over whether France could find the money to continue the war have prevented anyone from thinking about his pension. The royal patronage of the French king was not forthcoming. In disappointment, Descartes renews ties with old friends. As he puts it in his opening compliments, "Even though I know well that the place and the condition that I am in gives me no occasion to be useful to your Highness, I would not be fulfilling my duty, or true to my zeal, if after having arrived at a new home, I failed to renew to you my offers of very humble obedience." If things do not settle down, he will return to Holland in six weeks or two months and wait "until the sky of France is more serene." With stoic sighs at the inconvenience and futility of the trip, he shows himself virtuous by the terms of his morality.

> I believe that those who have good fortunes differ from others, in that when they have displeasing things happen to them, they are more sensitive to it, not only in that they have more pleasures, but because all the contentments that they can have, being a usual thing for them, do not affect them like afflictions, which come to them when they expect them the least and when they are not prepared; all of which might serve as consolation to those whom fortune has accustomed to disgrace.

Perhaps somewhat exaggerating the difficulty of his situation, Descartes again is putting his prudence to work.

Elisabeth answers with loving acceptance, flavored with undertones of irony.

Krossen
July 1648

Monsieur Descartes,

You could not be in a place on earth where the trouble that you take to give me your news would not be to my satisfaction. For I persuade myself that events will always be to your advantage and that God is too just to send you unhappiness so great that your prudence would not know how to get out of it, just as the unexpected disorders in France conserve your liberty in obliging you to return to Holland. Otherwise the Court might have seduced you, whatever care you would have taken to oppose it. For me, I look forward to the pleasure of seeing you again in Holland or elsewhere.

I believe that you have already received the letter in which one spoke to you of another trip which had to be made if friends approved it, believing that in this connection there would be some service to them. Since then, they have asked it and have furnished the expenses. Nevertheless, there are those who are where she must begin from who have prevented the preparations that would be necessary from day to day, and are moved to do so by such feeble reasons that they themselves will not confess them. Meanwhile at this point there is so little time that the person in question could not possibly be ready. And on one side she would have badly wished to have said nothing; on the other, her friends believe that she has not the will or the courage to sacrifice her health and peace for the interest of her house, for which she would still sacrifice her life if required. That makes her a bit angry, but does not surprise her, since she is well accustomed to suffering blame for the faults of others (even on occasions in which she would wish to rid herself of them) and to finding her satisfaction only in the witness that her conscience gives her that she has done her duty. Always, this turns her thoughts away from matters that are more agreeable. Even though you are right to say that those who have great fortune are different from others in that they are more sensitive to the displeasures that happen to them—not that they enjoy more pleasures, but because there are few that give true objects to their pleasures—if what gives them pleasure is to give good to the public and particularly to persons of merit, being in a condition which would give them more power would also give more pleasures than those to whom fortune refuses this advantage. I ask nothing greater of fortune than to be able to witness in effect the esteem which I have for your kindness to

Your very affectionate friend at your service,
Elisabeth

Finally Elisabeth is angry. It is hard not to applaud. Even Descartes, preoccupied as he is with his troubles in France, might have read veiled criticism of his own attitudes between the lines of this letter. Was he, unlike her, in danger of being seduced by a royal pension, of dancing attendance on royal courts, of becoming an intellectual flunky? Was he really able to see, as Elisabeth did, the narrowness of his escape from France and the real advantage in his "misfortune," now that he was again "free" of obligation and could travel at will, saved from the renown that he craved? But still how indulgent this older and wiser Elisabeth is with her old friend. She will be happy to see him in France, or elsewhere, she says with the magnanimity of someone pressed by important affairs but still able to reassure a friend.

As for the trip to Sweden, many readers of her letters ignore what Elisabeth herself says about it. Again a familiar scenario is conjured up. Elisabeth, a woman in love, jealous as women are, wants to follow her famous lover to Sweden. When the trip falls through, she is devastated and angry, even though Descartes's own trip to Sweden has not yet been planned and she has warned him against it. The truth is less romantic. Poor Elisabeth, always the negotiator trying to do what is good for the public and for those of "merit," is maneuvering adroitly and painfully in the midst of plots, unspoken motives, secret designs. She has been told by her relatives to visit Sweden with the queen mother, a difficult woman with whom she has no rapport. She has been told to attempt some personal diplomacy. In the meantime, the German wing of the family mysteriously delays her departure, preventing her from making the needed preparations. Maybe they do not want to give up her help and good counsel; maybe they have doubts about what can be accomplished in Sweden. As usual Elisabeth is blamed. It is she, the others say, who drags her heels because she is worried about her health or does not want the trouble of a trip.

From the point of view of Descartes's prudence, she might have taken stoic advantage in her impotence and so inured herself to inevitable disappointments. But to Elisabeth, living with and responsible to others, power of action is desirable not to ensure her own convenience but because she wants to do public good and help those who deserve it.

She writes again at the end of August.

23 August 1648
Krossen

Monsieur Descartes,

    I spoke to you in my last letter of a person who, without having done anything wrong, was in danger of losing the good opinion and perhaps the good wishes of most of her friends. Now she finds herself delivered in an extraordinary fashion, since that other, to whom she had devoted the time necessary to try get herself near to her, has responded that she would have better waited, since her daughter has changed her mind, judging that one would take it amiss if she were approached so closely by someone of a different religion. This is behavior that, in my opinion, does not correspond to the praise which your friend has given to the person involved, at least if it is entirely hers and does not come, as I suspect, from the weak spirit of her mother, who has been accompanied, ever since this affair has been afoot, by a sister who supports a party opposed to the house of the person mentioned above. Your friend could shed light on this for you, if you find it appropriate to inquire about it. Or perhaps he will write to you of it on his own, since they say that he governs completely the spirit to which he gives so much praise. I do not know anything to add to this, since it is not that I judge that the above accident is one of misfortune for the person to whom it has happened, since she got out of having to take a trip in which the bad that would have come out of it (such as the loss of health and peace, joined to the angering things that it would be necessary to suffer in a rough country) is very much assured, and the good that others hoped to get from it very uncertain. And if there is any insult in the affair, I think that it falls entirely on those who have made it, since it is a mark of their inconstancy and lightness of spirit, and all those who have knowledge of it know also that she has not contributed to any of the caprices involved.

    As for me, I maintain that I will live here until I learn the issue of affairs in Germany and England, which seem to be now in a crisis. We had here an interesting encounter three days ago, in a time otherwise very unsettling. While we were walking under a chestnut tree, Madame l'Electrice with those of her court, there came to us in an instant a sort of rash over all the body, except the face, without fever or other illness than an insupportable itching. The superstitious ones thought they had been bewitched, but the peasants told us that there is sometimes a certain venomous dew on the trees which, coming down in dust, infects the peasants in the same way. And it is notable that all the remedies that anyone thought up for a malady so new, like baths, bleeding, leeches, and purges did nothing. I tell you the story because I presume that you would find something there to confirm some of your doctrines.

I am perfectly, M. Descartes,

Your very affectionate friend at your service,
Elisabeth

Interesting juxtaposition. A venomous dew descending from the trees that cannot be relieved by baths, salves, or purges, and continual storms that descend on Elisabeth's family, with Elisabeth bathed as usual in poisonous politics. Sober, moral, mercilessly intelligent, always in the middle, used and blamed by those who have neither her understanding of the situation nor her clear estimates of human character. Would the trip to Sweden have been useful? The rigors of the undertaking are clear to Elisabeth: Swedish winters are punishing, nor would there be the comforts that could be obtained even in backward Berlin. Further, it is rapidly becoming clear what she already suspected, that the character of the Swedish royal family leaves something to be desired. Certainly she has had an opportunity to observe and judge the loose tongue of the queen mother and her susceptibility to treasonous influences. Nor is she sanguine about Queen Christina, whose role in events is far from clear. Did Christina go along with the proposed visit thoughtlessly, just until she realized who was coming? Is it really the clash between her Lutheranism and Elisabeth's Calvinism that is bothering her? Or had she developed an animosity for the brilliant, learned princess when she discovered this was the patroness of her latest conquest, the philosopher Descartes? Had she, regardless of affairs of state or the old friendship between her father and Elisabeth's father, comrades in arms who died on the same battlefield, seen no particular advantage in having a rival nearby? Had she already promised the French that she would not interfere in favor of the Palatines? Whatever the motives, she seems guilty of at least "inconstancy and lightness of spirit," casting doubt on the praise lavished on her by Chanut and Descartes. Although Christina wrote to Charles-Louis, Elisabeth's brother, promising to do what she could for the Palatines, in the end she made no effort on their behalf.

Elisabeth's warning about Christina may be less for herself than for Descartes, a warning about this queen who has so impressed him, a warning that does not come from jealousy but rather from worry that he might undertake a trip and risk danger to his health and peace, all for so little gain. Only to escape the toothless attacks of Dutch theologians, and for what? Another dubious pension, the seductions of court life, and this time a court that does not have the finesse of its French counterpart but offers a punishing winter of snow and ice? And all for the friendship of a politician who has for the moment power over the Swedish queen, a representative of a country that is busy undermining the interests of the Palatines at the peace conference? Is it really worthy of him to think of such a trip? Would it not be better for him to retire to Egmond and his old life, even without the chance that she will return, which is not completely ruled out? She is too respectful to say it outright. He should suspect Chanut's motives. Christina is not to be trusted. Peace and health should not be risked for a royal whim.

Descartes did not reply to this series of letters until after he had returned to Holland. In a fit of anger, disappointed not only in the missing pension but also in the small extent of a legacy he had been expecting, Descartes left his friend Mersenne on his deathbed in Paris. Back home in Egmond at the end of March, he again reflected bitterly to Chanut on his reception in France. "What is most disgusting to me is that no one there showed that they wanted to know more of me than my face, so that I had reason to believe that they only wanted me in France as they might an elephant or panther—because of its rarity but not really to be useful for anything."[1] Perhaps in the end it was more gratifying to be condemned in Holland than ignored in Paris. In October he writes to reassure Elisabeth that he has received her letters and that they did not fall into bad hands. He agrees that she should be glad "not to have made a trip in which the inconveniences would be inevitable and the advantages uncertain." Yes, he is glad to be living the retired life again, having given up other ambitions and resigned himself to the happiness of "mediocre fortune."[2]

As usual he urges prudence on Elisabeth.

> If your Highness compares her situation with those of Queens and other Princesses of Europe, she will find a contrast between those who are in port at anchor where they can rest and those who are on the open sea, blown by the winds of a tempest. Even when one has been blown into port by a storm—provided that one does not lack the necessities of life—one must not be any less content because one has arrived in this fashion. The angering encounters which happen to those who are in the action and whose happiness depends completely on others penetrate even to the depth of the heart unlike that poisonous dew, descending from the trees under which your Highness was peacefully walking, which would have touched, as I hoped, only the exterior of the skin.

Descartes takes the occasion to add a little more medical advice. As for the dew, if they had just washed with a little eau de vie, the irritation would have gone away.

Did he think that washing away the troubles of the Palatines was so easy? That if she could only take the right attitude, she could will into existence the rebuilding of the Palatine, the restoration of the University at Heidelberg, the restoring of peace and prosperity to her people? That she should let the negotiations on which such possibilities depend simply touch her skin and not her heart, easily washed away by a little diversion, a walk in the woods, pleasant thoughts, a good dinner?

25

On the Advantages of Partition and Death by Beheading

∿

Certainly Descartes had his own reasons to be wary of the Swedish affair. For five months, he tells Elisabeth in his October letter, he has heard nothing from Chanut or from Christina, nothing in response to the forwarded letters, nothing about the long letter on the sovereign good that he so carefully and diplomatically drafted. He excuses his friend Chanut. No doubt Christina was busy or not interested and Chanut was too ashamed to write that he had heard nothing from her on the subject of Descartes. Descartes does not want to write first for fear of seeming to cast blame, especially since he knows from one of Chanut's relatives in France that all is well with him. He promises Elisabeth that when he does get back in communication with Sweden, he will ask about her affair. He ends on a note of affection; how could those who do not know her value her as he does?

There is no answer from Elisabeth. Complaining of exhaustion, Descartes rests at his country retreat. If he was troubled by her silence, no doubt he attributed it, as he did Christina's, to preoccupation with affairs of state. In the meantime, the Palatines were taking some heavy blows. In the autumn Elisabeth fell ill, this time with smallpox, and was completely immobilized. Again there was fear for her life. Gallantly she joked to her brother, busy with the peace negotiations, that although the doctors assured her that she would not be disfigured, it hardly mattered because it would only be a matter of time before age took away the last of her looks anyway.

On 24 October 1648 the Peace of Westphalia was concluded; for the Palatines the terms were a great disappointment. The Peace of Augsburg was reaffirmed; the princes of some three hundred principalities were granted the choice of established religion for their territories. But the Palatines recovered only half of the Palatine—the Lower Palatine, or Rhineland. The Upper Palatine, along with the electorship, was given over to their hated enemy, the duke of Bavaria. Although a new electorship was to be established for Charles-Louis, to have Bavaria ruling even part of the Palatine was especially galling. Bavaria was at the center of the Catholic Reformation, with Jesuits in charge of schools and a long tradition of political autocracy. In the early stages of the war, murderous hired guns included those of Maximilian of Bavaria, who plundered as they drove through Protestant lands, indiscriminately killing civilians.

Regardless of Palatine hopes, much of the settlement was inevitable. Years before, Maximilian was persuaded by the emperor to be an ally in the ousting of Elisabeth's father from Bohemia in return for the promise that in the end he would get Frederick's electorship and at least some of the Palatine land. Although neither Maximilian nor the Palatines were happy with the outcome—Charles-Louis's acceptance of the deal was held up for a long time while Maximilian demanded that he abjure any right to the Upper Palatine, which Charles-Louis refused to do—to the major players in the game it seemed a fair compromise. Although there were promises to restore other properties due the Palatine children, including Elisabeth, most were never kept. But even disappointment in the terms of the peace settlement could not compare to the "tragedy of England."

On 9 February 1649, King Charles of England, Elisabeth's uncle, was beheaded in London. None of the disasters that hit the Palatines was quite as final as this. With the Treaty of Westphalia decided, the only hope of recovering the entirety of the Palatine was England and the power of the Stuart king; also from England came the last hope for pensions, properties, and dowries. But Charles's autocracy, his refusal to deal with or accommodate opposition, had brought about his final downfall.[1] This was the uncle who had stood as father to Elisabeth, to whom demands had been made for her hand in marriage, who had sheltered and parented her brothers. And there were the larger consequences: the threat of upheavals that might affect even the enlightened democratic administration of rulers like the princes of Orange.

The news of Charles's death reached The Hague on 14 February and Descartes in Egmond a few days later. About a week later, on 22 February 1649, Descartes received the long-awaited letters from Sweden with the news from Chanut that Christina finally would probably try to "tempt" him to Sweden. Immediately, Descartes sat down to write to Elisabeth, beginning by expressing sorrow at her pain and joy at her recovery. Tactfully omitting any mention of marks left on the body, he commiserates that such an experience can leave "traces of sadness on the spirit, which cannot be so easily erased." Referring to a mention she must have made in a letter (now lost) of writing verse while incapacitated and fearful for her life, he flatteringly compares her to Socrates writing poetry in prison, adding, "I take this impulse as the mark of a spirit stronger and more elevated than what is common."[2]

All of this, however, is only a convenient bridge to the main subject of his letter, the death of her uncle:

> If I did not know your spirit for such, I would think that you might be extraordinarily afflicted by the sad conclusion of the Tragedies of England. But I promise myself that your Highness, being accustomed to disgraces of Fortune, and having herself,

just a little before, been in life-threatening danger, will not be so surprised, nor so troubled, to learn of the death of one of her relatives as if she had found out about it before her other afflictions. And even though this death which was so violent seems more horrible than anything one might have expected at your sickbed, nevertheless, in actuality, it is more glorious, more happy, more gentle, in that what afflicts the common man particularly in such an event must rather serve as consolation to your Highness. For there is much glory in dying in such a situation, so that one is universally grieved, praised, and regretted by all who have any human sentiment. And it is certain that without this proof, the clemency and the other virtues of the recently dead King would not have been so much remarked nor so esteemed as they are and will be in the future by all those who read his history. I assure myself that his conscience gave him more satisfaction in those last moments of his life than indignation, which is the only sad passion which one is said to have noticed in him, nor for him would it have been a cause of anger. As for what there might be of pain, I would not worry on that account, for beheading is so short, that, if executioners could use fever or some other of the sicknesses which nature is accustomed to use to take men from the world, one would have reason to judge them more cruel than they are who kill with a stroke of the hatchet. But I will not dwell long on a subject so sad. I add only that it is worth more to be entirely delivered from false hope than to be uselessly maintained in it.

Such was Descartes's comment on the pitiful death of Charles I, the downfall of the Stuarts, and the impoverishment of the Palatines.

Immediately, he moves with excitement to the subject of Sweden. He has heard, he announces, "from that place from which I have not had any news for seven or eight months" and from "that person to whom I had sent the *Treatise on the Passions* a year ago." He assures Elisabeth: "Since this person has remembered a man as inconsiderable as I am, one must believe that she will not forget to respond to the letters about your Highness, even though she has waited four months to do it."[3] She has not, however, made any mention of Elisabeth to date, nor has she said anything about the peace treaty. Descartes does not hesitate to go on to explain why he thinks that might be. "The conditions of the Peace of Germany not being so advantageous for your house as they could have been, those who have contributed to it may be in doubt whether you would wish them ill and restrain themselves from witnessing friendship for you." Then he offers Elisabeth and her brother some sage advice.

I have always been troubled, ever since the conclusion of this Peace, to learn that Monsieur the Elector, your brother, would not accept it, and I would have taken the liberty of writing my feeling about this to Your Highness, if I imagined that it would have had any weight in the decision. But, although I do not know the particular reasons which moved him, it would be rash of me to make any judgment. I can only say in general that, when there is a question of the restitution of a state occupied or disputed by others who have force of arms, it seems to me that those who have only the equity and justice of those who plead for them on the other side should not count on obtaining all their demands, and that they rather have reason to be grateful to those who gave them a part of what they asked for, no matter how little, than to wish ill on those who keep back from the rest. And although one cannot hold it against them that they claim their right as much as they can, when it is those who have force who are deliberating, I think that when decisions are made, prudence obliges the claimants to witness that they are content, even if they are not; and to thank not only those who have given them something, but also those who do not take everything away, in order to acquire by this means the friendship of one and the other, or at least to avoid their hate: for that could very much serve afterward to perpetuate it. Other than that it is a long road from promises to effects, and that if only those who have force are in accord, it is always easy to find reasons for dividing between them that which perhaps they would not have wished to give to a third party because of jealousy one of the other, and to prevent that one who is enriched with spoils does not get too powerful.

This is an uncharacteristic discourse for private citizen Descartes "down on the plain," who usually keeps out of politics. Certainly he seems unaware of much that has been going on: Maximilian's demands, Charles-Louis's hesitation to sign over forever the land he inherited from his father and grandfather, worries about the restitution of the Palatines' other properties, worries about Protestant subjects trapped in Catholic territory, the desperate impoverishment of the Palatines.

The sentiments he expresses are pragmatic. Right and good have no power against force. Base motives rule. The weak with only right on their side had better ingratiate themselves with the strong. It was a view of the world that he might have known Elisabeth would never accept, no matter how many tragedies fell on the Palatines, any more than she would accept Descartes's God, the supposed regulator of this "trading of favors" between those with power.

Is Descartes afraid that bad feeling against "his friends" the Palatines accounted for the silence from Sweden? That the intransigence of Elisabeth's brother might possibly ruin his own chances of safe harbor? Is he asking now, in effect, for a service from Elisabeth: for his sake would she please not offend the Swedes who did not support her family at the peace talks? Perhaps. But as always, it is not so simple.

Descartes goes on:

The least part of the Palatine is worth more than all the Empire of the Tartars or of the Muscovites, and after two or threes years of peace, living there will be as agreeable as living any other place on earth. For me, I am not attached to the inhabiting of any place; I would have no difficulty in leaving the Provinces, or even France, for a country like that, if I could find there a repose sufficiently assured, even if no other reason than the beauty of the countryside made me go there. But there is no place in the world so rough, so inconvenient, where I would not count myself happy to pass the rest of my days, if your Highness was there, and I was capable of doing her service, because I am entirely and without any reserve . . .

Another mirage has materialized out of the cold North Sea: not Sweden warmed by the illumination of its Snow Queen but Heidelberg restored. If the Palatines would only be realistic, with Elisabeth and her brother back in their own lands, he might leave Holland, leave France, for such a country as the Palatine. Certainly its temperate climate and fertile lands would be preferable to a land of ice and snow, if only for the beauty of the countryside. But even without that, he would leave, because there is nowhere so rude, so uncomfortable, that he would not be happy to pass the rest of his years with her.

Camelot restored, the brilliant University of Heidelberg, the opulent castle in its former glory, science accepted and rewarded, eager students, a loving patroness, the philosopher and his princess together at last, no longer watched by spies or skulking in the hall to avoid frivolous courtiers, fending off the calumnies of jealous theologians, but at home in their own precious kingdom, center of learning and progressive ideas. It could happen. Yes, at that moment, it seemed it could happen. But only if the Palatines did not make trouble, if they ingratiated themselves with all parties, as Descartes's ethics dictated, if they graciously forgave their enemies.

Talk about the peace treaty had been intense that winter in Holland. Some deplored the fact that the Palatines' interests had been neglected; others thought that they had gotten about as much as could have been expected. Some suspected that France and Chanut put undue influence on Sweden not to champion the Palatine cause. As usual Elisabeth's mother was the subject of gossip. Her dejection at the death of her uncle, her low opinion of her son's judgment, a rumor that she had advised him not to accept the treaty—all were hotly debated and discussed. Back and forth the talk went, with the queen deploring Charles's willingness to deal with Parliament at the same time that she complained of his weakness. But there was no doubt in anyone's mind that the execution of Charles was a "fatal misfortune" for the Palatines. As one observer put it: "The confusion that one sees [in England] for many long years, would take away the means from those whom [Charles-Louis] had counted on as friends to give him any support for his complete and general reestablishment."[4]

As for the Swedes, they had little interest and perhaps little power in the matter. More important to the Swedish negotiators than one small piece of the Hapsburg empire was the establishment of religious freedom in Catholic territories and indemnity for their own war damages and costs. Back in Germany the ravages of war might never be made right. Bad as the early pillage and looting had been, wholesale destruction characterized the later stages of the war when, afraid of a solid phalanx of Catholic autocracy and absolute monarchy, Sweden and France joined forces to defeat the imperial army. One-third of the population was lost, seven or eight million dead, few of them combatants. In Germany the war was a disaster, fought to little benefit for anyone, bloody, irrational, a stunning example of the danger of religious fervor and hired armies.

To his letter Descartes received no reply. Elisabeth was still at Krossen, weakened by illness. What she thought of Descartes's advice can only be imagined. Take what you can get; beggars can't be choosers; it is natural for those in power to divide the spoils; don't try to drive a wedge between France and Sweden; do not protest that at the peace negotiations the French and their representatives, including my friend Chanut, worked against your interests behind the scenes; do not do anything to harm French interests or to sour the possibility that a Frenchman like myself will be well received in Sweden. To have responded positively to such advice could have been taken as treason, or at least as some degree of complicity with the enemy. Perhaps most difficult would be any response to Descartes's "positive bias" on the event of Charles's death, a death that horrified not only royalists but also many democrats.

Details of the trial and execution were well known. Charles was a pitiful figure as he tried ineptly to argue the illegality of the proceedings against him and insisted on giving the signal himself for the ax to fall on his head. Intimations of mob violence, the breakdown of civil order, summary justice, the king's confusion on the block as his thoughts wandered, all struck fear in the hearts even of those who were opposed to absolute monarchy. Many now feared that the alternatives to monarchy might be worse. In the circumstances, Descartes's fantastic description of the comfortable state of mind of Charles as he stood before his executioner, easy in conscience, happy to be dying a death that brings him fame, was grotesque.

But after all the self-serving, though perhaps well-meant, advice and the bumbling condolences, there was still that sweetness at the end. For one moment hovered a fragile vision of happiness: regular, fruitful intercourse between friends flourishing in a peaceful, prosperous country where neither malice, pretension, nor force of arms rules.

26

A Royal Summons

~

The letter Descartes received from Christina on the day he wrote to Elis-abeth about her uncle's death had been mailed in December but delayed because it was sent to Paris and had to be forwarded to Egmond. Christina wrote:

Stockholm
2 December 1648

Monsieur Descartes,

A while ago, my curiosity caused me to ask by way of M. Chanut your feelings on the question of the sovereign good: on that subject, Monsieur, you have declared yourself in a letter that you have taken the trouble to write to me, for which I wish to thank you, as well as for the *Treatise on the Passions* which you have attached to it. I assure you, Monsieur, that these pieces have confirmed me in the good opinion which the gentleman Chanut has given me of you. I know already that to be his friend it is necessary not to have not the least of virtue, and knowing that God has given you that, I judge that the rightness of my judgment as to his merit obliges me to have the same for you, especially as you are known by the beautiful books you have written, I thank you from all my heart that you have confirmed this for me and augmented the esteem that I have for one and for the other, and I pray you to believe that I embrace with pleasure all occasions which will permit me to witness to you that your merits have won the esteem and affection of

Christina

In this stiff little note, Christina acknowledges Descartes's attentions. There is no showing that she has read his letter on the sovereign good or his *Treatise on the Passions* with any care. It is also clear that Chanut has judged it untactful to pass on to her letters written to another woman.

In his cover letter, Chanut gives Descartes his own account of the evolving situation in Stockholm:

I had the honor two months ago of going with the Queen on a trip to the silver and copper mines. At leisure on the road, she gave herself entirely to reading. I had taken along your *Principles of Philosophy*. I read her the preface. She opened the book at places, and remained quite pensive for a few days. I thought I knew the cause, and when I dared to say to her that it seemed to me that she was caught between desire to be instructed in this Philosophy and the difficulty of it, she confessed that I had divined what was bothering her. My advice was to work at her leisure at some of the other studies which had been proposed to her and in the meantime to ask M. Freinshemius, her historian, a very honest man and learned too, from whom she gets help with her reading, if he would instruct her in the *Principles* as well as it was possible for him, so that when Her Majesty came to read them, she would be saved from difficulties that would annoy her if she applied herself to their study by herself. My advice pleased her. On her return she gave the order to M. Freinshemius. And because he recognized that he himself would need a companion on this road, I was asked to read at the same time. So it is, Monsieur, since one of the principal parts of my office is not being disagreeable to the Sovereign at whose court I serve our Master [the French King], that I announce to you that today one of the functions of the Embassy in Sweden is to read and study your philosophy. I confess to you that I needed duty to be joined to my curiosity in this endeavor, because, finding myself engaged in the civil life, I had scruples in diverting my thoughts to abstractions. The plan of the Queen of Sweden is to take your book as soon as we have finished with it and when, in the course of reading, we are not strong enough or adroit enough to untie the knots that hold us up, we will have recourse to you. Her Majesty has strenuously enquired about your fortunes, and the care they are taking of you in France, and I do not know that, when she has gotten a taste of your Philosophy, she will not tempt you to Sweden. I will be, if it pleases God, before long in France, where I will be able to tell you several things which will be important for you if you put this affair into the works. Meanwhile, I can assure you that this Princess, who values nothing in the world but truth and virtue, judges you very highly for the love of both one and the other. You see that I am not at a Court where malice and disguise are in credit.

Side by side one might imagine them riding, this faithful representative of France, a thoroughly civilized man, and the young Swedish queen. It would be early winter, cold as they drive though the north country on their way to the mines. The roads would be rough, the houses they pass little more than log huts, the frozen ground covered with a thin crust of snow. To pass the time, the Queen brought books. The diplomat takes the opportunity to offer to her his friend's major work. He reads to her from its preface. She takes the book from him, leafs through it, opens at a few pages, puts it aside. Says nothing. Points at something out the carriage window. Picks up another book.

But Chanut is clever. "I know what is bothering you about this," he says, "the problem is the difficulty of it, isn't it?" He himself, he confesses disarmingly, has similar scruples. He understands the concern that in a life dedicated to civil affairs, perhaps it is wrong to take time for philosophy, to indulge "curiosity" about such abstruse matters. He proposes a compromise. Her librarian can read the book and then explicate it for her. And then—it's so hard not to like this man—he gets caught in his own trap. He is roped into reading Descartes's *Principles* too, something that up to then he has managed to avoid. So it was that a French diplomat found speculation about the "structure of the world" part of his official duties.

Chanut, always urbane, does not complain, although he does manage to communicate the irony of it all. But it is for such a good cause. He is certain that the groundwork is now laid for Descartes coming to Sweden. He and Freinshemius will not be up to the task; they will need Descartes's help in unraveling the knots. Descartes will be flattered; Christina will send for him. One can almost see him rubbing his diplomat's hands in satisfaction at a job well done.

A few days later, Descartes writes to Chanut, enclosing a letter to Christina. Echoing his first responses to Elisabeth, he is again the rapturous courtier: "If ever a letter was sent me from Heaven, and I saw it descend from the clouds, I would not be more surprised and could not receive it with less respect and veneration, than I received what it pleased your Majesty to write to me."[1] He describes himself as amazed that a great monarch with so many responsibilities would have shown such an interest in his work. He ends with the assurance: "Even if I am not born Swedish or Finnish, I could not be with more zeal or more perfectly at your service."

To Chanut he is equally gracious.

You are right to think that I have much reason to wonder that a Queen, perpetually busy with affairs, would have followed up, after a few months, on a letter that I had the honor of writing her, and that she has taken the trouble to answer so soon. I was surprised to see that she wrote so precisely and easily in French—all our nation is obliged to her—and it seems to me that this Princess is much more created in the image of God than are the rest of men, inasmuch as she can take care of a great number of matters at the same time. For there is no one in the world except God whose spirit does not get tired, and who is not less exact in knowing the number of hairs or in taking account of the smallest worms, rather than in moving the Heavens and the Stars.

Leaving aside what the pious Voetius might have said about this daring comparison of Christina to God moving heaven and earth, the reference to the importance of his own work is surprisingly humble. Biology, zoology, his treatise on animals. Hair and worms? Perhaps he judges that in all courts, after all, some degree of humble pie is necessary.

He goes on in a more characteristic vein. It is not surprising that she wants to read his *Principles*, because there are truths there that she will not find anywhere else, truths that are relevant to public life because they are the foundation of morals. Yes, he will answer questions about his work with pleasure, although of course he is so far away that his responses will not get there before those in Sweden have resolved the matter for themselves.

To facilitate the reading, he writes to give Chanut some idea of what might be left out and some of the main points to keep in mind. He again describes his depressed state of mind after his disappointment in Paris. It was as if he had been invited to dinner by people he thought were his friends but on arriving "found their kitchen in disorder, and their pot turned over." He will never go anywhere else on promises alone. Even though there is nothing keeping him in Holland except having nowhere else to go, he is in danger of having to spend the rest of his life there. From day to day he suffers more and more, so he doesn't think he could make any voyage anyway. On a brighter note, certainly Chanut will be passing through soon on his way to France; Descartes hopes to see him. He adds a hesitant apology: the letter to Christina did not deal with anything of substance but contained only compliments because he was afraid of discouraging her even further from philosophy.

Even before he received these letters from Descartes, Chanut had accomplished his aim. With her usual impetuosity, Christina demanded to see Descartes in Stockholm immediately and learn his philosophy from his own mouth. Quickly, Chanut sent letters both to Paris and to Egmond. Getting no reply, he wrote again in early March, sending as many as three short notes via Hooglande in Leyden urging Descartes to come. Once the queen made up her mind, her will had to be done quickly. In fact, Christina had already dispatched one of her admirals in a ship to pick the philosopher up and bring him to her.

Poor Descartes. This is no rash man. And certainly, after his experience in Paris, he is not a man to rely on promises. He stalls. Christina wants him to come in the spring so that he can travel home in the summer and avoid the cold. But the prospect of another ocean voyage exhausts Descartes. Wouldn't it be better to wait, travel in the summer when travel is easier, and then stay a year, over the winter? Give him time to breathe, to think, to communicate with Elisabeth, to let her know what is happening.

The thirty-first of March was another big day of letter writing. First he wrote to Chanut with compliments to the queen and assurance that of course he will obey her very wish. Respectfully, he argues for delay. With all due deference, can he really teach her philosophy in a few months? Wouldn't it be better to come later and spend more time? He is not so young anymore and he is tired from his last trip. Should he really undertake the trip now, when the weather is still unsettled? Even when Christina's admiral, disguised as a common sailor, arrives at his door with orders to bring him immediately, Descartes is adamant. No, he must wait and come later in the summer. So he drags his feet. He will not leave until he hears again from Sweden, although, of course, he will obey whatever are her commands.

Once he drafted this official communication meant for Christina, Descartes wrote a second letter to Chanut, this time for his eyes only, expressing more serious reservations. In fact, he confesses, he is having a lot of difficulty deciding whether to take the trip at all. First, he has worries about whether the queen is really willing to take the time to learn philosophy; his experience has been that so few are. Then, once people do understand his ideas, they often find them so simple and obvious that they do not admire them anymore. He has not been appreciated. He has not been admired. His work has been cast aside. Why should he think it will be any different in Sweden? "It seems," he told Chanut, "as if fortune is jealous that I never wanted anything from her and that I tried to live my life so that she had no power over me, because she never fails to disoblige me whenever she has an occasion." Clearly, his power of positive thinking has for the moment failed. The mistress of fate, fickle like his absent mother, resents his apparent independence.

He gives Chanut more details of the trip to France, breaking a silence he preserved in his last letter so as not to "offend" any one. The pension that was to have been given to him, he was supposed to pay for. His supposed supporters were indifferent to his work. He knows that nothing like this will happen in Sweden, but, he writes with some exaggeration, "the poor success of all the trips which I have taken in the last twenty years makes me fear that nothing more remains to me but to find en route thieves who will rob me, or a storm which will take my life." He does not want to appear disrespectful to Chanut's queen; he repeats his assurance: even thieves and shipwreck will not keep him away if the queen really wants him to come and will take the time to examine his opinions, but he begs: if the queen "only has some curiosity that will pass," he can do without this journey.

Finally, the last letter was for Elisabeth, telling her about the summons from the queen to visit and his decision to delay the trip until summer.

Egmond
31 March 1649

Madame,

It has been about a month since I wrote to your Highness, to let her know that I had received several letters from Sweden. I have just received more, in which I am invited, by the Queen, to make a trip there this spring, so as to return before winter. But I have answered that, even though I do not refuse to go, I believe nevertheless that I will not leave from here until toward the middle of the summer. I have asked for this delay for several reasons, and particularly so that I can have the honor of receiving the commands of Y.H. before I leave. I have already so publicly declared the zeal and devotion that I have in your service that one would be justified in having a bad opinion of me if they noticed that I was indifferent to anything regarding you, which they would if they saw that I look for occasions to avoid my duty. So I ask very humbly Your Highness to do me the favor of instructing me in all that she judges I can render her or her relatives service, and to assure her that she has over me as much power as if I have been all my life her footman. I ask her also to let me know what it would please her that I respond if it happens that anyone remembers the letters from your Highness on the Sovereign Good, of which I made mention last year in my letters, and is curious to see them. I am resigned to spending the winter in that country and to not returning until the next year. It is likely there will be peace then in all of Germany, and if my desires are accomplished, on my return I will take a route through the place where you are, so as to be able to more particularly witness that I am . . .

How different is this letter from the one to Christina, intimate, respectful, without inflated compliment. There is only the one false note—the letters again—creating a suspicion that Descartes may be angling for permission to make use of more of his to Elisabeth, even those that will not make sense unless it is known to whom they are addressed, even though Chanut has clearly put aside the first batch, not at all sure that the queen would want to see letters written to another woman. Descartes asks for Elisabeth's orders. Is there anything he should say or do for the Palatines in Sweden?

Again the mirage of reunion is evoked. On the way back from Sweden, with peace restored, he will come to her. How might he have imagined it? An extended visit, even a rented house in the country, close again to his friend, lecturing to receptive students, part of a community of scholars. Did he look up from his letter out his window at fields just beginning to green and feel a rush of vitality? Perhaps, after all, life is not over. He is as much in her power, he writes, as if he were her servant, her footman. Once the year in Sweden is up and peace is established, he will come to her, wherever she is. He will make the trip through a Germany restored to peace and prosperity.

April comes. He explains the reluctance he still has to go to Sweden to his friend Brasset.

> I confess that a man, born in the gardens of Touraine, and who is now in a land where if there is not as much honey as in that land which God promised to the Israelites, it is believable that there is more milk, cannot so easily decide to leave to go to live in another country among rocks and ice. Nevertheless, since this same country is also inhabited by men, and the Queen who commands them has, alone, more knowledge, more intelligence, and more rationality than all the doctors of the Cloisters or the Colleges that the fertility of the country where I have been living has produced, I persuade myself that beauty of place is not necessary for wisdom and that men are not the same as trees that one can observe grow not so well when the land where they are transplanted to is less rich than that in which they were sown.[2]

Milk and honey, the mother's milk denied him as a child, the hunger that makes him sad even as an adult. Can this orphan be finally nourished among the ice and the snow by the wise, queenly mother with more intelligence than all of the theologians of Holland, by someone who will see him for what he is, cherish him for that alone? Will he be transplanted so that no more painful uprooting is necessary? Or might he still end up at home in gentle Heidelberg with his princess, whose interest in philosophy is so much more assured. Chanut, passing through on the way to France, seems to have finally put away Descartes's doubts with important considerations of what he may gain in Sweden—a college of learned men with himself at the head, the possibility of an estate, and even a pension.

Elisabeth writes inquiring about the trip with some concern, although what her arguments are we cannot know, because her letter is lost, or perhaps discarded because it is too personal, shows too much feeling for his health and peace on a trip that she herself was unwilling to make, even when the interests of her family demanded it.

Descartes answers her letter in a short note in June. No, he is determined to go. Chanut has visited on his way to France, has spoken so glowingly of "this marvelous Queen that the road does not seem to me so long nor so upsetting that it did before." He assures her that he will try to put in a good word for her while he is there.

> I will count myself very happy, if while I am there, I am able to render some service to your Highness. I will not fail to search for occasions, and will not fear to write openly what I will do or think on this subject, because not having any intention which would be prejudicial to those for whom I would be obliged to have respect, and taking as a maxim that the way that is just and honest is the most useful and most sure, I hope that what I write or think will not be wrongly interpreted nor fall into hands of persons who are so unjust as to find it wrong that I acquit myself of my duty and make open profession to be . . .

Is it Elisabeth who has warned him that in Sweden he may be watched closely and not able to communicate freely? Nevertheless he is busy preparing for the trip, his sartorial preparations causing some amusement to his friends.

Throughout his life, Descartes was known for plainness of dress. His usual attire was a plain dark wool jacket relieved only by a white linen collar trimmed with a small amount of lace. At Amsterdam, ready to embark for Sweden, his friends were surprised to see not the soberly dressed philosopher but a courtier, dressed up, dolled up, in a new wig from France freshly curled and washed, with beard and mustache elegantly trimmed, sporting long pointed shoes and white gloves. On 7 September, Brasset reported naughtily to Chanut, "when he came to say goodbye with a hairdo in curls, shoes ending in points, and great white gauntlets, it reminded me that this Plato was not so divine that he did not know about the human, and I thought the recluse of Egmond will emerge in Stockholm a courtier shod and vested."[3] In addition to preparing a good appearance for his new patroness, Descartes was mindful of philosophy. Before he left he took to his publisher *The Passions of the Soul,* fruit of the long correspondence with Elisabeth, the last of his published works.

There could be no more procrastinating. Winter was approaching. Giving up the hope that Chanut would return from France in time for them to sail together, Descartes set out for the north, accompanied only by a borrowed servant.

27

Reason in the Service of Sense

~

As Descartes was arriving in Stockholm, a momentous event was occurring in the life of the Palatines. With Elisabeth watching and waiting in Berlin, her brother Charles-Louis marched back into Heidelberg, the capital of his ruined kingdom. As he entered, the Catholic clergy left by another gate. Given the state of the Palatine and the wearying negotiations that still dragged on over the terms of transition, his return was not triumphal. The Bavarian ambassador waited to press Maximilian's demands for compensation for the harvest the Bavarians had gathered and for the heavy cannons that had been used to mow down Palatine citizens. The castle was uninhabitable. Wolves roamed the grass-grown streets. Public buildings were in rubble. A once-thriving economy was moribund, with no crops and no trade. Part of the territory was still occupied by France, another part by Spain.

Taking rooms in town for himself and his new wife, Charles-Louis set to work with the small amount of funds at his disposal. He opened the quarries to mine stone for building materials, restored the postal service, replanted vineyards, and gave licenses to the inhabitants to shoot on sight the wolves that haunted the streets. He offered asylum to all those who had lost their lands by religious persecution. He reestablished the school system, which had been the pride of his ancestors, releasing teachers from all but instructional duties. Unfortunately there was no possibility yet that Elisabeth or any other family member could return to be with him, not until there was a place for them to live. From Berlin, Elisabeth remained in close contact with Charles-Louis. This was the brother who had stayed behind with her when the family had been driven out of Bohemia, who had been her playmate in Krossen while they waited out the war, who made the long journey with her to The Hague. In the next decades, he would often turn to her for advice and help in the work of rebuilding the Palatine.

He consulted her in particular on the question of reopening the university. While Descartes waited on the Swedish queen in the frozen north, Elisabeth and her brother planned the restoration of an intellectual institution that before the war had been a center for freethinking scholars and students. Repairs were begun on the university building, negotiations opened for the return of looted manuscripts stored in the Vatican, a fund was set aside for books. A list of scholars was drawn up to be invited to come to teach and live at Heidelberg. Descartes was on the list, as was Spinoza in Geneva and others whom Elisabeth suggested. The conditions to be offered once building was complete were favorable: good compensation and religious freedom. No more "beard and bite" of theologians, no more courtiers more interested in influence than learning, no more draining struggle to flatter aristocratic egos, only solid learning in a progressive community dedicated to knowledge.

With Elisabeth's good advice and Charles's insistence on economy and sound investment, a small miracle seemed to be the works. With Charles resisting his mother's ill-tempered requests from The Hague for money and insisting on the priority of trade and education, the old Heidelberg was reemerging.

In the meantime, Elisabeth was deeply involved in a project close to her heart—the marriage of her young sister Henriette. Whether Henriette had accompanied Elisabeth to Brandenburg or come to join her sister sometime later, it is clear from Elisabeth's letters that Henriette was with her in Germany by the winter of 1646. This youngest sister, frail in health and with a sweet disposition, was the darling of the family. Her delicate features, halo of ash blond hair, and fair complexion were much admired. Several times Elisabeth had nursed her back to health from dangerous illnesses. Now she saw a chance for Henriette to be settled in her own home. There had been an offer for her hand from the second son of a Transylvanian prince, Sigmund Rakoczy. It was an offer that Elisabeth, as well as her aunt the dowager electress, believed should be accepted.

The single life to which Elisabeth and her sister Louise were resigned was difficult for any woman; it was impossible, it would seem, for the gentle Henriette, always unsure of her own mind and waiting to be governed by others' opinions. The problem was Charles-Louis. Puffed up with his newly restored status, not much excited by a match with the second son of a minor prince, he wavered, delaying decisions and making inconsistent demands while hoping unrealistically for a grander offer for Henriette. He was so difficult that Elisabeth and her aunt the dowager electress removed to Krossen to conduct negotiations further away from Heidelberg and Charles's bad temper, arguing that Krossen was more convenient for ambassadors who passed back and forth from Transylvania.

Managing her brother in this affair required all of Elisabeth's powers of argument. Even as a contract favorable to the Palatines, who could offer little in the way of dowry, was concluded by Elisabeth and her aunt, Charles-Louis threatened to withdraw his consent. He cited as reasons that Henriette's suitor did not have the rank of prince and that he had no assurance that the Rakoczys would carry out financial arrangements in case of Sigmund's death. Elisabeth wrote back refuting his points one by one.

The two things which you urge against the Transylvanian marriage are that he is not esteemed a prince and that one must trust to his honesty to observe the conditions. For the first we have the testimony of all those who have served in the Swedish army, of Comenius, and now of Courtland, which I send you herewith, and I think the authority is quite as good as that of Lesley. One may well believe that in a Court where they try to lower the Palatine House, they do not want it to make good alliances. Besides, the Ambassadors of the Prince of Transylvania would not have ventured to give a false title to his brother if it did not belong to him, and we have the original of that which they sent you written in their own hand. On the second point I do not think you can bring forward a single instance of a marriage where the dowry was advanced before the death of the husband, and if one believes one is deal-ing with people without honesty one should not give them a daughter. . . . If the Elector Palatine did not wish the said marriage he should have informed his relations here, who could have refused with better grace than by demanding conditions quite unheard of.[1]

The importance of evidence, the reliability of testimony, consistency in judg-ment—Elisabeth's logic was more in keeping with the empiricism of later modern philosophers than with Descartes's rationalism. It was also informed by her sensi-tivity to some of the motives behind her brother's wavering. Realizing her broth-er's reluctance to incur expense, she lays out a plan for meeting the costs of the wedding out of her own meager funds and small contributions from the rest of the family. Understanding her brother's inability to grasp the state of mind of poor, timid Henriette, she describes at length to him and with eloquence Henriette's tearful happiness at the prospect of marriage and her nervousness at going to live with strangers in a new country. Sensing her brother's underlying wish to do well for his sister, she works to make him see how his indecision drags Henriette's emo-tions painfully back and forth.

She [Henriette] assures me she will not press for more (expenditures) if only she may be furnished with a trousseau that will not put her nor her relatives to shame, that she may be respected from the start; and she begs to send humble thanks to her papa [his sisters were in the habit of calling Charles papa as the head of the family] for the care he has for her, but since the thing has gone so far she cannot draw back with dignity, and hopes he will continue his kindness in the way mentioned. She would write herself but is so melancholy she cannot.[2]

Elisabeth also reminds Charles of the elderly aunt who had worked so hard on the marriage contract and whose reputation was on the line if the marriage fell through. "I forgot to tell you that I have not shown what you said about the full power (of attorney) to the Electress, knowing that it would vex her."

Elisabeth closes with an appeal to principle. "One should not cavil at a thing done, but try to draw all the advantage possible from it."[3]

As usual Elisabeth is the reasonable intermediary between opposing forces, feeling out solutions, dealing with other's emotions, and looking for some common ground that allows affairs to go forward. As usual she is bitterly accused of "meddling," this time by a bullying and irascible Charles-Louis, at the moment more intent on venting his irritation than on producing a favorable result. There are no angry and defensive answering letters from Elisabeth. Instead she shields others from irrationality, carefully doctoring her accounts of Charles-Louis's letters for her aunt and concealing from Charles-Louis her aunt's harsh judgments on his undiplomatic behavior.

By the next December things were still not settled. Charles Louis writes to invite Elisabeth to come home to Heidelberg. With irony, she refuses. "The Elector Palatine does Elisabeth too much honor in thinking of offering her a lodging which would be too good for her, and she will try to repair thither as soon as possible, but she cannot yet make an assignation with my lord . . . [W]hile the Electress (Dowager) is so out of temper with him she dares not propose the journey."[4] Again and again she writes to Charles about the marriage. Even on Christmas Eve, she is inquiring whether he has received the marriage contract, giving him more evidence of the princely status of Henriette's suitor, and citing many witnesses to honors paid him by others. She defends herself against Charles's charges that she is interfering.

> If you had told me not to meddle in the matter I would have obeyed you gladly, for it is not my humor to push myself into affairs; I am too used to being charged with the faults of others in such business to seek it, but not having your orders for an excuse I could not oppose myself to the desire of the Electress that I should be present at all that was done—but enough of this matter.[5]

Charles's immediate angry response tested all of Elisabeth's virtue. Twelve days later, after two hostile letters from her brother, she writes:

> The reason I did not answer you last week was that your examples showed me the wrong one may do by writing in a passion, and one must be more apathetic than a stoic to receive such cruel reproaches from the person one loves best in the world without an extreme perturbation. Still, my sense of what you do to me is not so great and afflicts me much less than the harm you do yourself by your passions, and if you do not accustom yourself to control them or at least not to make decisions while they possess you, I foresee that you will not only lose success but health of body and mind. Consider, I beg you, that all those who have maintained or advanced their interests by conduct and not by force of arms have been people of moderate passions, the Duke of Bavaria, old William, and Prince Henry,[6] the Count de Schwartzenberg and numbers of others. While on the contrary those whom they ruined were the slaves of their passions or those of others.[7]

As for her brother's unjust attack on her and his complaints that she has not come to help him in Heidelberg, Elisabeth's stoicism has a touch of humor to it.

For my own part I would not only bear the imputation of all your faults and past misfortunes, but make the journey to Heidelberg to take upon me those you have or may have in the future if that could ease your mind, but while I am here there is not any means of verifying your accusations touching the marriage, since all who have assisted know my innocence. My only fault has been to speak the bare truth as I learned it, and it is with regret that I will correct myself, but I will do it from the respect that I owe you. My former letters have amply answered the things you accused me of, so I will not weary you with repetition, but only beg you to read them over in cold blood, and you will see I could not have acted otherwise.

Again she protects her aunt. "I have not shown your letter to the Electress for fear of vexing her, believing that you did not intend to reproach her, but only me."[8]

Finally Elisabeth and her aunt triumphed. The date for the marriage was fixed. They had proved too much for Charles-Louis. Elisabeth worked hard with little money to provide a respectable trousseau. She wrote to Holland for bargain lace, she wheedled horses from her relatives, she borrowed money to buy nightdresses. There were more delays. News arrived that Elisabeth's brother Philip, whose unfortunate temper had been the occasion for her exile from The Hague, had been killed fighting for Spain as a soldier of fortune. Mourning did not prevent Charles from continuing to vent his anger. His tirades continued. The marriage was delayed until May but finally took place without incident. The elector could not be present but sent a gift and a blessing.

Henriette traveled to Transylvania to her prince and was well received. Although she died a short time after her arrival and her brokenhearted bridegroom a year later, Henriette's first letters from her new home show her to be happy with a devoted and loving husband. In her childish way she describes to her brother her situation. "Both the Frau Mother and the reigning Princess have greatly caressed me, as the former still does, and my lord is very good to me and sees that I have nothing to complain about except being so far from all my relations."[9]

28

In the Land of Ice and Snow

⌇

In the meantime Descartes had arrived in Stockholm without encountering thieves or shipwreck. With Chanut still gone, he was received as a houseguest by Madame Chanut in Stockholm and wrote to Elisabeth a few days after his arrival to let her know he had arrived safely.

Stockholm, 9 October 1649

Madame,

Having arrived four or five days ago in Stockholm, one of the first things I considered to be my duty was to renew the offers of my very humble service to your Highness, so that she can know that the change of air and country can never change or diminish my devotion and my zeal. I have only had the honor of seeing the Queen two times, but I think I already know her enough to dare to say that she has no less merit and more virtue than people have attributed to her. With the generosity and majesty that brightens all her actions, one sees there a gentleness and a kindness which obliges all those who love virtue and who have the honor of approaching her to be entirely devoted to her service. One of the first things that she asked me was if I have any news of you, and I did not neglect to say directly what I think of your Highness. Remarking the force of her spirit, I have no fear that this would give her any jealousy, as I also assure myself that your Highness would not have any, if I write freely my feelings about this Queen. She is extremely taken with the study of letters, but, because I do not know if she has seen anything of philosophy, I cannot judge whether she will take to it, or whether she will be able to take the time, and in consequence whether I will be able to give her any satisfaction and to useful to her in anything. This great ardor which she has for the knowledge of letters is spurring her on now to cultivate the Greek language and to collect many ancient books, but perhaps that will change. And if it will not change, the virtue which I remark in this Princess obliges me always to prefer usefulness in her service over the desire to please her, so that this will not keep me from saying frankly what are my feelings. If they fail to be agreeable to her—which I don't think they will be—I will take away in any case the advantage that I have done my duty, and that will give me the opportunity to be able, all the sooner, to return to my solitude, without which it is difficult for me to be able to advance at all in the search for truth. It is in this that consists my principal good in this life. Monsieur Freinshemius has found it good for her Majesty that I only go to the Palace at the hours it pleases her to give me to have the honor of speaking to her. Thus I do not have much trouble in paying my court and that fits well my mood. After all, nevertheless, even though I have a very great veneration for her Majesty, I do not believe that anything will be capable of keeping me in this country any longer than just to next summer, but I cannot absolutely answer for the future. I can only assure you that I will be all my life . . .

Descartes maneuvers, but there is a weariness to it all. One of the first things Christina has asked is for news of her, he tells Elisabeth—truly or not truly is hard to tell. He has well-founded doubts that Christina has any sustained interest in philosophy or that he can satisfy whatever interest she has. Will she have a taste for philosophy when she finally gets down to reading it? Will she take the time? Can he really be useful to her? The queen has her own scholar, Freinshemius, her librarian and historian. At the moment, her enthusiasm is for learning Greek and collecting old books, subjects in which he is hardly of much help, given that most of what was written in the past he judges to be worthless.

Elisabeth would have read this ambivalent little letter closely, read it word for word and words between words, to try to make out what really was the situation of her friend at the Snow Queen's court. With all her struggles with her family at home, she must have worried for him, worried for his health, worried for his virtue. She knew this queen by reputation, knew of the fierce struggle of wills between Christina and her powerful chancellor Axel Oxenstierna, knew of her hot temper, her eccentric habits, her addiction to sport and the hunt, the strength of her will. She might have winced when she read that Descartes was determined to speak freely. Would this pupil take Descartes's corrections with as much equanimity as she had?

But images of a happier future for her philosopher also must have been present, with the restoration of the university under way and the list drawn up for its distinguished and progressive faculty. Descartes's visit had been promised as early as the next summer, and it might be through a revived and free Heidelberg.

As Elisabeth read Descartes's letter, in Stockholm the hours for Christina's philosophy lessons were still not set. Christina was not so eager to learn philosophy as Elisabeth. Take a month, take six weeks, she told Descartes, get to know Sweden. For weeks, he did not see the queen at all. It gave him time to get settled and to try to work, but he found it difficult to concentrate in Chanut's busy household where he was still a guest. There were unpleasant rumors; he had not been to the queen's taste, she did not like his looks or his manners. At court he was resented, even ridiculed, as a foreigner. To make it worse, when it did come, the queen's summons made rather a court jester of him. He was to compose verses for a ballet to be presented at court, the queen much liking such entertainments. She herself would perform in the role of "Diana victorious over love."

Descartes obeyed and must have acquitted himself to the queen's satisfaction, because soon afterwards he was asked to write verse again, this time as part of a celebration of the peace treaty that had resulted in the partition of the Palatine. This time Descartes organized the dancing, a chorus of crippled soldiers and ragged peasants singing :

> He who knows how we are made
> and thinks that war is beautiful
> Or that it is better than Peace
> Is crippled in his mind.[1]

After this less-than-memorable comment on the war, Descartes ended his poetic career. While he waited for Christina's philosophy lessons to begin, she assigned him more academic tasks. He should put his unpublished manuscripts, which he had brought with him, in order. He could advise her on the formation of an Academy of Learned Men.

In mid-January the time for his tutoring of Christina was finally arranged. He was to go three times a week to the palace, which was some distance from Chanut's house, and he was to go at five o'clock in the morning, the only time that Christina was willing to give him. Descartes, always weak in the lungs, got up well before dawn, shivered in the corner of a carriage borrowed from Chanut, and presented himself before the twenty-four-year-old queen, her long pale hair tied back with a ribbon. The room was cold, Christina professing to be above such niceties as heat. After only a few lessons, Chanut fell ill. Descartes hurried back after each morning session to nurse him and then drove back to the palace at Christina's command to advise her on her academy. In a few days, Descartes was ill also.

By the end of February, Descartes, faithfully tended to the last by a recovered Chanut, was dead. There would be no last words to his patroness, only silence from the land of ice and snow. In the early spring of 1650, Elisabeth received Chanut's notice of Descartes's death. The news could not have counted for much among the people around her. Her friendship with Descartes had been a subject of jokes rather than reverence. Her aunt was still preoccupied and "vexed" by the Henriette affair. There is no record of what Elisabeth thought or felt as she looked out over the snow-covered hills at Krossen. Nor have we copies of the letters she wrote to Chanut the following summer in reply to his request that her letters be published in Sweden. Only snatches can be gleaned from Descartes's biographer Baillet, who had access to the letters.

In her June letter to Chanut, Baillet noted, Elisabeth spoke of Descartes's piety, a piety that was "sincere and solid, but neither extreme nor factious." She spoke of Descartes's never-lacking "zeal" for her, a zeal that yet was never "blind or uncontrolled." Yes, she said, she had challenged the philosopher with the problem of reconciling God's omniscience and foreknowledge with free will, but Descartes approached the issue philosophically, keeping, she said, to a prudent "resolution never to produce anything that the Theologians could pretend to be under their jurisdiction."[2]

If Descartes, in the dedication to Elisabeth of the *Principles of Philosophy,* had generously attributed his virtue to her, Elisabeth returned the favor. Piety and service to others all too often bring in their train zealotry and imperiousness. Her Descartes was guilty of neither; he was faithful to their friendship and reasonable in his opinions. Just as the virtue of mental detachment for which Descartes praised Elisabeth was more his than hers, so the fidelity and the reasonableness that Elisabeth attributed to Descartes were inherent in her own character and practice.

Whatever she suffered, she suffered alone. By the next spring, with her sister's marriage accomplished, she was ready to go to Heidelberg to take upon herself her brother's "misfortunes." Sophie, who had noted in her *Memoirs* the change in her sister's appearance, went on to give hints of what some of those misfortunes would be.

> The Electress [Charles's wife] made much of me out of dislike of my sister, and Elisabeth at once asserted such authority over me that I began to prefer Madame, who could be charming when she wanted to be; for at times she had some very gracious times which I profited by. Still I was wrong not to submit to a sister who had obviously much more sense than myself. My friends, on the other hand, were well pleased to foster my ill-humor in order to draw me closer to themselves.[3]

Poor Elisabeth. In the past year she had lost her best friend and one of her favorite brothers, as well as the companionship of her beloved sister Henriette. Now she was walking into a hornets' nest of tangled feelings that would take all of the force of her philosophy to manage. Ungovernable Sophie was much in need of discipline and guidance from an older sister. Charles's embarrassing and obsessive jealousy of his wife and her bad temper would lead to the ugly deterioration of their relationship and his alliance with another woman. Elisabeth would play a major role in resolving the situation by organizing his wife's removal to a separate home, again to the criticism of carping relatives. Charles's mocked-up proclamation of divorce and irregular second marriage would bring disgrace on the family and make it impossible for Elisabeth to continue to live in Heidelberg. But there were also happier matters: the repaving of the roads, ruins cleared away, the castle rebuilt. Best of all was the reopening of the university, the appointing of its faculty, and the refurbishing of its library, made bitter only by the absence of the man who might have been its leading scholar.

As far as we know, Elisabeth never worked up her doubts about the separation of mind and body into a treatise. She never systematically spelled out the philosophy of science that might have resulted from a nondualist metaphysics. She never worked out a practical ethics suitable for bodily life in time. She never described in analytic terms the emotional intelligence that comes when thoughtful body and embodied mind learn to work together nor specified the ways grief and shame can spur moral regeneration. After life in her brother's chaotic household became impossible for her, she negotiated a home and position for herself as canoness and then abbess of Herford, with ample scope for administrative and judicial skills. From that secure seat, over the next thirty years of her life, she actively governed a small kingdom and supported and counseled religious dissidents who championed freedom and self-government.

Did she regret the restricted life of a woman? Regret that she had not been able to do battle with Descartes for Cartesianism in the universities or that she would not herself be named professor at Heidelberg? There is no way to know. Only one last short note to Descartes must stand as a final statement of the fruit of their philosophical collaboration.

Elisabeth answered Descartes's last letter from Sweden as soon as she got it in early December.

4 December 1649

Monsieur Descartes,

Your letter was forwarded from Cleve, but even delayed it was very agreeable and a strong proof of your continued kindness to me, and it assured me also of the happy success of your trip, since the thing was worth the trouble and you found even more marvels in the Queen of Sweden than her reputation would have made evident. I must say, you are better able to recognize those marvels than those from here who are taken to proclaiming them. And it seems I know more of her, in the little you have said, than in all I have learned elsewhere.

Do not ever think that a description so advantageous gives me reason for jealousy; rather it makes me value myself a little more than I did before, to have the idea of a woman who is so accomplished, an idea which acquits our sex of the imputation of imbecility and weakness pressed on it by Messieurs the pedants.

I know that when the Queen has tasted your philosophy, she will prefer it to their philology. But I am impressed that it is possible for this Princess to apply herself to study as she has been able to do at the same time that she must attend to the affairs of her kingdom, two occupations so different and which each requires a whole person. The honor she has done me in your presence of remembering me I attribute entirely to the aim of pleasing you, in giving you the pretext to exercise a charity which you have witnessed to exercise on many other occasions and I owe to you this advantage—as well as that I might also obtain some part in her approval—that I will be able to retain all the more the honor of never being known to her other than you represent me. I feel myself always guilty of a crime against your service, being at ease in thinking that your extreme veneration for her will not oblige you to stay in Sweden. If you do leave there this winter, I hope that it will be in the company of M. Kleist, with whom you will have the most convenient way to give the pleasure of seeing you to

Your very affectionate friend at your service,
Elisabeth

Might some of what is in this letter serve as philosophy after all? What could be more exemplary of goodness than to want to be known as you are known in your friend's mind? What more perfect adjustment of self and other than to trust a friend enough so as to be willing to understand yourself as he represents you? Is this not virtue, to feel guilt for missing a friend's presence when he believes his advantage is elsewhere? Should a woman be jealous when another woman is praised? Should a woman see herself as the rival of another woman for a man's attention so that the excellence of one must be an insult to the other? Or should she take pride in the fact that another of her own sex has with her achievements belied once more the wisdom of "Messieurs the pedants" that a woman is less than a man?

Descartes might not have found much that was "angelic" in these remarks, drawing from them at most a sigh of relief that he had not burnt all his royal bridges behind him. But for me, evoked in Elisabeth's last letter is a kind of heaven after all, an attitude above personal hurts, above past betrayals, certainly above changes in royal allegiance, even above a judicious adjustment of the interests of self and public, a stance from which the goodness of others has become so linked with one's own that the two are inseparable.

Epilogue

The Abbess of Herford

❧

The convent at Herford had a distinguished history as a religious community for women. Catholic at its inception in the ninth century, later endowed with considerable territory, in 1220 it became an imperial free abbey with jurisdiction over the surrounding countryside. A large church was built. Later, when a vision of the Virgin Mary appeared on a nearby hill in the form of a dove, a second church and a sister convent were founded. During the Reformation, Herford continued with only a change of denomination as a refuge for aristocratic women. At the time of Elisabeth's tenure as abbess (1667–1680) it was the third among the four female ecclesiastical principalities with votes in the Imperial Assembly and a flourishing agricultural and commercial community.

Thirty years after Descartes's death, Elisabeth would have had reason to feel satisfied with her own part in that history. As abbess and princess and prelatess of the Holy Roman Empire, she had for a long time been the successful administrator not only of a convent but also of a bustling town, vineyards, farms, mills, factories, and a healthy and prosperous population of seven thousand. She had been largely responsible for ensuring that the abbey and its territory retained a degree of independence after the Treaty of Westphalia and kept its vote in the Reichstag. She had skillfully and patiently mediated conflicts and jealousies. She had enlarged the convent's library, contributing many of her own books; she had supplemented classics with works of modern philosophy and science of which Descartes would have approved. She had continued and enlarged the tradition of the abbey as a place of learning and independence for women.

Perhaps we might evoke her as William Penn described her in the epitaph that opens this volume, in the courtyard of her house at Herford, looking out over its fertile fields to the town below. On this day, perhaps business is slow. With few decisions to make, there would be time to remember and contemplate. Sitting, quietly knitting, an activity she found calming, listening to birds singing in the trees against the more distant, prosperous buzz of the mill or the noise of a cart, heaped with prunings from the vineyards, rumbling by on the road. Elisabeth is free for a moment from affairs of the abbey to take stock of her life and accomplishments.

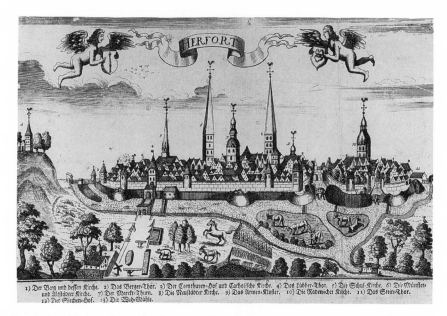

1) Der Berg und dessen Kirche. 2) Das Berger-Thor. 3) Der Comthuren-Hof und Catholische Kirche. 4) Das Lübber-Thor. 5) Die Schul-Kirche. 6) Die Münster- und Altstädter Kirche. 7) Der Marckt-Thurn. 8) Die Neustädter Kirche. 9) Das Armen-Kloster. 10) Die Radewicher Kirche. 11) Das Stein-Thor. 12) Der Siechen-Hof. 13) Die Weh-Mühle.

Fig. 1. An old print shows the thriving community at Herford as it was during Elisabeth's rule. To the far left is the convent on the hill, to the far right the prosperous town. In the foreground are depicted various agricultural and animal husbandry activities.

At Heidelberg, where her brother ruled, with her help and advice the university had flourished. Spinoza had refused her and her brother's invitation to teach, but Freinshemius, Descartes's supporter and Christina's librarian, accepted, along with others. Another, she thought sadly, would have been Descartes himself, who did not live to see the realization of his dream of an education informed by science. She had met, philosophized with, and corresponded with the leading intellectuals in Europe: the German philosopher Leibniz, the English philosopher Anne Conway, the Cambridge Platonist Henry More, the Quaker William Penn, and the mystical Kabbalist Franciscus Mercurius van Helmont, who would attend her in her last illness.[1]

Her sisters were all settled one way or another. Pretty Henriette was long dead, but only after Elisabeth had won for her a short time of married happiness. Louise, the artist, finished with escapades, lived out her days chastely in a Catholic convent—not so terrible, it seemed now, after all. Little Sophie was well married. Charlotte, Charles-Louis's difficult first wife, was comfortably removed from the humiliation of Charles's open liaison with another woman. Charlotte was better on her own, Elisabeth was sure.

Most important, Elisabeth had made Herford a refuge not only for unmarried aristocratic women but also for freethinkers of all classes and genders. What a stir it had caused when she answered the plea of her old friend Anna van Schurman to let her and her Anabaptists come and make a residence in Herford. It was the one affair in which she angered her subjects. Providence—that was one point on which she would never budge, not with Descartes or with anyone. It was the undeniable core of religious faith. And about how Providence might be tapped or approached, there could be no closed mind. So she had welcomed to Herford Anna's protégé, the notorious Jean Labadie, a heretical Catholic converted to evangelical Protestantism, who had, she smiles to herself, also tangled in Holland with Descartes's old enemy, Voetius.

She looks up from her knitting. Indeed, between these two, Descartes and Labadie, there was a strange commonality. She remembers Labadie's assertion in one of his lectures that "the soul must judge of all things by its own inward light to the exclusion of outward impressions produced by mere sense and of all illusions of the imagination."[2] Descartes might almost have written those words. She wonders what Descartes would have made of Labadie's egalitarianism, his community of equals living simply together, giving up private property and rank. Of course that had been the shocking thing for the family and for the town. She laughs aloud this time. No, it was not so much Labadie's religion but what they called his "community of wives" that really upset the officious assemblymen, so convinced were they that a woman's place is as wife and mother, and that making money is the way to salvation.

Yes, the coming of the Labadist community to Herford had caused a storm of protest, laughable in retrospect, angering at the time. The Labadists had a right to worship as they pleased. They provided business for the town, they kept to themselves and bothered no one. So what could have been more sensible? But no, there were letters of protest, charges that Elisabeth had gone senile, false stories about the Labadists' promiscuity, rocks thrown in the Labadists' window. In the end, she had to remove the community to her own summer house for safety.

And that dreadful day when Sophie brought the delegation of inquiry. Elisabeth breathes an amused sigh. Countering extravagant opinion with reasoned argument was something she had been so often called upon to do. She invited them all to dinner. She exhibited her usual patience. They were being unjust, she said, to a genuinely spiritual man. Her guests cried out that everywhere Labadie had been, there had been trouble. Elisabeth replied that the charges made against Labadie and his group were false. But Labadie attacks the church, they said. Incorrect, she answered, he had never attacked the church; on the contrary, it was the church that had attacked him. They said he had no clerical authority to establish a church. But, she reminded them, it was she who had invited this man, she who had episcopal rights and possessed the power of authorizing such associations and dissolving them. So the wrangling went on and on until everyone was tired and went to bed.[3]

Eventually, the Labadists left, and she was sorry to see them go. The women in their simple loose dresses without adornments or cosmetics—marvelous strange habiliments, said Sophie and her delegation, van Schurman busy with her statues—ungodly icons, the bishop said. Gatherings of people from all walks of life—common riffraff, said her relatives.

But isn't it this—strange that after all these years she still has the habit of referring her thoughts to him—isn't it this, my dear friend Descartes, this freedom of association and freedom of thought, this, and not a physiology of the passions, not the exercise of obdurate will, not obedience to law, that is the real moral flowering of your science? She wonders what Descartes, with his provisional morality of obeying authority and following established custom, would have said. She pictures them together, him and Labadie, maybe Anna's lover, although she would never inquire about such a thing. What would Descartes have thought of that strange assembly of women and men of all kinds, all classes, mixing freely, speaking among themselves openly? In the end, wasn't that the dream they both had, of a free-thinking community in which women are prominent and honored; in which women and men are free to be artists, philosophers, spiritual leaders, scientists; a community dedicated to piety, study, the simple life; a place where one can live without pretension, pursue without censorship the search for truth.

And it hadn't ended with the Labadists; the Quakers, too, had come: Mistress Keith, the stepdaughter of George Fox; Robert Barclay, with whom she had such lengthy and amicable correspondence; her friend William Penn, who visited the abbey twice, engaging in rounds of conferences, discussion groups, and services. She had intervened in England on the Quakers' behalf, writing to her brother Rupert and other friends and contacts to help them in prison, an intervention that proved successful in a number of cases. But of course they could not make her a convert. She had no intention of allowing any religious establishment at Herford. When Penn wanted to hold a conference that would combine the Labadists and the Quakers, she diplomatically refused, not willing to give up involvement in life for pietist "interior illumination" any more than she would have for Descartes's rational illumination. When her friend Robert Barclay preached quietism to her in place of attention to administrative duties, she put him off with the words—she remembers them exactly—"silent waiting is no more in my power than flying through the air, since my calling gives me some diversions."[4] When Barclay continued to implore her to give up worldly concerns, it might have been Descartes's own voice that answered in hers: "I cannot submit unto the opinion or practice of any other though I grant that they may have more light than myself." She added a wry comment on Anne Conway's conversion to Quakerism: "The Countess Conway doth well to go on the way that she thinks best, but I should not do well to follow her, unless I had the same conviction, neither did it ever enter into my mind to do so."[5]

She had been no docile disciple, with Descartes or with anyone else. With William Penn, too, kind as he was, she had to be stern. She wrote him when he pressed her to become a Quaker: "I am deeply touched by the interest you take in my eternal welfare and I will seriously reflect upon every line of your advice to me, and try as much as in me lies to follow your counsels; but God's grace must assist me, for, as you rightly say, He will only accept that which He has Himself inspired."[6]

Is it really that different, she would have asked her friend Descartes if he were still alive, this insistence on one's own reflection, one's own inner light? Neither faith nor reason is a thing purely of the mind. Whatever dangers and pain are risked, a mind shaped by passion is what makes a life satisfying and useful to others. No, she had written no great works. But still, giving comfort and support to the Labadist women, advising and leading her sisters, counseling her brother on policy at Heidelberg, encouraging the nuns to read the books in the library: couldn't the flowering of her life be favorably compared to the untimely withering of his, as he shivered in the early light of dawn in a temperamental girl-queen's boudoir?

Notes

Preface

1. A reproduction of the painting discussed in the preface can be found in any collection of Vermeer's work. See, e.g., A. Blankert, J. M. Montias, and G. Aillaud, *Vermeer* (New York: Rizzoli, 1988), plate 23. For a specific treatment of the subject of letter writing in Dutch painting, see Svetlana Alpers, *The Art of Describing: Dutch Art in the Seventeenth Century* (Chicago: University of Chicago Press, 1983).

Prologue

1. All of the translations of Elisabeth's and Descartes's letters in this volume are mine from the French texts (Elisabeth, proficient in several languages, wrote to Descartes in French) in the standard edition of Descartes's works, *Oeuvres de Descartes*, ed. C. Adam and P. Tannery (Paris: Librairie Philosophique, J. Vrin, 1972). Letters from 1642 and May and June 1643 can be found in vol. 3; from July 1643 to April 1647 in vol. 4; and from May 1647 until Descartes's death in 1650 in vol. 5. Letters from Chanut are in vol. 5.

2. *Memoiren der Herzogin Sophie* (Leipzig: Verlag von Herzel, 1879), summer 1651, 48–49.

3. How the letters came to be in the baron's possession is something of a mystery. Rosendal is near Rhenen, where Elisabeth's family had a country house. When the house was sold and torn down, the baron may have purchased the library or bought an old secretary in which the letters were secreted. There they remained until recovered and published by Foucher de Careil. Who saved the letters is not known. Foucher de Careil speculated that Elisabeth's favorite brother, Rupert, who inherited Rhenen, might have preserved the letters after her death.

Chapter 1

1. Carola Oman, *Elisabeth of Bohemia* (London: Hodder & Stoughton, 1938), 33. Criminal records for The Hague show Maurice being brought in at seventeen for rowdyism and assaulting citizens, including local dignitaries. See also Baroness Suzette van Zuylen Nyevelt, *Court Life in the Dutch Republic: 1638–1689* (London: J. M. Dent, 1906), 27.

2. Letter to Pollot, 6 October 1642.

3. This is from Sophie's description in her memoirs. Although she, being considerably younger, came to the nursery house at Leyden after Elisabeth had left, there is no reason to think that her detailed description of the daily routine in her memoirs would not have held true for the older children as well. The Plessens ran the house as they might have a

strict boarding school, with early hours for waking, strict protocol at meals, and a rigorous schedule of classes.

Chapter 2

1. Anna van Schurman was known as "the Dutch Minerva." Elisabeth met van Schurman, who was ten years older, at the studio of Honthorst, where both were taking lessons. Although women were not allowed to attend university lectures openly, van Schurman was in the habit of watching dissections and listening to lectures behind a screen. There is some evidence that she acted as mentor for Elisabeth, urging on her the study of history, the classics, and the Bible, subjects which for Elisabeth were never of primary interest.

2. René Descartes, *Discourse on Method*, in *Philosophical Works*, trans. Elizabeth Haldane and G. R. T. Ross (New York: Dover, 1955), 100.

3. A classic study of French residents in Holland in the seventeenth century is Gustave Cohen, *Ecrivains français en Hollande, dans la première moitié du 17ème siècle* (Paris: Librairie Ancienne Edouard Campion, 1920).

4. Sorbière, *Sorberiana, ou bons mots, rencontres agréables, pensées judicieuses, et observations curieuses de M. Sorbière* (Paris: Chez la Veuve Mabré-Cramoisy, 1732), 85–86.

Chapter 3

1. Several biographers have suggested that Descartes's removal from The Hague in the beginning of May 1643 was a retreat before unwelcome visits from Elisabeth and her friends. Some have even suggested that she may have been privately tutored by him at Chateau Endegeest. See, e.g., Elizabeth Godfrey, *A Sister of Prince Rupert: Elizabeth Princess Palatine and Abbess of Herford* (New York: J. Lane, 1909) and the sly hint in Cohen, *Ecrivains français*, 607. This suggestion is picked up in more recent works, such as Jack Vrooman, *René Descartes: A Biography* (New York: G. P. Putnam, 1970), 171. There is no evidence of any such visits, nor are any mentioned by either Descartes or Elisabeth in their correspondence. Given that clandestine visits would have been highly improper, the more likely reason for Descartes's removal was the dispute at Utrecht, which had escalated beyond university debate to reciprocal charges of slander and threats of arrest.

2. Descartes to Vatier, 22 February 1638, *Oeuvres de Descartes*, vol. 2. Elisabeth's spare, reasoned style is in sharp contrast to the later French *cartésiennes*, who used the précieux poetic language of the salons to express their admiration for Cartesian philosophy. See Erica Harth, *Cartesian Women* (Ithaca: Cornell University Press, 1992).

3. Cohen, *Ecrivains français*, 605.

4. Descartes's famous argument, "cogito, ergo sum," known as "the cogito" for short, was an argument for his own existence. Of what can we be certain? After rejecting every other possibility, including the evidence of his own senses, Descartes finds his own existence undoubtable. "Cogito, ergo sum." I think, therefore I am. Descartes's notion of autonomous reason has often been criticized by contemporary feminists as exemplifying a distorted, masculinist view of the self.

Chapter 5

1. See my article on their relationship, "Philosophy: A Woman's Thought or a Man's Discipline? The Letters of Heloise and Abelard," *Hypatia* 7, no. 3 (Summer 1992): 1–22.

Chapter 6

1. Letter to Pollot, 8 April 1644.
2. The problem of the three circles, dating from antiquity, was regularly used by geometry teachers to illustrate the application of algebraic techniques to geometry. Descartes solved it and used it in the scientific works appended to his *Discourse on Method*.

Chapter 7

1. Descartes had been acquainted with van Schurman for some time. They had a falling out when Descartes scoffed at her reading of the Scriptures in Hebrew. To van Schurman's horror, he said that he had tried to read Genesis but found nothing there that was clear and distinct and therefore nothing of value. Van Schurman's consequent rejection of Cartesianism and her stern warning to Elisabeth that Cartesianism was a dangerous, irreligious doctrine caused a rift between the two women friends that lasted until late in their lives, when they were reunited at the Abbey of Herford.

Chapter 8

1. When Charles dissolved Parliament in 1629 for a "personal rule," the main opposition to his plan among his advisers came from those sympathetic to the interests of his sister, the queen of Bohemia. They saw Parliament as the only hope of raising enough money to recover the Palatine. Charles, however, was quite willing to forgo any such ambitions in return for not having to deal with an increasingly recalcitrant Parliament. When in 1638 Parliament had to be recalled, dissident or not, it still was the only hope for significant funds to recover the Palatine, including some of the property of Elisabeth's mother. In addition, Charles-Louis, always at his uncle's side in the early days of his stay in England, more and more came to the conclusion that his uncle was inept.
2. *Oeuvres de Descartes*, 4:221.

Chapter 11

1. From a conversation with Clerselier in 1644, reported by Baillet and reprinted in *Oeuvres de Descartes*, 12:576–77.

Chapter 12

1. Details can be found in a letter from Conrart to Rivet, 10 November, quoted in *Oeuvres de Descartes*, 4:337–38. The marriage occurred on 24 April but was kept a secret,

either so it would not be known before Edward's formal abjuration in November or so as not to rock the boat until after Marie's marriage to Wladisaw on 5 November. Earlier in June, however, there had been pamphlets in Holland publicizing the affair; Elisabeth either did not know about them, did not credit them, or ignored them in her letters to Descartes. There was no less consternation in France, where the marriage of a Catholic princess to a foreigner and a Protestant was thought to show a lack of respect for, and obedience to, the monarchy. Whatever political humiliation the marriage may have caused, it was a relatively happy one, and Edward was eventually forgiven and back in contact with his Protestant relatives. Rather a lightweight and a playboy, he played little or no role in public affairs.

Chapter 13

1. Quoted in *Oeuvres de Descartes*, 4:337.

2. In his *Meditations*, Descartes removes the doubt that God is a deceiver with a series of deductive arguments. First, from the supposedly obvious premise that we all have an idea of God, Descartes deduced that God had to exist because the idea neither came from the senses nor could be made up. Second, from the fact that we exist as a mind, Descartes deduced that God had to have caused us because we cannot be thought to have caused ourselves and our parents cannot be thought to cause us except as dispositions in the physical body in which the mind is housed.

Chapter 15

1. Descartes, *On the Passions*, in vol. 1 of *Philosophical Works*, 2:137.
2. Descartes, *Passions*, 2:145–46; 3:153.
3. Descartes, *Passions*, 3:156.
4. Descartes, *Passions*, 3:186.
5. Letter of 20 May 1637.
6. Descartes, *Passions*, 3:212.
7. Descartes, *Passions*, 3:190.
8. Descartes, *Passions*, 2:147.
9. Descartes, *Passions*, 2:148.

Chapter 16

1. The letter in which he talks about a "mistake" was undated. Adam and Tannery suggest two possibilities. One is that the letter was written soon after the May letter to Elisabeth. The other, which in my view is less likely, is that the letter dates back to the middle of March, just after he has left his manuscript with Elisabeth.

2. Letter of May 1646.

3. Descartes, *Passions*, 2:119–20.

Chapter 19

1. November (day not given) 1646. In Plato's Apology, Socrates explains that the divine voice that sometimes talks to him tells him when he is doing something wrong. Some said that Descartes actually wrote a treatise on the subject, called *De Deo Socrates*. No such treatise, however, was found among Descartes's papers in Sweden after his death. (See *Oeuvres de Descartes*, 2:408.)

2. See Adrien Baillet, *La Vie de Monsieur Descartes* (1691; reprint, Paris: Table Ronde, 1946), 1:91–92, for Descartes's denial of any connection with the Rosicrucians. *Fama Fraternitatis* is reprinted in Francis Yates, *The Rosicrucian Enlightenment* (Frogmore, England: Paladin, 1975), 238. Yates makes much of the Palatine and Bohemian origins of Rosicrucianism and the degree to which Frederick and Elisabeth Stuart's wedding was invested with the symbolism of a mystical Protestant Enlightenment.

Chapter 21

1. Quoted by Cohen, *Ecrivains français*, 656.
2. Cohen, *Ecrivains français*, 464.

Chapter 22

1. 11 May 1647.

Chapter 24

1. 31 March 1649.
2. 31 March 1649.

Chapter 25

1. The downfall of the Stuarts began with James, Elisabeth's grandfather. Bumbling and rather crude, he demanded money from Parliament and was free with royal monopolies, which he gave to incompetent favorites. Although hopes ran high when Charles, his son, inherited the throne, Charles turned out to be even more difficult. Wanting more than anything to simply live a royal life apart from wrangling with his subjects, in 1629 he dissolved Parliament, which did not meet for eleven years. High-church, he infuriated Puritans and other reformist Protestants by making all churches use the Anglican prayer book. The resulting civil war ended when Cromwell engineered a coup and instituted a "Puritan Republic" with himself as Lord Protector. It was the republic's rump parliament that ordered Charles's execution.

2. Descartes gives a rather odd account of this poetry business. Feeling obliged to explain the "impulse" to write verse, he gives a physiological account, tracing it to the nervous system. In some people, whose brain is impressionable, a strong agitation of bodily spirits can trouble the imagination, an effect that he takes as the mark of a spirit that is stronger and more elevated. Plato reports Socrates as giving a different explanation of his

verse-writing in prison: he has often had a dream in which a "genie" came to him and said, "Practice the arts." He is thus taking his last chance to conform to this secret sign.

3. The reference to letters here is rather puzzling. Although some have taken the sentence "elle n'oubliera pas de répondre aux lettres de votre Altesse, bien qu'elle ait tardé quartre mois à le faire" as referring to letters that Elisabeth wrote to Christina, Elisabeth does not mention in her letters having written to Christina directly, nor is it likely she would have taken the first step in that regard. More likely, in my opinion, is that Descartes is referring to letters "about" Elisabeth that he had written to Chanut. In fact, Descartes mentions Elisabeth in his letters only twice, and only in passing.

4. The observer was Brasset. *Oeuvres de Descartes*, 5:287–89.

Chapter 26

1. 26 February 1649.
2. 23 April 1649.
3. *Oeuvres de Descartes*, 5:411.

Chapter 27

1. Quoted by Godfrey, *Sister of Prince Rupert*, 231.
2. Godfrey, *Sister of Prince Rupert*, 232.
3. Godfrey, *Sister of Prince Rupert*, 232.
4. Godfrey, *Sister of Prince Rupert*, 233.
5. Godfrey, *Sister of Prince Rupert*, 235.
6. Elisabeth is referring to William the Silent and Henry of Orange.
7. Godfrey, *Sister of Prince Rupert*, 235–36.
8. Godfrey, *Sister of Prince Rupert*, 236.
9. Godfrey, *Sister of Prince Rupert*, 243.

Chapter 28

1. Quoted by Vrooman, *René Descartes*, 238.
2. See Baillet, *Vie de Monsieur Descartes*, 2:438, 502, 515, 526.
3. *Memoiren*, summer 1651, 48–49.

Epilogue

1. Elisabeth visited Sophie in Hanover in the winter 1678, where she introduced Sophie's friend Leibniz to Malebrache's *Conversations chrétiennes*. Leibniz wrote to Elisabeth explaining his reactions and his view of Cartesian proofs of the existence of God. (His argument was that the Cartesian proof failed for want of an adequate idea of individual substance.) In 1679, Leibniz traveled to Herford to see Elisabeth, who was then very ill. Sophie and van Helmont, who was treating Elisabeth, were there (E. J. Aiton, *Leibniz: A Biography* [Bristol, England: Adam Hilger, 1985], 90–91; and Robert Merrihew Adams,

Leibniz [New York: Oxford University Press, 1994], 192–93). More mentions answering one of Elisabeth's letters in a letter to Anne Conway (10 May 1659); also he apparently received messages from her to Anne Conway (*The Conway Letters*, ed. Marjorie Nicolson, rev. ed., ed. Sarah Hutton [Oxford, Oxford University Press, 1992], 158, 323). More thanks Conway for sending his writings to Elisabeth, remarking that it would have been "too great a presumption to have sent them myself." (June 1671 and July 1671, *Conway Letters*, 340).

2. Godfrey, *Sister of Prince Rupert*, 314–15.
3. Godfrey, *Sister of Prince Rupert*, 314–15.
4. Godfrey, *Sister of Prince Rupert*, 319.
5. Letter to Robert Barclay in *Reliquiae Barclaianae*, (London, 1870), 27, quoted in *Conway Letters*, 435.
6. Godfrey, *Sister of Prince Rupert*, 330.

Bibliography

Adam, Charles. *Descartes, ses amitiés féminines*. Paris: Boivin, 1937.

Adam, Charles, and Gérald Milhaud, eds. *Correspondance*. Paris: Félix Alcan, 1936.

Aiton, E. J. *Leibniz: A Biography*. Bristol, England: Adam Hilger, 1985.

Alpers, Svetlana. *The Art of Describing: Dutch Art in the Seventeenth Century*. Chicago: University of Chicago Press, 1983.

Baillet, Adrien. *Vie de Monsieur Descartes*. 1691. Reprint, Paris: Table Ronde, 1946.

Barene, Arvede. *Princesses and Court Ladies*. New York: G. P. Putnam, 1906.

Benger, Miss. *Memoirs of Elizabeth Stuart, Queen of Bohemia*. London: Longman, 1825.

Birch, Una. *Anna van Schurman: Artist, Scholar, Saint*. New York: Longman, 1909.

Carlton, Charles. *Charles I: The Personal Monarch*. London: Routledge & Kegan Paul, 1983.

Cohen, Gustave. *Ecrivains français en Hollande, dans la première moitié du 17ème siècle* . Paris: Librairie Ancienne Edouard Campion, 1920.

Descartes, René. *Oeuvres de Descartes*. Edited by C. Adams and P. Tannery. Paris: Librairie Philosophique, J. Vrin, 1972.

————. *Philosophical Works*. Translated by Elizabeth Haldane and G. R. T. Ross. New York: Dover, 1955.

De Vries, A. B. *Jan Vermeer van Delft*. London: Batsford, 1939.

Foucher de Careil, A. *Descartes et la Princesse Palatine*. Paris: Auguste Durand, 1862.

Gaskell, Ivan. *Seventeenth-Century Dutch and Flemish Painting*. London: Sotheby's, 1990.

Geyl, Pieter. *Orange and Stuart*. Translated by Arnold Pomerans. New York: Charles Scribner, 1969.

Godfrey, Elizabeth. *A Sister of Prince Rupert: Elizabeth Princess Palatine and Abbess of Herford*. New York: J. Lane, 1909.

Harth, Erica. *Cartesian Women*. Ithaca: Cornell University Press, 1992.

Kahr, Madlyn Millner. *Dutch Painting in the Seventeenth Century*. New York: Icon, 1978.

Kroll, Maria. *Sophie Electress of Hanover*. London: Victor Gollancz, 1973.

Lougee, Carolyn. *Le Paradis des Femmes: Women, Salons, and Social Stratification in Seventeenth-Century France*. Princeton: Princeton University Press, 1976.

Masson, Georgina. *Queen Christina*. New York: Farrar, Straus & Giroux, 1968.

Memoiren der Herzogin Sophie. Leipzig: Verlag von Herzel, 1879.

Nash, J. M. *The Age of Rembrandt and Vermeer*. San Francisco: Holt, Rinehart & Winston.

Néel, Marguerite. *Descartes et la Princesse Elizabeth*. Paris: Editions Elzévir, 1943.

Nicolson, Marjorie, ed. *The Conway Letters*. Oxford: Hutton, 1992.

Nye, Andrea. "A Woman's Thought or a Man's Discipline? The Letters of Abelard and Heloise." *Hypatia* 7, no. 3 (Summer 1992).

Nyevelt, Baroness Suzette van Zuylen. *Court Life in the Dutch Republic: 1638–1689*. London: J. M. Dent, 1906.

Oman, Carola. *Elizabeth of Bohemia*. London: Hodder & Stoughton, 1938.

Osler, Margaret. *Divine Will and the Mechanical Philosophy.* Cambridge: Cambridge University Press, 1994.

Parker, Geoffrey. *The Thirty Years' War.* London: Routledge & Kegan Paul, 1984.

Sorbière. *Sorberiana ou bons mots, rencontres agréables, pensées judicieuses, et observations curieuses de M. Sorbière.* Paris: Chez la Veuve Mabré-Cramoisy, 1732.

Thomson, George Malcolm. *Warrior Prince: Prince Rupert of the Rhine.* London: Secker & Warburg, 1976.

Vrooman, Jack. *René Descartes.* New York: G. P. Putnam, 1970.

Yates, Frances. *The Rosicrucian Enlightenment.* London: Routledge & Kegan Paul, 1972.

Index

Aristotelianism, 5, 12, 120, 121
Arminians, 75

Barclay, Robert, 172
body: and emotion, 67–68, 89–90, 93–95, 96; nature of, 57, 60
Bohemia, 7

Calvinism, 75, 77
Careil, Foucher de, 3, 17, 175
Catholicism, 77, 84–85
Chanut, Hector-Pierre, 1–2, 125–31, 132–34, 138, 145, 151–57
Charles I, king of England, 3, 23, 34, 179; execution of, 146–47, 150
Charles-Louis, elector Palatine, 2, 8, 34, 43, 54, 146, 147–48, 149, 158–62
Christina, queen of Sweden, 2, 125–31, 132–33, 135, 137, 139–40, 143, 145, 147, 151–57, 164–65, 170, 180
Conway, Anne, 170, 172
Cromwell, Oliver, 5, 43

depression, 40–42, 44–46, 48, 55–56, 91
determinism, 74–75, 80, 95
Digby, Kenelm, 42, 44
dualism, xi–xii, 9–10, 12–13, 19, 21–22, 23, 24–25, 26, 42
Dutch: culture, 13, 27; government, ix, 13–14, 122, 123–24; painting, ix, 175; theologians, 121, 122, 124; trade, 13, 27; universities, ix, 5, 13, 124

Edward, prince Palatine, 3, 76–80
Elizabeth, queen of Bohemia, x. 2–3, 6–9, 22, 27, 43, 54, 80, 100–101, 149
emotions. *See* passions
Epicurus, 54, 55
erudition, treatise on, 136–37

ethics, 36–37, 51–53, 61–62, 67–70, 81, 102–8

Frederick, elector Palatine, 3, 7, 8, 77
free will, 73–75, 79; and God's foreknowledge, 86
Freinshemius, Johann, 152–53, 164

generosity, 91–92
God, 129, 178; existence of, 61–62, 63, 67, 72–76, 79; blasphemy against, 120–21
good: deeds, 86–87; and evil, 86; the highest, 130–31, 133; knowledge of, 94–95; life, 48–53
grief, 92–93
Gröningen, University of, 30

happiness, 48–56, 65–66, 79, 90, 132
health, 123–24
Heereboord, 120–21, 124
Heidelberg, 7, 149, 158–59, 170
Helmont, Fredericus Mercurius van, 180
Henriette, princess Palatine, 2–3, 114–15, 159–62
Herford, Abbey of, v, 169
Hogeland, 117, 118, 122, 123
Honthorst, Gerritt van, 6, 11, 27
House of Orange, 7, 14, 27, 31, 35

Jesuits, 5, 75, 77, 80
joy, 92–93, 97, as good-luck genie, 109–11
Juliana of Orange, 3, 8, 37

Krossen, 8, 117, 123

Labadie, Jean, 171–72
languor, 96–98
Leibniz, Gottfried Wilhelm von, 180
letter writing, ix–x, 135

185

About the Author

Andrea Nye's previous books include *Feminist Theory and the Philosophies of Man; Words of Power: A Feminist Reading of the History of Logic; Philosophia: The Thought of Rosa Luxemburg, Simone Weil, and Hannah Arendt;* and most recently *Philosophy and Feminism: At the Border.* In these books, she explores many aspects of the relation between feminist theory and mainstream philosophy. She has also been interested in reviving and making accessible the work of woman thinkers and writers such as Elisabeth. Currently professor of philosophy and religious studies at the University of Wisconsin at Whitewater, she received a B.A. degree from Radcliffe College and a Ph.D. from the University of Oregon.